Media Power: A Sociological Introduction

Media Power

A Sociological Introduction

Ciaran McCullagh

Consultant Editor: Jo Campling

palgrave

First published 2002 by
PALGRAVE
Houndmills, Basingstoke, Hampshire RG21 6XS and
175 Fifth Avenue, New York, N. Y. 10010
Companies and representatives throughout the world

PALGRAVE is the new global academic imprint of
St. Martin's Press LLC Scholarly and Reference Division and
Palgrave Publishers Ltd (formerly Macmillan Press Ltd).

ISBN 0–333–64340–2 hardback
ISBN 0–333–64341–0 paperback

This book is printed on paper suitable for recycling and
made from fully managed and sustained forest sources.

A catalogue record for this book is available
from the British Library.

Library of Congress Cataloging-in-Publication Data
McCullagh, Ciaran.
   Media power: a sociological introduction / Ciaran McCullagh;
   consultant editor, Jo Campling.
      p. cm
   Includes bibliographical references and index.
   ISBN 0–333–64340–2—ISBN 0–333–64341–0 (pbk.)
      1. Mass Media—Social aspects. I. Campling, Jo. II. Title.
HM1206. M38 2002
302.23—dc21   2001060260

10   9   8   7   6   5   4   3   2   1
11   10 09 08 07 06 05 04 03 02

Printed in China

To Damian and David

Contents

Preface

This book is aimed at students and other newcomers to the sociology of the mass media. It sets out to discuss a range of topics that arise in the study of media power. The intention is to do so in a manner that is both accessible and introductory. In keeping with this the text is written in a direct and relatively non-technical manner, but it is hoped that this has not been achieved at the cost of simplification of the ideas involved.

It begins with a discussion of what is often regarded as the traditional model of media effects and looks at how this has structured and limited research into violence in the mass media. It proceeds from this to formulate an alternative that focuses on three aspects of the communication process: media content, media production, and media reception. These become the focus of subsequent chapters. Chapter 2 discusses issues of bias, selectivity and framing as central elements in debates about media representation. Chapter 3 looks at the range of arguments about the relationship between media content and social power. It examines the degree to which there is a common structure in media framing and how this might relate to or be reflective of the nature of power in society. Chapter 4 looks at the social influences on the content of news, such as the power of ownership, the influence of sources, the politics of media personnel, and the effects of organisational routines on media output.

Chapter 5 asks if new forms of media (such as talk television) and new forms of communication (such as the Internet) widen access to the public sphere? Chapter 6 discusses the sociological study of television fiction and, in that context, looks at the representation of gender and race in the media. Chapter 7 considers the research on media audiences and through that addresses the issue of reception of media messages. The conclusion (Chapter 8) discusses the future of media sociology.

The object throughout is to introduce as wide a range of issues as is consistent with this framework and to bring together a range of research on the media from the USA, Britain and, to a lesser extent, continental Europe. This material often figures prominently in the respective national debates but seldom appears at introductory text level. Thus while the work of someone like Robert McChesney figures prominently in the American literature, it is less well-known in Britain. Similarly, while British audiences know the work of Jenny Kitzinger, it is less familiar to American ones. This book attempts to bridge this kind of divide.

There are a number of limitations that arise in writing a text within these parameters. The first and most important is that while the text deals with the mass media in general, there is inevitably a certain bias towards television. This is a recognition of the centrality of television as the mass medium of our time and also of the degree to which it dominates the environment in which other media operate. A longer book would give more space to newspapers and radio.

The second is in the examples that are used in the text to illustrate arguments. There is pressure, for pedagogic purposes, to make these as contemporary as possible so that they will have the necessary resonance with the intended audience. The problem is that for the most part the research literature on the media is not so much a history of the present as of the recent past. For this reason there has to be a trade-off between examples of the researched and attested and the immediate and the contemporary. As is appropriate in a sociology text the balance is struck in favour of the research literature.

CIARAN McCULLAGH

Acknowledgements

This book was drawn from courses I have been teaching to under-graduate and postgraduate students at University College Cork over a number of years. Its final shape owes much to their comments and responses and to their stubborn refusal to being easily impressed or convinced by the material much presented. The book also owes much to a number of colleagues who, while they did not comment direct on this particular book, encouraged and supported the writing in ways that they may not have been always fully aware of. These include Linda Connolly, Ethel Crowley, Mary Daly, Damian Hannan, Tony McCasnin, Jim McLaughlin, David Rottman and Hilary Tovey. Jo Campling was also important, not least through her patience and tolerance for a project that she may sometimes have doubted would ever be completed. Keith Povey was a courteous and intimidatingly efficient editor. My thanks to all of them.

I would also like to acknowledge the financial assistance of the Arts Faculty Publications Fund at University College Cork. This helped defray the cost of the production of the index.

CHAPTER 1

Introduction: Media Power: From Simple Answers to Complex Questions

No escape

It has become both a truism and a commonplace to observe that we live in media-saturated societies. The mass media – and particularly television – have become 'the cultural epicenter' of our world (Castells, 1996:336, 333). At the level of everyday life it has become routine and normal to encounter the media. Just as offering a cup of tea or coffee is a method of making people feel at ease, the provision of some form of media is rapidly becoming complementary to it. We accept without question the availability of newspapers in dentists' waiting rooms, bank managers' offices, the waiting rooms for job interviews, and in aeroplanes. Similarly access to television is not limited to the domestic sphere. It can be encountered in supermarkets, hair salons, bars, lounges in airports, buses, schoolrooms, and in the local take-away restaurant. We live in a media-saturated world, and for the most part are no longer surprised by it.

Media production is now one of the largest and most lucrative industrial sectors in the global economy. According to Nichols and McChesney (2000), 16 of the world's largest corporations are in the communications sector. Thirteen of the 100 richest people in the world are media magnates. Almost all households in the Western world own at least one television set, and many have one for each household member. In 1992 there were over 1 billion television sets in the world; 55 per cent of these were in Europe or North America, and 1 per cent in Africa. Media consumption is the predominant activity in the domestic sphere in industrialised societies, and second only to work in terms of the time spent on it. According to Preston (2001:205), average daily television viewing time at the end of the 1990s ranged from 150 minutes in Asia to 230 in North America and around 200 minutes a day in Europe. It is generally accepted that children will, for example, spend more time watching television than they will in class.

The power to deprave and corrupt?

Yet for all of its commonplace nature and for all its dominant presence in our lives, there is a feeling that this kind of media saturation is not a 'good' thing. As Connell (1988) says, the media, and in particular television, have been credited with 'fabulous' powers to change people and have been blamed for contributing to most social ills. An Irish politician, for example, suggested that there was no sex in Ireland before television. This implied that, prior to this, the Irish had a unique method of population reproduction. In the USA in the 1950s television was regarded as a health hazard, and as such responsible for a range of ailments including radiation sickness, crooked eyes and 'buck teeth'. Children got this last condition from watching television for long periods with their chins supported in their hands (Root, 1986:10). At a more serious level, it has been blamed for the decline of religion, the undermining of trust in politics, the increase in crime and violence in society, the dumbing down of popular culture, the growth of permissiveness, and as, generally speaking, having the power to corrupt and deprave. No politician or public figure has ever lost votes or reputation by attacking the media. None has become famous by defending it.

There is little that is new in this level of antipathy to the popular media. Every new medium with the potential to reach a mass audience has been a source of concern over its potential impact and this has usually been conceptualised in negative terms. New media are seen as disrupting existing relations of communication between powerful and powerless, and so threatening existing hierarchies of power and control. In societies 'so thoroughly shot through with class division and class dislike', Barker and Petley (1997:7) tell us, 'every new means of communication...has been greeted in much the same fearful fashion'.

When newspapers first developed in mid-seventeenth century Britain there was a concern that the public might 'become too familiar with the actions and counsels of their superiors' (quote in Eldridge, Kitzinger and Williams, 1997:18). In the mid-nineteenth century the concern was with music halls, which featured re-enactments of notorious murders and violent crimes. These attracted youthful audiences and were held to be responsible for an increase in juvenile crime (Murdock and McCron,1979).

At the turn of the twentieth century the concern was with radio and the cinema. In Britain it was feared that the emergence of radio would have 'incalculable significance for political stability' (quoted in Eldridge, Kitzinger and Williams, 1997: 13). The growth of audiences for the cinema was considered an epidemic that would have serious consequences. An American writer of the time claimed, 'the road to delinquency is heavily dotted with movie addicts' (Henry James Forman, quoted in Gilbert, 1986). There was also apprehension about the conditions in which films were viewed. These were referred to as the 'moral dangers of darkness' (Pearson, 1983:32). In 1908 the Mayor of New York tried to close cinemas because he felt they threatened the virtuous well-being of its citizens (Eldridge, Kitzinger and Williams, 1997:16).

By the late 1940s and early 1950s crime comics had become a major villain in the USA. They were accused of predisposing children to delinquency, and the issue of banning comics was seriously considered. Frederic Wertham, a liberal-minded psychologist, felt that the juvenile violence provoked by the comics was a new phenomenon. In addition, he argued, the comics were a health hazard. They encouraged 'linear dyslexia', a disease found in children whose eyes were damaged by having to read up and down rather than across the page to follow the dialogue balloons of the comics (see the account in Gilbert, 1986).

By the 1960s television had come into its own as the major antisocial medium. This is exemplified by the book entitled 'Television: The Plug-in Drug' (Winn, 1985). This blamed the medium for most forms of childhood and adolescent misbehaviour, (it was dislodged by violent videos in the 1980s). These videos, it was claimed, had replaced the magician at children's birthday parties (see Brown, 1984). They were also held to be responsible for a series of violent incidents. These included high-school shootings in the USA, and the murder of two-year-old James Bulger by two children in Liverpool. The latest form of communication technology, the Internet, is increasingly beginning to displace all of the others as the source for social anxiety and social concern. The risks of exposure to pornography and of encountering paedophiles have led to demands for its control and regulation.

What is the point of history?

Though these concerns came at different times and focused on different media, they have a number of features in common. The main one is the massive simplification of media effects. These are seen as direct and powerful and there is assumed to be a direct relationship between exposure to the media and subsequent behaviour. The implicit model underlying all of this is that of imitation. People will imitate what they see in comics, films and on television screens. If what they see is violent behaviour then that is what they will imitate. In some accounts this imitation is extended to include addiction. Viewers repeat and re-enact what they see in the media not because they wish to, but because it is something over which they have little control.

Violence in the media: into a dead end

These concerns structured what is the best-known topic in the study of the media. This is the attempt to find links between the amount of violent material in the media and the level of violence in society. It has spawned one of the most extensive bodies of research in the social sciences (for a review see Gauntlett, 1995). Laboratory experiments, field studies, and longitudinal and correlation based methodologies have been applied to the issue. The results have been reviewed by government-sponsored researchers in Britain (see Cumberbatch and Howitt, 1989), by the Surgeon General in the USA (1972) and by various bodies of accredited experts such as the American Psychological Association (1993). The results are largely inconclusive. For each review that finds a positive relationship between the two, there is equally one that does not. To the extent that there is any consensus it is that any link between violence in the media and violence in society is not a particularly strong one.

Friedrich-Cofer and Huston (1986), for example, argue strongly for the causal effects of viewing television violence but say that the relationship is a small one. Hughes and Hasbrouck (1996:140) also claim that the research findings show consistently that there is a relationship between television viewing and later aggression, but they also accept that the 'amount of variance in aggression accounted for by television viewing is small'. Freedman (1984:378), a trenchant critic of this research tradition, says, 'if there are effects, they are rather small'. Finally Cook, Kendzierski and Thomas (1983:193), also critics of much of the existing research, say it is unlikely that 'television plays more than a minor role in directly producing violence and violent crime'.

Cumberbatch argues that the lack of definitive results is a product of a series of conceptual and theoretical inadequacies in the research. These include the assumption that violence has clear and unambiguous effects, and he refers to the 'crude nature' of the models through which media violence is supposed to operate on viewers (Cumberbatch and Howitt, 1989:49). Viewers may imitate what they see in the media but precisely why they do so is never fully clarified. It is unclear why seeing violence in the media should become a motive for engaging in it.

Back to the communication process

The traditional approach to the study of the mass media has been informed and shaped by the range of concerns about the effects of the media on society, most persistently in attributing violence in society to violence in the media. This approach has essentially run itself into a dead end, though many of its leading practitioners would not necessarily recognise this. It is, in the words of Marvin (2000:143), 'stymied'. This has come about largely because of the narrow model of media effects with which it works and its limited understanding of how people are influenced and affected by the media. It is largely a common-sense view of the media in which the viewer or reader is a passive recipient of media material and in which there is a direct relationship between media content and audience behaviour.

The way to transcend this approach is to focus attention on the communication process and to abandon the notion that the application of the term 'mass' necessarily carries with it negative implications. The mass media are simply the means through which content, whether fact or fiction, is produced by organisations and transmitted to and received by an audience. As such the process of mass communication involves the three fundamental factors: content, organisation, and audience. It follows from this, as John Thompson (1990) points out, that there are three dimensions to the analysis of the mass media.

The first is the content of media messages. It is necessary to look at how stories, whether fact or fiction, are put together and how, (to use the language of a later part of this book), they are selected and framed. The media are the means through which information and entertainment is diffused in society, so it is important to know what exactly is being communicated to audiences and it is important to ask whether it meets certain socially acknowledged criteria, such as informativeness and representativeness.

The second is the production and transmission of messages. Media content is increasingly the product of complex bureaucracies and large commercial organisations, so it is essential to look at the institutional contexts in which media messages are assembled. We need to ask how characteristics such as their ownership and control, their level of regulation by the state, and the kinds of assumption they make about audiences influence the nature of the end product. Advertising is, for example, credited with an important role in the production process, so we must ask whether it influences the nature and shape of media content and what the nature of that influence might be.

The third is the reception of the media message by the audience. The separation of the contexts of production and reception means that while audiences may have little control over the production of media messages, they have a lot of control over their reception. This requires us to examine the contexts within which messages are received and to look at how factors such as gender and class influence the interpretation of media messages. The objective, according to John Thompson (1990:306), must be to look at how people 'make sense of media messages and incorporate them into their daily lives'.

What is being suggested here is that media analysis is essentially about the three 'Xs' – texts, production contexts, and reception contexts – and about the relationships between them. Its objective is to consider all three levels to see if the messages and meanings produced by the mass media confirm or contest existing power structures or, in John Thompson's (1990:307) words, 'sustain or challenge the structure of relationships in society'.

Using the approach: applying the argument to media violence

The utility of this approach can be illustrated by applying it to the issue of media violence. It will be seen to generate more interesting and more sociologically relevant questions than the traditional effects perspective.

Representing violence, symbolising social control

If the mass media is the central means through which ideas and information circulate in society, and if violence is a central part of media schedules, then, according to Marvin (2000), this should prompt a question. We need to examine 'how cultures represent and circulate notions of what violence is and what purposes such violence serves' (Marvin, 2000:143). This means we need to consider what the media represents to us as violence, and why such representations occur so frequently in their programming.

In most media research the assumption is that the term 'violence' covers acts of interpersonal aggression, such as physical assault and rape. This locates the violence that television is alleged to cause at an individual level and as a problem of criminal behaviour. But arguably the major problem of violence in the world is that of collective and legal violence in the form of war and the actions of states and their armies. Halloran (1978:288), for example, says that collective violence 'is much more normal, central and historically rooted than many of us believe'. There is little suggestion in the research that collective violence is caused by television or by the mass media. Indeed, the various research agendas that exist for the mass media do not include studies of the viewing habits of army generals.

Thus the violence that is represented as problematic by television and the cinema is of secondary importance in an overall consideration of the nature of social violence. The focus is exclusively on interpersonal violence as it is perpetrated by certain kinds of people. Given the class-specific nature of much of this violence, it may well be that lurking behind this concern is middle- and upper-class fears of 'the dangerous classes' (see Gans, 1978).

In this context it is convenient to use the media as the scapegoat. It is certainly more attractive than confronting other social explanations of violence. Indeed, one of the curiosities of this debate is that if interpersonal violence is approached from the perspective of criminology then television and the media generally disappear as relevant factors. Criminologists emphasise the role of frustrated expectations and the sense of relative deprivation over material and economic circumstances as primary factors in such violence (see, for example, Beirne and Messerschmidt, 1991).

As an extension of this, Gerbner (1994) argues that we must not treat and count all acts of violence as if they were the same; instead, we need to look more closely at the dramatic contexts in which these are shown in the media. We need to ask who engages in violence, who is it used against, is it successful, and how is its use justified? Approached in this way, it becomes clear that there is a consistent underlying structure in media presentation of violence.

Minority groups are, for example, more likely to be shown as perpetrators of violence. Women, children and old people are most likely to be its victims. Their status in society as 'helpless' and 'in need of protection' provides the dramatic context for the violence of good characters and gives it its legitimation. The use of violence against such villains is justified because of the threat they pose to vulnerable groups. In this way villains 'deserve' the violence that is used against them.

Gerbner (1994) contends that this manner of depicting violence has important social functions. It symbolises for us which groups represent threats to social power and it shows how to deal with these threats. In this way it highlights the necessity of state violence in the maintenance of the established order. In addition, what he terms the 'symbolic overkill' of violence is designed to intimidate viewers and to create an atmosphere of fear and insecurity in society; he referred to this as the notion that we live in a mean and dangerous world. This makes audiences less likely to oppose and resist conservative law and order policies. Thus, he argues, violence in the media is symbolic of social values and a demonstration of social power. It serves as an instrument of social control.

Murdock (1994) is broadly in sympathy but argues that Gerbner's model is limited by an exclusive focus on acts of violence. As a result it ignores how violence is talked about in the media. When this is included the picture is somewhat more complex. Drawing on research on urban riots in Britain, Murdock (1994:176–7) argues that the media used three discourses or ways of talking about violence. One was 'authoritarian populism', which located the causes of violence in the decline in traditional values. This was the discourse of the then government. The second was a 'labourist' discourse, which presented mass unemployment as the cause. The third was a 'radical' discourse, which explained the violence in terms of established tensions between the police and inner-city communities. Each of these discourses explained, understood and evaluated the violence of rioters in different ways and accorded it different degrees of moral and political justification, ranging from total condemnation to reluctant justification.

The important question was which discourse the media drew on most often to explain the riots. Murdock found that the discourse depended on the programme involved. The news was more likely to utilise the official discourse of 'authoritarian populism', whereas documentaries were more open to the discourses that he characterised as 'alternative' and 'oppositional'. He argued that the media's representation of violence is not as one-dimensional as Gerbner suggests: in certain circumstances, and in certain kinds of programme, other views can gain public airing.

Manufacturing violence

Von Feilitzen (1998) poses the second topic. She asks why the level of violence in the media continues to increase if everyone is supposed to be against it? The search for an answer directs attention to the production process in the media and to the factors that influence and shape it. Gerbner (1995), for example, argues that private ownership and the search for profit is the key factor shaping media content. The centrality of violence is 'a product of a complex manufacturing and marketing machine' (Gerbner, 1995:552), which is rooted in the organisation and ownership structure of the US-based television industry and in the competition for profit that this generates. The industry has been forced to go global in search of profit, and as it seeks global markets it must give its products global appeal. This means that violence has become a staple of the business as, to put it at its most simple, violence sells. As an American media executive says, 'kicking butt plays everywhere' (quoted in Herman and McChesney, 1997:44). It gets around the problem of language barriers to the dissemination of programmes, as, by its nature, violent material requires little dubbing and its meaning is readily understood in most cultural contexts. Violent content is, for the American media industry, 'as close to risk-free as anything they produce' (Herman and McChesney, 1997:44).

Rowland (1982) has extended the analysis to suggest that the power of the industry is the key factor in understanding why nothing has been done to regulate the level of violence in the American media. He has characterised the policy-making process as a 'continuing ritual of public debate and policy avoidance' (1982:399). There are regular reviews of the evidence, new research is commissioned, public debate is encouraged, and reports are published. But at the end of the process no radical proposals for change (such as the extension of public service television or the restructuring of the television industry) are ever seriously contemplated.

The issue of media ownership is important but cultural values also play a part. Von Feilitzen (1998) has pointed out that the level of violence is much higher in American television than is the case in Europe. This may be due to different cultural attitudes to the use of violence and to the ideology of public service rather than the unrestricted profit that exists, somewhat precariously as we shall see, in many European media systems. Murdock (1994) has argued that this ideology has been important in allowing the media in Britain to give space to alternative accounts of the dynamics of violence and the motivations for it. However, he argues that market dynamics in the form of globalisation and conglomeration, combined with increasing pressure from the state, is steadily eroding this space.

Finally it is useful to mention the case of Japan. Statistically it has some of the most violent television in the world. There are seven acts of violence per hour on Japanese television, compared to 5.5 in the USA and 2.5 in the UK (Milne, 1988:22). Moreover, the kind of violence shown is different. In Japan the male hero is more likely to be the victim of violence than is the case in American television. His suffering is shown more clearly and it goes on for a longer period of time. Clearly this is a reflection of Japanese cultural values and of attitudes to violence and suffering. Such values also have a complex relationship to behaviour. Despite the violent nature of its media culture Japan is a major anomaly for criminologists because the level of crimes such as murder and assault, is very low (see Beirne and Messerschmidt, 1991).

Watching television and not seeing violence

The final element in the communication process is the audience. Researchers who believe that the media influences the level of violence in society base their arguments on particular measurements of violence. But what happens when viewers differ with the researchers on what constitutes violent material: do the inferences of researchers continue to have any validity?

A number of studies have found that there are considerable differences between viewers' perceptions of violence and those of researchers (see, for example, Gunter and Wober, 1988). Viewers' perceptions in turn also show significant differences by class, culture, gender, age, and extent of familiarity with real life violence (see Schlesinger, Dobash, Dobash and Weaver, 1992). In general their perceptions do not depend on the number of violent incidents in a programme. According to standard methods of measuring violence, cartoons are four times as violent as other kinds of programmes but, as Gunter and Wober (1988) show, viewers do not perceive them in this way. Similarly while many crime dramas are regarded as violent by researchers, viewers do not necessarily feel they are.

Their responses to violence are complex. Many claim to have difficulty with violent television programmes and argue that there is too much violence in the media, yet the majority told Gunter and Wober (1988) that they enjoyed watching violent programmes. Parents said they watched the kinds of programme that provoke concern about violence in the media, such as tough crime series, with their children. They would be disappointed if many of these were taken off the air as they felt they were not really that violent.

Morrison (1999) asked groups of viewers in Britain to talk about what they considered to be violent media material. The ensuing discussions confirmed the complex and varied nature of viewers' definitions. Among the findings were that many viewers did not regard the film *Pulp Fiction* as violent. This film provoked intense debates in the media about its violent content and it was given an 'adult only' rating by the film censor; however, viewers felt that because the violence was surrounded by humour, it was less serious, less threatening and less 'violent' as a result.

These kinds of findings point to the need to incorporate viewers' interpretations and understanding into the way in which the power of the media is analysed. The media does not operate on naive and innocent audiences: viewers come from a variety of backgrounds and bring a range of social experiences and cultural knowledge to their viewing. These influence how they interpret and respond to the media and intercede in the relationship between the media and the effects it is supposed to produce. It is not possible to infer media effects from media content. We need to know how viewers engage with what they see and how they receive and interpret the media material they select to use.

Conclusion

In this introduction we have looked at a range of issues relating to the study of media power. We considered the way in which this power is often conceptualised in terms of imitation and in terms of a direct link between exposure to media material and subsequent behaviour. This approach has, we argued, been unproductive and the research on the effects of violence in the media on society illustrates this.

A sociological approach has to transcend this tradition by considering the three principal features of the mass media. These are content, production and reception. We need to look at how the world is represented to us in media content. We need to look at how this material is produced and how the context of its production shapes its nature and content. Finally we need to examine the ways in which audiences interpret and understand the material that is presented to them. These issues are developed further in the rest of the book.

CHAPTER 2

The Media as Definers of Social Reality

Introduction

It has become a cliché to say that we live in increasingly more complex societies and in a more complex world; but this statement has implications for the manner in which we think about and understand the power of the mass media. As the societies and the world we live in grow more complex, the range of information that we 'need' also increases. If we wish to function as informed and competent citizens, or even to pass as such, then we need to know about events happening in geographically distant places. Northern Ireland, the Middle East, Eastern Europe and Iraq, everyone's favourite enemy, are pertinent examples. We also need to know about events in socially distant places in our own society, such as the inner cities and the inner sanctums of power.

The range of issues with which we are expected to be familiar is also increasing rapidly. The complexities of the politics of Afghanistan were not a key issue in the West a few years ago; now they are. The issue of drugs and the related gang violence in inner cities was not an urgent issue 20 years ago; now it is. But as the range of issues grows, the number of them that we can learn about at first hand declines. Many of us, for example, have never been, or are ever likely to go, to Iraq or to the Middle East. Equally, the inner cities are places that most of us travel through rather than live in. They are, in effect, as foreign to us as many distant societies.

Information delivery

So, if we need to know about these places and issues, and if these are outside the scope of our personal experience, how do we find out about them? The answer is through the media. Radio, news-papers and television carry information to us about events that we do not witness personally and that happen in places to which we have no access. Through this they make us indirect witnesses of the events of the world. In this way, the role of the mass media in contemporary society is that of information delivery.

In this capacity they bring us two types of information. The first is about events outside our own society. This is the sense in which Marshall McLuhan claimed that the media made the world into a 'global village'. We are now familiar with a range of countries, and of issues and the lives of the people in these countries, that previous generations were not. The time taken for information to reach us has also been significantly reduced. It took three weeks for the details of the Charge of the Light Brigade in 1854 to reach London (Knightley, 1975). Nowadays it would be live on our television screens.

The other type of information they bring us is about our own society. There are many places where socially significant events occur and in which important issues arise, are debated and are resolved. For the most part we do not have easy and routine access to them. These include social and political institutions such as Parliament, the law courts, and the boardrooms of powerful corporations, and also geographic locations such as urban ghettos and rural farmyards. As John Thompson (1990) argues, the media increase the visibility of these institutions and locations through the coverage that they give to what happens in them.

However, there is nothing particularly profound about saying that the media provide us with information. Where the argument gets interesting and sociological is when we focus on the quantity and quality of the information that the media transmit. How reliable and accurate is the information that the media deliver to us? If we base our attitudes and action in the world on information derived from the media, how predictable and successful would these be?

A window on the world

There are two views on this. The first is that of journalists and the media generally. This characterises the media as the 'window on the world'. Its job is to provide us with a window through which we can see out into the world. Like the glass in the window it should be clear and must not distort or refract what we are looking at; it must allow us to see the world as the world really is.

The metaphor of a window should not, of course, be taken too literally. It is not possible for the media to tell us everything that is going on in the world. Media space and time are limited so only so much information can be carried. The media have, in Zha's (1992) phrase, a 'limited carrying capacity', and this means that some element of selectivity is inevitable. The important issue is how the process of selection works. The topics selected for media coverage should be a representative cross-section of what is going on in the world. As Herman (1985:135) has pointed out, the issues and events covered in the media must be those that it is important for us to know about. If a significant number of facts and perspectives is left out then a central condition of an adequate democratic media – that of 'meaningful diversity' – is not achieved.

Fractured glass

The second view on the information in the media comes from media sociologists. They argue that the media are selective in what they tell us about the world. The media tell us about some events and issues but not about others, and the ones they bring to our attention may not necessarily be the most socially or politically significant. This kind of selectivity means that the media can control and shape the knowledge and understanding that we, their audience, develop about the world.

Put in formal sociological language, this argument contends that our images and knowledge of social reality are formed and shaped by the images and information that the media deliver to us. If these images and information are selective and partial, then our images and information will also be selective and partial. Thus the power of the media is the power to define our sense of the social reality of the society and the world that we live in; they achieve this through control over the information that they present to us.

Selective or not?

This means that when we think about the media and the information they carry to us we have two arguments to consider: one is that the information is a direct reflection of the world or of social reality; the other is that the media account of reality is a selective one. It is selective in terms of what it tells us about the world and also it is selective in terms of the way in which it chooses to tell us about events and issues. This pattern of selectivity constitutes a distortion and a misrepresentation of significant events and issues in the world.

If we wish to choose between these arguments then we must ask whether the media are selective in their coverage or not? Are they the clear windows (as suggested by the media themselves), or are they a distorting lens illuminating and magnifying some parts and some events in the world and ignoring, neglecting and diminishing others?

Researching media selectivity

Sociologists have developed a number of research strategies to address these questions. We look at three of these below. What they have in common is that they compare media coverage of an event or issue with some outside account of the same event or issue. The outside account is chosen because it is believed to be a more objective and impartial one and so constitutes an independent standard against which the accuracy of the media account can be tested. If the media account differs in a consistent and systematic way from this then we have evidence of media selectivity. Where these strategies differ is in what they use as the impartial and independent standard.

Using official records

The first and most common strategy is to compare the media account with an official record of the event or issue. Two examples illustrate how this works.

The coverage of crime.   The first is the media coverage of crime. Researchers in a number of different countries have looked at the pattern of crime recorded in official statistics and compared it to that presented in the media (for a review, see Reiner, 1997). According to official statistics and victim surveys, property crimes such burglary and robbery are the most common types of crime in industrialised countries. These can account for as much as 95 per cent of the crimes recorded by the police. Media coverage, by contrast, tends to high-light crimes of assault and interpersonal violence, particularly those that happen in the street. These are consistently over-reported con-sidering their low incidence, whereas property crimes are, despite their high incidence, consistently under-reported. The extent of the coverage of violent crime varies somewhat by the medium in-volved, with the popular or tabloid press highest followed by local news bulletins on television and then by the self-styled 'quality press'. There is also further selectivity within the coverage of violent crime. The most common focus in, for example, media reports on sexual violence against children is on child abduction, whereas incest is more likely to occur (Eldridge, Kitzinger and Williams, 1997:170). Accordingly, researchers have concluded that media ac-counts of crime are biased and selective.

Environmental risks.   A second example is the media coverage of environmental risks. According to a growing number of social analysts we live in societies that are increasingly threatened by environmental hazards, such as nuclear accidents, which are ex-tensive in the level and extent of the destruction they can cause. Yet these risks are somewhat remote from our everyday experi-ence and understanding (see, for example, Beck, 1992). The media carry information to us about risk and are central to the kind of 'risk consciousness' that is created in a society. So how do they cover these issues?

If media coverage is a direct reflection of reality then the cover-age of environmental risk should be related in some consistent way to the established levels of danger associated with different hazards: those that pose the greatest level of risk should get the highest level of coverage, yet for the most part this is not what happens. Kitzinger and Reilly (1997) looked at the level of media attention given to different kinds of risk over a period in the early to mid-1990s in Britain. They found that the media gave more attention to some risks than others, and the amount of coverage was not proportionate to the levels of risk involved. Thus although genetic research poses considerable risk to a wide range of people, most notably the disabled, it attracted relatively little media atten-tion. Most newspaper articles, for example, tended to be one-off features, and the issue generated no long-term coverage. False memory syndrome, by contrast, attracted considerable attention and a high media profile. Yet it was, they argued, at best a minor-ity issue and a phenomenon whose actual existence was a source of considerable dispute. 'Mad Cow Disease' fell somewhere in between. It attracted considerable media attention at two points in their research period, the first in 1990 and the second in 1996. Yet although the disease and the risks that it posed did not go away in the intervening period, media attention did.

The ideal media: fair and informative?

The second research strategy uses a yardstick of a more political or citizenship-style nature to assess the nature of media coverage. It sets out how the media should operate in modern democratic societies. Media coverage is then compared to this yardstick to see if the media are fulfilling their role in an adequate and appropriate manner.

A Fair Media?   The most common yardstick used here is that of fairness or equality. A fair medium is one that gives equivalent or proportionate amounts of time or space to the range of viewpoints or political positions in a society. This is felt to be essential if citizens are to have the kind of information necessary for making the responsible choices on which democratic societies depend. So if, for any reason, one or other of these gets more time or emphasis then the media is being selective and failing in its responsibilities.

If we apply this standard to British and American newspapers they do not generally pass the test. Many are biased and make no apologies for it. The type of coverage they give is shaped by their political affiliations, and this coverage is intended for the particular section of the audience that shares their political perspective. However, there are some important differences between the print media in Britain and the USA in this regard.

According to Norris (2001:178), the British press is more partisan that that in the USA. Traditionally, the Conservative Party has had what Scammell and Harrop call (1997:183), a press 'surplus' over Labour. This averaged out at 15 per cent in the pre-Thatcher period and rose to 45 per cent during Margaret Thatcher's premiership. In the 1992 general election, for example, seven of the eleven daily newspapers supported the Tories.

There is some evidence of a disruption in this long-standing partisan bias. In the 1997 election, the Labour Party had the support of six out of the ten daily newspapers and five of the nine Sundays. This was unique and regarded by some as a landmark, as prior to this the party had only once had the support of 'as many as three national dailies' in 14 general elections from 1945 to 1992 (Seymour-Ure, 1997). Most writers characterise this as a dealignment of the press from their traditional links to particular parties, rather than as a realignment to new ones. This is driven by a commercial need to broaden their appeal to audiences who are increasingly detached (in a politically partisan sense at least).

However, unlike the printed media, television is required by law to be fair to the political parties. The close monitoring by the parties or formal inter-party agreements on equality of time ensure that this standard is met. In Britain, for example, television coverage is structured by the requirements of a 'stop-watch' balance (Semetko, Scammell and Goddard, 1997). News programmes keep count of the time allocated to the various parties to ensure that they give equal or proportionate time to the parties. The parties in turn check to see that the media get it right.

In the USA, there is little evidence of clear favouritism on television towards Republican or Democratic candidates in presidential elections (see Graber, 1980). The tone of reporting about candidates has changed considerably. Negative stories are now far more likely than positive ones (see Hallin, 1992), which does not produce biased media as good and bad news was distributed fairly equally between the parties. Similarly, there is no strong evidence of a liberal bias in the selection and distribution of soundbites among the candidates in elections (see, for example, Lowry and Shidler, 1995). In any direct sense of the term, then, television is generally not politically partisan.

An informative media?   If we move from formal equality as a criterion to that of informativeness, then claims about media selectivity are more fully documented and substantiated. Thomas Patterson and Robert McClure (1976), for example, argue that the role of the media is to facilitate the electorate in making informed political decisions. This means that they should provide information on the policy positions of the candidates and on where they stand on key political issues. The failure to do so represents selectivity by the media. A number of writers have used this as a standard to evaluate television coverage of presidential elections in the USA.

Lichter, Noyes and Kaid's (1998) work is typical of the genre. They looked at the nightly new bulletins of the three national networks during the traditional election period, from September to November 1996. They found that the election coverage had three features. One was the decline in the time given over to election issues, which went down from 25 minutes a night in the 1992 presidential election to 12.3 minutes a night in 1996.

The second was the continued decline in the amount of news time given to the words of the candidates, or to what are known as soundbites. This is the time a candidate is allowed to speak directly to the audience without interruption by journalists. The average soundbite in the 1968 election campaign was 42 seconds. By the 1992 campaign, it had fallen to 10 seconds and, in 1996, it fell again to 8.2 seconds.

The third, and most crucial, feature was the amount of this time devoted to policy issues. In 1996, around 37 per cent of election stories were about policy issues. This represented a decline over previous years in the 'absolute amount of coverage devoted to issues' (Lichter, Noyes and Kaid, 1998). Moreover, most of the coverage of policy issues was very brief. Sixty per cent of the 'mentions of policy' lasted less than 20 seconds. These were not for the most part about the substance of policies but about the political and electoral implications of the particular policy positions adopted by the candidates.

The decline in the time given to the candidates was balanced by a rise in the amount of time given to journalists. As Thomas Patterson (1994:75) points out, 'for every minute that the candidates spoke on the evening news in 1988 and 1992, the journalists who were covering them talked for 6 minutes'. It might be anticipated that the bulk of this time would be given to conveying information to the public, but this was not the case. Most of it was spent offering opinions, evaluations and analyses of candidates' performances and strategies. In other words, there has been a decline in the role of the journalist as information giver, and increasingly this role became one of 'arbiter, passing judgement on campaign events and strategies' (Steele and Barnhurst, 1996:198).

Research on television coverage of British elections indicates a number of differences from this pattern but also evidence of some growing similarities. In general, television in Britain tends to give more coverage to its national elections than is the norm in many other countries (Semetko, Scammell and Goddard, 1997), but research on the 1997 election confirmed the proliferation of soundbites and the denial of direct voice to politicians. According to Harrison (1997:145), 'only 17 per cent of election news coverage reported what politicians had said and only about 10 per cent was clips of direct speech'. The main evening news had 50 sound-bites of less than 10 seconds, with just ten lasting more than 50 seconds (Harrison, 1997:142). The average soundbites on the main evening news on the BBC was 16.5 seconds, whilst that on ITV was 14.7 seconds. Tony Blair, leader of the Labour Party, made a speech in which he spoke of 'the seven pillars of a decent society'. As a then aspiring Prime Minister, the precise nature of these might be of some interest to the electorate, yet his speech received 'only 13 seconds of coverage in an 80 second report' and only three of the pillars were mentioned (Harrison, 1997:142).

The decline in direct access to the words of candidates was accompanied by the increase in the commentary by political corres-pondents. According to Harrison (1997:145), 'they were heard as often and at greater length than the party leaders'. Their comments and those of 'experts' formed an increasing significant part of media coverage and resulted in a style of coverage 'heavily struc-tured or "framed" by journalists and experts' (Harrison, 1997:145).

When we combine these features – little overall time devoted to elections, little direct voice given to politicians and little coverage of issues – we are left with a situation in which 'voters in search of information about their candidates and their issue positions re-ceived little assistance from the nightly news' (Lichter, Noyes and Kaid, 1998:11).

Equality of argument?

The third way of looking at media selectivity is a variant of the second. It takes media coverage of controversial policy issues and asks if media coverage fully represents the range of expert views on the topic, or the range of arguments in society about the issue. If it does not then, according to this argument, we are looking at media selectivity.

An example of this approach is in the work of Lichter, Rothman, Rycroft and Lichter (1990). They surveyed the views of scientists, engineers and members of what they called the 'energy' community on the issue of nuclear power. They then looked at its coverage in the major newspapers, news magazines and television networks in the USA. They found that the aspects of nuclear power that the media emphasised diverged from those that experts considered significant and important. The experts believed that the safety risks of nuclear reactors were acceptable, and that they knew how to solve nuclear safety problems. The media, by contrast, focused on the issues and problems that had not yet been resolved, and this kind of coverage reflected in an adverse way on nuclear power and on the nuclear industry. Most energy specialists saw nuclear power as a positive force, while the media regularly presented it in a negative light.

Media power as selectivity

These kinds of research result suggest that media accounts differ in significant ways from the reality of events and from certain standards of adequate media performance. If we return to our initial question, 'Are the media selective?', then the answer from these researchers is 'Yes, they are.' The media do not provide a reliable and accurate guide to the range of important events in the social and political world.

On this basis many media sociologists argue that the source of media power lies in its ability to be selective in what it tells us about the world. It tells us about some issues and events and not about others. Thus it controls the information that is available to media audiences and so has the potential to shape or to set limits to their social knowledge and to the images that they can construct of the world in which they live.

This model of media power can be characterised as 'agenda-setting', after the formulation of McCombs and Shaw (1972).[1] They argue that people learn two things from the media: one is factual information, and the other is the salience or importance to attach to issues. If an issue or event gets extensive coverage then the audience is being told that it is an important one. If it gets little or no coverage then it is not important. This means that while the media 'may not be successful in telling us what to think', their power lies in that fact that they 'are stunningly successful in telling us what to think about' (McCombs and Shaw, 1972:66). The media's selection of news items and the differential emphasis given to them sets

---

1   It is important to point out that many accounts of agenda setting conflate two separate processes: that of *agenda setting*, in the sense of the media's selection of items for coverage and for differential emphasis, and that of *agenda transfer*, which is the process through which audiences may acquire the same set of saliences as those present in the media. This confuses the nature of the message being sent with the manner of its reception by audiences. This chapter deals with the issue of agenda setting in the above sense, while agenda transfer is dealt with in Chapter 7.

limits to what people know and what they talk about. Thus the ability to be selective is the source of the media's considerable power in society.

The problems of objective description

There is considerable agreement on issue of media selectivity, but a significant group of media sociologists believe that the notion has an important limitation, and this prevents it from fully encompassing (or, indeed, fully identifying) the nature of media power. The limitation is that the kind of research studies that we have considered are based on a central and unsustainable assumption: they assume that social reality exists in a concrete external manner. This makes it possible to describe and report on the social world in a neutral, balanced and comprehensive way; all that is required is the use of of appropriate objective journalistic techniques. This assumption is essential to concepts such as distortion and bias. Without it they have no meaning as they imply the possibility of undistorted and unbiased journalism. In principle, the media could be less biased or distorted if their accounts mirrored the nature of social reality more closely and objectively.

The issue, for many media sociologists (see Hackett, 1984), is that the problems of objective description are extensive. Where the print media are concerned it involves the assumption that language is a tool through which the events of the world can be described in a impartial and neutral fashion, but this is not that simple. Language, as Hackett (1984:236) tells us, is not 'a neutral transmission belt which can refer directly to a world of non-discursive objects'. The use of particular words to describe events and issues represents not merely the choice of a descriptive phrase but also the choice of an attitude towards the event or issue.

To characterise a trade union, for example, as making 'demands' and management as making 'offers' is to convey very different meanings about what are generally comparable negotiating strategies. Similarly, describing an attack as a 'mugging' conveys and mobilises a different range of associations and emotions from the use of the word 'assault'. There are also significantly different social and political implications involved in describing someone's death as a 'killing' or an 'assassination' rather than as a 'murder' (see Parenti, 1981:222).

Television: the (more) real thing?

These kinds of linguistic problem often appears to be solved on television, part of whose power comes from what Stuart Hall (1982:75) calls the 'naturalistic illusion'. The pictures that we see on our screens seem to be raw unmediated reality, and this appearance of authenticity gives them their particular power and influence. But appearances are deceptive. These pictures are, in a number of important ways, the products of human decision-making. These include decisions about the events to send television cameras to, the distance to put them from the people or events to be filmed, the selection of parts of the resultant material for transmission, and decisions about the content of the accompanying voice-over.

The meaning of television footage depends, for example, on the position from which the filming takes place. In riot situations the police generally insist that television crews and press photographers position themselves behind the police lines. Their intention may be to ensure the physical protection of media personnel but, as Hansen and Murdock (1985:251) point out, these angles encourage the viewer 'to see the situation through police eyes and by extension to share their perspective on events'. Hence what the cameras record is the police view of the riot and not that of the rioters.

The kinds of camera shot used are also important. Different kinds of attitudes are conveyed by different camera angles. 'Tight' camera shots reproduce the kind of closeness that either indicates respect for the people being filmed or, alternatively, can be construed as the form of aggression conveyed by the invasion of private space (see Tuchman, 1978). The medium-long shot, by contrast, includes people's heads and shoulders and so appears to be more objective in that the camera adopts the spectator's perspective on events. Through placing the viewer in the position of onlooker, it represents what might be termed 'cultural neutrality' at a visual level.

A number of studies show important differences in the distribution of camera shots between the different participants in television news. Loshitzky (1991), for example, has pointed out that there were very few 'close-ups' or 'zoom-ins' on Palestinians in Israeli television coverage of violent incidents in the Intifada. One of the few individuals shown in close-up was an Israeli general. A 'medium-long' shot would have seen him amid scenes of disorder surrounded by microphones, journalists and camera crews. The use of the close-up, by contrast, conveyed the impression of order, of respect and, most importantly in the circumstances, of control.

For these reasons, the 'realism' of television is deceptive. It is not 'raw' reality that unfolds before our eyes, but a mediated and selected version of it. This means that bias and selectivity are not accidental features of the media: they are inevitable features of the language we use to describe the world, of the visual technology that we use to capture images of it, and of the communication process through which newspapers and television convey their accounts of the world. Accordingly the important question for media studies is not the presence or absence of bias or selectivity; it is the nature of the perspective from which the media describes and interprets the social world. To understand this more thoroughly requires us to give consideration to the notion of 'framing'.

Getting beyond the issue of media selectivity: the idea of framing

The basic argument about framing is that the media do not simply provide us with information on certain issues and events: they also provide us with perspectives on them. These place the events and issues within particular contexts and encourage audiences to understand them in particular ways. In effect, the media do not simply select events to cover; they also offer interpretative frameworks through which these are to be understood.

These frameworks or perspectives are what media sociologists refer to as 'frames'. They are the 'persistent patterns of cognition, interpretation, and presentation, of selection, emphasis, and exclusion, by which symbol-handlers routinely organize discourse, whether verbal or visual' (Gitlin, 1980:7). They enable audiences, Goffman (1974:21) tells us, to 'locate, perceive, identify, and label' the information that is coming at them about the nature of the social world.

The coverage of illegal drug use provides a useful illustration of how media framing works. McLeod, Kosicki and Pan (1991) have pointed out that there are a number of perspectives through which the issue could be framed. It could be told through a 'public or social health' frame, which would look at the issue from the point of view of the users. It would consider the quality of users' lives and how this influences their drug taking. This would lead to a particular set of questions, such as what is it in their lives that makes drug use seem such an attractive option? Equally, the story could be told as an 'economic' one, treating illegal drugs as simply another consumable good and as such on par with legal drugs, such as tobacco and alcohol. This would raise issues about the legalisation of drugs such as cannabis and the use of taxation policy to control consumption. The third possible frame is 'crime' one. Illegal drugs could be presented as a criminal matter, which in turn would raise issues about legislation, law enforcement and punishment. The main point is that each frame positions the problems in a very different way and so has different implications for how we understand the nature of, and the solutions to, the drugs problem.

How does this differ from media selectivity?

At first sight this idea may not appear to be significantly different from that of media selectivity. In the selectivity model the media have the power to select the events and issues that are given coverage; however, in the framing argument they have the power to be selective about what is covered but also the power to interpret events and issues for us. Media frames do not simply include some issues and events rather than others but they also, as Entman (1993:52) puts it, 'define problems ... diagnose causes, make moral judgements and suggest remedies'.

The example of the media coverage of conflict in Northern Ireland may clarify the difference. The perspective of media selectivity would lead us to look at the kinds of issues and events that get covered, and in particular those which do not. Thus we might consider, for example, the alleged failure of the British media to give coverage to police and army harassment of the civilian population. The framing argument would accept this, but it would go further and suggest that the perspective from which the media cover the issues is also important. Presenting Northern Ireland through the frame of the British state as an independent adjudicator between two warring and not entirely rational 'tribes' is not simply reporting the conflict: it is also suggesting a particular and limited way of understanding it (see Miller, 1994).

Framing: the heart of media power?

The notion of framing, media sociologists argue, brings us to the heart of the problem of media power. It provides the study of the media with a concept that William Gamson (1992:384) says is 'indispensable'. It also suggests the central questions in the study of media power. If media power is the capacity to present issues and events within particular frames and so potentially limit and control how these are understood, then the following are important questions. What frames do the media bring to bear on events and how can we identify them? Is there a consistent pattern to the frames that are used to represent the world to us? Do some groups and institutions have a greater capacity than others to influence and shape the frames used by the media? Do audiences accept the frames used and the meanings they are intended to convey?

Questions about the consistency and sources of frames are taken up in the next chapter. Questions about audiences are dealt with in Chapter 7. In the remainder of this chapter, however, we look further at how frames might be identified.

A fractured paradigm?

The concept of framing is a central one in media sociology but, as William Gamson (1992:384) has pointed out, its precise meaning is 'elusive'. There is broad agreement on its importance in that all who use the term share the assumption that media power is the power to frame events and issues in particular ways. But there are considerable differences in how sociologists use the idea, and there are different ways through which they identify the frames in media material.

These difficulties arise because frames in media texts do not announce or highlight themselves but appear as natural and obvious ways of telling stories and of relating events to us. Thus when, for example, the media tell the story of US presidential elections as a 'horse race' story – which candidate is currently ahead in the polls – rather than as an 'issue' story – where do the candidates differ on matters of policy – they do not signal this in advance to readers or viewers. They do not forewarn them that it is going to be that kind of story, or indeed that the same events could be told as a different kind of news story. The responses of researchers to this dilemma can be classified into two distinct research strategies (see Semetko and Valkenberg, 2000). The first is inductive and involves setting criteria, generally fairly loose ones, for the identification of frames. These are then applied to particular media texts to draw out the underlying frames that are structuring the text, or are latent in it. The examples we use here are from research on Western intervention in Kosovo, the media portrayal of mental illness, and the work of Robert Entman (1991).

From text to frame

The reluctant bombers: the West in Kosovo.   The first example of the search for frames is typical of the inductive approach. Researchers begin with what Semetko and Valkenburg (2000:94) describe as 'loosely defined preconceptions of these frames', and through an analysis of the stories they 'reveal the range of frames used'. Using this, three central frames or interpretative frameworks were identified in the Western media's coverage of the conflict in Kosovo in 1999 (Vincent, 2000), and particularly in that of CNN (Thussu, 2000). The first was the framing of Serbian action in Kosovo as 'terrorist' and Western intervention as 'humanitarian'. The bombing by the West was framed as a necessary but reluctant act of the last resort by benign and well-intentioned Western governments, aided by their military wing, NATO. Two subsidiary but complementary frames supported this. The first was the demonisation of the Serbian leader, Slobodan Milosevic. He was framed as the epitome of evil, thus turning Western actions into a moral crusade against a dictator who resorts to terrorist action. The second was the selective emphasis on atrocities committed by the Serbians and the exaggeration of their extent. One report of the mass rape of 20,000 women was, for example, based on interviews with four victims (Vincent, 2000:329).

This framing depended on the omission of certain items of information and the rationalisation of others. The portrayal of the Kosovo Liberation Army as a group of freedom fighters on the side of the West required the omission of key aspects of the army's recent past, most notably the fact that up to a year before this it had been seen in the West as a terrorist organisation and was widely believed by human rights organisations to be involved in drug smuggling (Thussu, 2000:351). The portrayal of the Serbs as evil aggressors required also that what Vincent (2000:337) saw as 'NATO-committed atrocities' (namely, the killing of Serbian civilians by Western bombing) had to be presented in media coverage as either accidental or justified.

Sick or psycho? The media and mental distress.   The Glasgow University Media Group (1997) wanted to find the dominant messages or interpretative frames that were used in the coverage of mental health and mental distress. They took an extensive sample of the media in Britain for one month in 1993, including the main evening news bulletins, local news programmes, current affairs and documentary programmes and eight national newspapers. They looked at the headlines over stories, the type of news language used in them, the kind of people that are identified in news stories as mentally ill, and the kind of behaviours that were associated with them.

From this they identified five main themes in media coverage. These were those of 'violence to others', 'violence to oneself', 'treatment and recovery' issues, criticism of accepted definitions of mental illness, and the use of images of mental illness for comic purposes. They found few positive images of mentally ill people, and few stories about the capacity of mentally ill people to recover. The dominant theme was that of 'violence to others'. It outnumbered the next most common category – treatment issues – by a ratio of at least 4 to 1. They concluded that the media world of mental illness is 'very much one that is populated by "psychopaths", "maniacs' and frenzied knife men" '.

Robert Entman: on innocent and not so innocent civilians.   Robert Entman's (1991) approach to framing, while still inductive, is somewhat more systematic in its methodology. He argues that there are five aspects of a media text that need to be considered in the search for media frames. Each aspect does not necessarily feature in every media story, and neither will it necessarily have the same level of importance and emphasis; but together they provide a framework through which the framing in media stories can be identified. The relevant categories are set out below.

1 'Sizing judgements': these are the amount of space and the degree of prominence given to stories by the media. The importance of a story is signalled by its placement on the front page of a newspaper or as the lead item in a news bulletin. A decisive statement of the media's belief in the 'irrelevance' of an event is its omission.

2 Agency: this refers to the media's use of particular words and images to suggest how and where responsibility for an event being reported should be placed.

3 Identification: this looks at the use of particular words and images that encourage or discourage identification with those most directly involved in the media story.

4 Categorisation: this is the way in which the media label events or issues. Different categorisations encourage us to look at events in very different ways. There are, for example, major differences between reporting an event as an 'accident' and reporting it as a 'crime'.

5 Generalisation is the degree to which the media generalise from an incident or issue in the news story to the nature of the political system in which the event occurred or the issue arose.

Entman applies these categories to the media coverage of the shooting-down of two civilian aircraft. One, Korean AirLines Flight 007, was shot down by the Soviets in 1983, and the other, Iran Air Flight 655, by a US Navy ship in 1988. In both cases, those involved claimed that the passenger planes were possible enemy targets, the relevant government officials defended the action, and in both cases 'deadly military force was applied against nearly 300 innocent human beings' (Entman, 1991:10).

He argues that although these events were similar in most respects, the major American media framed them in very different ways. The incident involving the USA was framed as 'accidental', while that involving the Soviets was treated as 'criminal'. It was given less space than the Russian one. It was described as 'ghastly' and 'tragic', whereas the Russian one was described as 'murder'. The victims of the American action were described as 'passengers' and 'travellers', those of the Russian action were described as 'loved ones' and as 'innocent victims'. Finally the Russian action was seen as the inevitable product of the Soviet system, while responsibility in the US incident was much more limited. It was confined to the officer in charge and to the US Navy.

From frames to media texts

In the second and more common strategy, the deductive one, researchers list the range of frames – or what Murdock (1994) calls 'the discursive formations' – that are available to make sense of events or issues in a society. Media texts are then analysed to see which of these frames are actually or predominantly used in the media account. The examples we consider here are from the Glasgow University Media Group (1997), Daley and O'Neill (1991) and Thomas E. Patterson (1994).

The Glasgow University Media Group: telling us about AIDS.   According to the Glasgow University Media Group (Miller, Kitzinger, Williams and Beharrell, 1998) there were four main political positions on the issue of AIDS in Britain in the late 1980s. The first of these was the conservative moralist position, which saw the problem as rooted in permissiveness and as being resolved by a return to monogamy and abstinence. The second was the libertarian view, which rejected the notion of a heterosexual epidemic of AIDS and regarded it as part of a conspiracy to justify state intervention in people's lives. The liberal/medical perspective regarded everyone as at risk of getting the disease through sexual intercourse, and argued that the solution lay in public education. This message was seen as a matter of common sense and, as such, beyond politics. The final position was the critical one, which rejected the view of universal risk: the problem was largely one of and for gay men. AIDS was being 'degayed', whereas the need was to 'regay' the problem. Media campaigns and coverage reinforced the stigma of homosexuality and medicalised many gay practices. It also reinforced racism through the association of Africa with the origins of the disease.

The researchers looked to see which of these perspectives was most prominent in British media coverage and particularly in television news. The period they analysed was from 1986 to 1990. They found that the dominant interpretative frame was the liberal/medical one. Television news 'displayed . . . an almost total acceptance of the orthodox line on the risks of heterosexual transmission' and 'supported the idea of an information campaign to change sexual behaviour' (Miller and Beharell, 1998:72, 75). The adoption of this frame enabled journalists to be critical of the government if its actions diverged from those demanded by the liberal/medical perspective; but it also meant that the views of the moral right were, effectively speaking, excluded. Similarly, alternative and more critical representations of the disease were comparatively rare. This kind of framing 'carried with it an implicit disregard for the impact of the epidemic on gay men' (Miller and Beharell, 1998:72).

Daley and O'Neill: the politics of oil spills.   The second example is
from the research of Daley and O'Neill (1991). The setting for their
study was the oil industry in Alaska, topical then and topical once
again in George Bush's America. By the late 1980s, it had become a
major economic and social force with almost 80 per cent of the
state's revenue coming from the industry, but its relationship with
the local population was an uneasy one. It was involved in disputes
with the local Indian population over the symbolic meaning of land,
and with the environmental movement over its potential for destruction. It was against this background that a giant oil tanker, the
Exxon Valdez, hit a reef in Prince William Sound on 24 March 1989
and began to leak over 25,000 gallons of oil an hour into the sea.
Daley and O'Neill looked at how the media responded to this.

They identified a number of frames, or what they call 'narratives', which the media could have used to make sense of the
incident. The first was the narrative of corporate responsibility,
which located the source of the accident in corporate pressures to
maximise profits. These require captains of oil tankers to keep
their ships running even if this means short-circuiting safety
standards. A second possible narrative was the disaster one,
which sees oil spills as the result of a natural, if unfortunate, set
of circumstances, such as the unpredictability of forces of nature
including the weather and the sea.

The third possible narrative was the criminal one. Here oil spills
are due to the criminal incompetence or negligence of some identifiable individual who is then blamed for it. The fourth narrative was
the environmental one, which stresses the environmental aspects of
the spillage and focuses on the political and administrative issues
posed by attempts to regulate the relationship between industry
and the environment. The final narrative frame was the subsistence
one, which presents the spill from the viewpoint of the groups most
directly affected by it (in this case the native Indian communities),
and focuses on the potentially devastating implications it had for
the balance of their subsistence economy.

They then looked at the media to see which of these narratives
structured their coverage of the issue and found that the predominant narrative strategy was the disaster one. This presented the
spill as a 'natural' disaster, and as such it had no obvious social
cause and no obvious group to whom responsibility could be
attributed. The effect of this kind of narrative was to 'naturalise'
the spill and move it into the context of technological inevitability
rather than those of corporate or political failure.

Other frames came into play in subsequent coverage, the first being the criminal one. The media drew attention to the past and present drinking history of the captain of the *Exxon Valdez* who was still drunk nine hours after the tanker had run aground. In the process he found himself the villain of the piece. The second was the environmental narrative. Follow-up stories looked at issues such as the trade-off between development through the oil industry and the environmental concern with the effects on the wilderness and on animal life. What is most significant is that two narratives were almost entirely absent in media coverage: that of subsistence, and that of corporate responsibility.

Thomas E. Patterson: story types.   The third way of moving from frames to media texts is through the notion of story type. According to this there are several types of story available through which we can relate the events of the world. The effect of telling an event as one kind of story is to give emphasis and prominence to certain aspects of the event and to marginalise others. In the case of a racial disturbance, for example, the media can tell us about it in a number of different ways using a range of different story types. It could be told as a crime story, as a social injustice story, or as a political one. As a crime story, responsibility would be attributed to the criminal inclinations of the rioters. In the injustice story, deprived social conditions would be held responsible, and in the political one the political authorities that allowed such conditions to exist would be held responsible.

There is a range of story lines or story types through which political campaigns can be covered. They can be told as stories about the policy positions of candidates or about their particular qualifications for leadership, although this sort of story line is seldom used in the coverage of US presidential elections. Thomas E. Patterson (1994), for example, argues that the 'game schema' or the 'horse race' story line has replaced them. This tells the story of elections through the excitement and spectacle of the campaign and through the tactics and manoeuvrings of candidates, rather than through accounts of their policies on major political and social issues.

In keeping with the 'game' theme, media coverage stresses which candidate is leading in the opinion polls and what the other candidates are going to do to remedy this. The success or failure of these strategies is assessed by whether candidates subsequently move up or down in the polls. The actions of candidates are also increasingly presented through the theme of manipulation. Candidates are portrayed as adjusting their positions on issues not because they believe in the changes, but because they feel the changes will improve their ratings in the polls. Similarly, media coverage of political debates between candidates does not focus on who has the most appropriate and workable solution to the problem of drugs or of free trade; instead, it centres on the much more limited question of which candidate won. This, Patterson (1994) argues, is the reporting of elections as if they are a spectator sport rather than the means through which voters democratically choose their leaders.

The British situation is not so clear-cut. Many of the trends identified by Patterson are also in evidence, but they have not gone as far as in the USA because the public service ethos acts as a constraining factor. After the 1983 general election Butler and Kavanagh (1983) argued that the increasing emphasis of the media on the results of opinion polls was diverting attention away from the issues. This was also a problem in the 1992 election where 12 per cent of television news was concerned with the polls. There was a decline in coverage of the opinion polls on the 1997 election, a decline attributed to the fact that Labour were so far ahead in them (see Norris, Curtice, Sanders, Scammell and Semetko, 1999:72).

This was not replaced or compensated for by increasing attention to the policy issues that separated the parties. The parties wanted to talk about education, welfare and health, but 'the top three stories on television news and in the press were the conduct of the campaign, the parties, and the opinion polls' (Norris *et al.*, 1999:83). There was less focus on the horse race aspects than in the 1992 election, but this was because there was little doubt over the result. Journalists focused instead on the day-to-day activities of the leading politicians and on the tactics being adopted by the major parties. As Norris and her colleagues say, 'these speak to a strategic focus of the news, rather than a policy focus' (1999:83).

Unresolved issues in the study of media framing

These examples show the importance of framing in the analysis of the media. It is a key concept through which the nature of media power can be understood. There are, however, a number of unresolved problems with it.

The first is that movement of the argument from media bias and media selectivity to media framing causes, as Matthew Kieran (1997) has pointed out, particular problems. Under the notion of bias it is possible to talk about issues such as accuracy of news and the control or removal of bias, but under the terms of the concept of framing it does not seem possible to ask similar questions.

If framing is an inevitable feature of news, then how can we distinguish between good and bad journalism or between accurate and inaccurate news reporting? In this way, the framing argument could be criticised for promoting 'a kind of relativism' in which there is ultimately no difference between one news account and another (Philo, 1990:199). As we shall see in the next chapter, this is exactly how post-modern theorists see the issue. For other theorists, the relevant criteria would be that the media should reflect in their content a meaningful diversity of interpretations or frames.

The second is the assumption that researchers can identify frames independently of the perceptions and responses of readers or viewers. This has been criticised by those who claim that media texts are, in a strictly formal sense, meaningless, and that the alleged structuring is an imposition of researchers. This means that their versions of media stories cannot claim to be the 'real' version. According to Anderson and Sharrock (1979:367), conclusions about meaning are not implicit in texts, and media material is 'amenable to other readings'. The validity of analyses of framing therefore depend not on the inherent meaning of media texts – they have none – but on the resourceful readings of these texts by researchers, so when researchers from different political and theoretical positions approach the same material they quite often come to different conclusions about its meaning. The response of those in the framing tradition has been to initiate studies of audiences to look at the degree to which audiences accept or reject the frames they have identified. This is discussed further in Chapter 7.

The third issue relates to the meaning of the term 'frame' and to divisions among theorists as to the number of frames that can be present in a media text. So, for example, there appear to be conceptual differences between the approach to framing of Robert Entman (1993) and William Gamson (1989). Where Entman is concerned, media coverage is structured around one particular frame. He argues that when a story is framed in a particular way, information that is not consistent with this framework can be included, but it is included in a way that renders it consistent with the dominant frame in the story or that reduces the dissonance it is likely to cause for readers or viewers.

However, Gamson (1989) has raised the possibility that there might be more than one frame present in news stories. He argues that we need to analyse the degree to which different perspectives on an issue or an event are given prominence in the same news report. In other words, a range of interpretations can be found in the one story. The important question, then, is not simply which frames are present in a story, but which one is given most prominence.

The differences between the two are important, as the power of a media text to shape audience perceptions of the issue or event may be dependent on the coherence of that text. A text organised around a single frame could be assumed to be a more powerful one than one that contains a number of perspectives on the same event.

Conclusion

In this chapter we have outlined and examined the argument that the power of the media is the power to represent the world to us in particular ways. As such, this power has two elements: one is the capacity to be selective in the events and issues that it covers; the other is the capacity to tell us about these events though particular frames or from particular perspectives. For some media sociologists, media power is restricted to the capacity to be selective (as, for example, in the theories around agenda setting). However, it is more common for media sociologists to combine both elements.

Thus many media sociologists would follow Robert Entman's (1993:52) definition of framing, or the closely related one of Todd Gitlin (1980). They see framing as the power to select events for coverage and to interpret these events in particular ways. This leads to a series of questions: do the media consistently favour, privilege and publicise a limited or a wide range of interpretations in their coverage of news and current affairs? And are there connections between the range of interpretations or frames present in the media and the power structures of a society? These issues are explored in the next chapter.

CHAPTER 3

Whose Frames?

Introduction

In the previous chapter we argued that selectivity and framing are central aspects of media power. We also identified a number of questions which need to be addressed if we wish to develop this argument more fully. Is there a pattern to the selectivity of the media? Is this one which is favourable to one or other particular political or social perspective? Alternatively, are the frames that are used specific to the stories being reported, or can we identify a pattern or a set of common or over-arching elements in them?

These issues are explored in this chapter, which has two sections. The first deals with the answers given by media sociologists to the questions raised above. For ease of presentation these answers have been categorised under five distinctive headings. The second section deals with the issue of assessing these perspectives, and criticisms of each are identified and discussed.

The answers from media sociology

The view from the left: the role of the dominant ideology

The first answer is from a broadly Marxist or critical position. This argues that the prevailing direction of selectivity and the predominant pattern of framing in the media is one that is compatible with the interests of the dominant class or power group in society. This means that a consistent and coherent range of oppositional or critical readings of situations and events is not available in the mass media. This deficiency, effectively speaking, sets limits to the range of information and interpretation that is available in society and this makes it easier for the powerful to secure their position.

The contemporary citizen as the new peasant.   Jürgen Habermas (1989) is one of the most prominent theorists to be identified with this position. He has argued that there is an area of social life in which public opinion is formed, and he calls this the public sphere. This is an arena to which, ideally at least, all citizens have access and in which all have the right to speak. As such, it is a social space in which private opinions can be communicated, debated and ex-changed and out of which 'a reason-based public opinion' emerges. It is also the arena in which public authorities can be called upon to debate and justify their decisions. The media have been central to this sphere in that an independent press has functioned as a vehicle for the exchange of ideas, information and argument.

Such a sphere, Habermas (1989) argues, emerged in Europe in the late eighteenth century. However, it no longer exists in what he calls 'mass welfare-state democracies'. The public sphere, and the ra-tional debate that characterised it, has been transformed by power politics. The world is increasingly dominated by large commercial and bureaucratic organisations which make agreements and deals with each other and with the state. Ideally they would like to do this behind closed doors, but in democratic societies they need the approval of the mass of the population for their actions. They use their control of the media to achieve this. This transforms the mass media from a sphere for open debate into the means through which this approval is produced and secured.

He characterises this process as the refeudalisation of society. Under feudalism the principle of open debate was denied in favour of the assertions of voices of authority. A similar problem now exists in contemporary society. The media no longer act as a centre for rational debate and discussion and for the presentation of the widest possible range of interpretations and arguments, but instead as a means through which the powerful can secure the consent of the masses. (Habermas has recently made significant modifications in his position: see Habermas, 1998. It can now be best characterised as a liberal pluralist one.)

Controlling the common-sense?   Habermas, however, was not pri-marily a theorist of the media but others have developed argu-ments similar to his. The work of Stuart Hall is important here. He argued that 'ideological power is the power to signify events in a particular way', and the power of the media is the power to represent the capitalist order in a way that makes it 'appear universal, natural and coterminous with reality itself' (Hall, 1982:69, 65). The media achieves this through framing events and issues in terms drawn from 'a very limited ideological or explanatory repertoire' (Hall: 1977:340) and in ones that are broadly favourable to ruling class versions of these events.

Striking news. He gives the example of industrial disputes, a form of social action that was more common in the 1970s but is not unknown in the contemporary period (Hall, 1982). There are a number of ways in which these could be portrayed by the media: they could be presented as examples of 'greedy' workers wanting more, as rational and justified attempts by employees to improve their working conditions, or as part of the wider defence of class interests by the working class. Each of these perspectives is available in society and each has very different implications for how disputes are interpreted and understood, and (most crucially) for how they should be responded to. However, the one most consistently and recurrently chosen by the media is that of 'greedy' workers which, given the low standing of greed in most catalogues of virtue, implies that their demands are probably illegitimate and most definitely to be resisted.

It is important to acknowledge that this argument does not imply that the media suppresses coverage of conflicts and social antagonisms: the central set of values that underpins the current social order is not a coherent one. The democratic shell, within which the oyster of capitalism thrives, brings with it many values to which ruling groups may have considerable difficulty accommodating. The commitment to equality and citizenship, for example, is central to democracy, but it sits uneasily alongside the notion of hierarchy and the restricted access to wealth and authority which capitalism creates. If the media is to retain its credibility, it must report on the range of issues generated by these kinds of value conflict. The problem, according to Gitlin (1980:257), is that these conflicts are presented 'within a hegemonic framework which bounds and narrows the range of actual and potential contending world views'. In this sense suppression is not the issue; it is the narrow frameworks provided by the media to interpret what is going on the world.

No guarantees.   It is also important to appreciate that while the
object of the framing process in the media may be to ensure that
audiences accept the dominant meaning, this acceptance is not
automatically assured. A media message may be intended to
have a particular meaning or to be interpreted within a particular
framework, but this does not ensure that it will be perceived as
such by audiences. However, while Hall (1980:135) accepts that
audiences have some freedom to 'misinterpret', they do not have
absolute autonomy to read what they like into media messages.
There must be some reciprocity between the meanings intended
by media producers and those taken up by media audiences,
otherwise communication becomes impossible.

In the terms of this argument, then, the role of the media is to
reproduce the definitions of social reality of the powerful. Contradictory ideologies and perspectives do occasionally appear in the
public sphere and there is no guarantee that audiences will interpret media messages in the anticipated manner. Thus, while the
dominant frames in media accounts typically favour the interests
of powerful groups, ideological consent or control is neither auto-
matic nor guaranteed.

Dominance in diversity: the new pluralism

The second perspective argues that the media form the arena
within which a range of viewpoints and interpretations contest
and compete for dominance and for control over how the issues
and events are defined and presented. In certain circumstances and
for certain issues and events, oppositional framings and critical
interpretations can secure a considerable – if not a dominant –
level of media coverage. Thus while the powerful may have certain
advantages in such contests it is not a foregone conclusion that they
will always win them. A number of writers can be included here:
William Gamson and his colleagues in the USA, and British sociologists such as Michael Gurevitch, Jay Blumler and Philip Schlesinger. They all agree on the comparative openness of the media
but differ on how the limitations on access to the media might be
conceptualised.

William Gamson.   William Gamson, writing alone (1989) and with
his colleagues (1987, 1992a and 1992b), for example, argues that

there is a variety of interpretative packages or frames available in the culture of a society through which events and issues can be understood. These are promoted by social groups and social movements who compete to get their particular insights on to the media agenda. In effect, there is a contest over whose interpretation will predominate and the media form the arena in which this goes on. The winner of the contest is the sponsor of the package or frame that succeeds in dominating news coverage.

Powerful groups have certain advantages in promoting their point of view, most notably a high level of material resources to devote to its dissemination. However, they are not guaranteed success. In certain circumstances and on certain issues, other groups can significantly influence media coverage. So, for example, the Peace Movement in the USA did not have the same advantages as its establishment opponents in promoting its perspective on the Gulf War; none the less, it had some success in getting it on to the media agenda.

Gamson and his colleagues (1992a) have developed this point: they see media discourse as having two separate dimensions. The first is the 'unproblematic' and 'uncontested', which is made up of issues and events that are felt by the media to be so obviously non-contentious that it is unnecessary to give space to opposing viewpoints or perspectives. Their examples include American media coverage of its foreign policy. This is regarded as such an 'uncontested' topic that its domestic critics, such as Noam Chomsky, get virtually no coverage.

The other dimension – the 'problematic' or 'contested' – encompasses those issues and events over which there may legitimately be conflicting points of view and differences in interpretation. It is in the coverage of these that alternative and competing frames are more likely to be found. These issues activate journalistic norms of balance and, while non-establishment groups may not have the same access, they still feature in the media contest for interpretative dominance. It may not be an equal contest but, as Gamson and his colleagues (1992a:382) put it, 'even an uneven contest on a tilted playing field is a contest'. According to this formulation, then, the degree of plurality of viewpoints and perspectives in the media will depend on whether the issue involved falls most readily into the 'unproblematic' or the 'contested' realms.

Blumler and Gurevitch: the sacerdotal and the pragmatic. The notion of a more diverse media is also proposed by a number of British writers, most notably Blumler and Gurevitch (1986), Blumler (1969) and Schlesinger (1990). Blumler and Gurevitch argue that media coverage can be considered as a continuum. At one end is the *sacerdotal*, in which particular groups, organisations and institutions are covered as of right. At the other end is the *pragmatic*, where coverage depends on those involved meeting media standards of newsworthiness. If the media orientation to an event or issue is sacerdotal then coverage is likely to be framed in the terms of the group or institution and the issues are likely to be portrayed in a manner that is favourable to the group. If, on the other hand, the media orientation is pragmatic, then coverage will be on the media's terms and the perspectives of those involved will not be given much recognition.

While most groups and organisations aspire to sacerdotal status, Blumler and Gurevitch argue that the attitude the media adopts to them will reflect their position in the social hierarchy. Thus the coverage of religious and political institutions in Britain, such as the established Church and Parliament, is generally respectful because they are felt to embody the central values of society. The activities of 'half-way' institutions, such as business organisations and trade unions, tend to be reported in a mixture of the sacerdotal and the pragmatic, with the balance of the coverage veering towards the pragmatic: that is, they are covered in terms of the relative newsworthiness of their actions. Finally, groups and organisations such as football hooligans, criminals and terrorists are seen as so opposed to societal values that coverage is totally on the media's terms and the opposing perspectives are not acknowledged or given any legitimacy.

Philip Schlesinger and the concept of doxa.   Philip Schlesinger (1990) also accepts that the dominance of the powerful is not inevitable. He argues that the media is an arena of contest between rival perspectives and that this contest can, within certain limits, be open. He conceptualises these limits through the term *doxa*. This is borrowed from the work of French sociologist, Pierre Bourdieu. It refers to 'the aggregate of the presuppositions which the antagonists regard as self-evident and outside the field of argument' (quoted in Schlesinger, 1990:78). These presuppositions constitute what might usefully be considered as the collective common-sense of a society, but they are also a reflection of the structure of power in that the perspectives of the powerful tend to be over-represented in the maxims of the collective common-sense. They influence media coverage in that if issues are considered part of the *doxa* of a society then coverage is on terms favourable to the powerful. When issues are not part of the *doxa* there can be a contest over whose frame will shape media coverage.

The view from the right

The third perspective is a mirror image of the first but from the opposite end of the political and ideological spectrum. It claims that the key elements in the selection and framing processes are drawn from liberal or left perspectives on the social and political world. These contribute to the creation and perpetuation of an 'adversary' culture which advocates scepticism about, and creates cynicism towards, all forms of authority, particularly that of a political nature.

This perspective on the media has had considerable influence at a political level, in the often uneasy relationships that exist between conservative political parties and social movements and the media. However, it remains somewhat under-developed at a theoretical level, though sophisticated versions of the position can be found in the work of Frederic Lynch (1993) and Austin Ranney (1983). Both are Americans, and their arguments have most direct application to that country's media. None the less, echoes of the argument can also be found in speeches of British Tory politicians.

Political correctness rules.   Lynch (1993) claims that the dominant perspective of the media in the USA is a liberal one and that an ideology of political correctness structures their selection of issues and events. Those that are compatible with this liberal ideology get extensive coverage, while those that are not are left out. This means, he argues, that issues such as the level of teenage pregnancies, the crack epidemic, illegal immigration, the rise in violent crime, the breakdown in inner-city family structures, and the true extent and the real causes of AIDS are almost totally ignored by the media.

Where is the Radical Right?   Ranney (1983) has also argued for this perspective, although he claims that the problem with the media is not its anti-establishment bias but rather its pro-establishment one. He believes that the media are 'extra-ordinarily uncritical' (Ranney, 1983:6) of the character of government in the USA. The media seem to be unaware of alternative economic policies, particularly those that are market-based and which involve a reduction in the role of the government and an increased role for the market and for the private sector. The media also quote government sources as if they were impartial experts rather than partisan participants in the making and defence of public policy. These tendencies are evident in a willingness to blame economic failure on the private sector and to see economic crises as ones which, if they are not engineered by big business, are certainly ones from which they benefit.

In this way, these arguments suggest, the selection and framing processes in the media are permeated with themes and interpretations that are drawn from the liberal or radical agenda or from the kind of adversarial culture that developed in the 1960s. Alternative perspectives, especially those of the radical right, do not have equality of access and the result is media that fail to reflect recent ideological changes fully, most notably the disenchantment with 'big' government.

The view from feminism: The media as a man's world

The fourth perspective comes from the feminist tradition. It embraces a variety of political positions but, broadly speaking, these share a belief in the centrality of gender as the structuring principle in media discourse. For them the media play a central role in the construction and justification of a society organised around gender divisions. As Dyer (1987:6) puts it, 'men own and control the media and it is their ideas, viewpoints and values which dominate the systems of production and representation'. A gendered production process inevitably produces a gendered representation of the world.

This perspective has been applied extensively in studies of the representation of women in television fiction and these will be dealt with in Chapter 6. However, as van Zoonen (1994:65) points out, the news has been 'relatively untouched by feminist research'. Their basic position is that the predominant media frames stress the insignificance of women and the degree to which their rightful place is in the domestic or private sphere. This inevitably produces news that is, in the words of Butler and Paisley (1980:217), 'more alien to the socio-political concerns of most women than of most men'.

The ways women get in. Few women are included in news and current affairs coverage. When they are there, they are, according to Rakow and Kranich (1991), limited to three roles. The first and most significant is to illustrate the private consequences of public events and issues. Thus, where crime is concerned they show up as victims of crime or relatives of victims, or as passive reactors expressing suitable levels of outrage. Carter (1998) found that the majority of sources used to explain the social sources of sexual violence were male.

The second role is as spokespersons for organisations and institutions, though typically these are ones that are close to the nurturing roles of women in the private sphere, such as crime victim support groups and child protection organisations. The third role is as feminists, and this is one in which they are typically on the defensive. They are present to defend political or ideological positions that the media are framing as unusual, unorthodox or simply bizarre. This is an aspect of the way in which issues that involve women are framed in terms of melodrama or soap opera. As Penley and Willis (1993:viii–ix) point out, they are 'trivialized as successive episodes of a spectacularized and romanticized battle of the sexes'.

A great wall or a media wall? This theme can be found in the media coverage of the United Nations Fourth World Conference on Women. This was held in Beijing, China, in September 1995. Its objective was to review the progress that had been made in advancing the concerns of women since the previous conference ten years before. These included issues of poverty, education, health, violence and human rights. Yet an analysis of the media coverage of the conference showed that there was little attention to these substantive issues (Danner and Walsh, 1999). Instead the media focused on its allegedly poorly organised nature and on disagreements between women's groups over issues of policy, referred to by the media as 'bickering'.

Violence against women. The area of violence against women is one in which research has identified a number of significant characteristics of news coverage. Over the past 30 years there has been an increase in the quantity of reporting of crimes of sexual violence, and this reporting has become more lurid and explicit in its attention to the detail of the offence. A study of British tabloids noted how such news tended to be placed on the pages immediately before or after pages with pictures of topless women, more popularly known as 'page threes' (Carter, 1998).

It has also been observed that coverage of incidents of violence against women is distorted and selective. Disproportionate emphasis is given to certain kinds of violence, most notably murder and rape. By contrast, much less coverage is given to the kind of violence that women are more at risk from, namely domestic violence (Carter, 1998). Within these categories, there is also selection. Meyers (1997) argues that the murders of certain kinds of women, white and middle-class ones, are considered more newsworthy than those of other women. Similarly, within media coverage of rape, the emphasis is on stranger rape, where the woman is raped by someone whom she does not know rather than on the more typical rape, where the victim knows the offender. Carter (1998) claims that the obsession with the 'extra-ordinary' makes other kinds of violence 'ordinary' and thus not worthy of media coverage. 'Such reports', she argues (1998:231), 'invite readers to accept that sexual violence is a "natural" seemingly inevitable feature in the daily lives of women and girls'.

Blaming the victim.   Meyers (1997) argues that when the media cover sexual violence against women the predominant frame within which it is reported is that of individual pathology rather than one which sees it as a consequence of the oppression of women in society. Lisa McLaughlin (1998), for example, argues that the media coverage of the O. J. Simpson trial framed domestic violence in personal rather than structural terms. Simpson was a celebrity footballer and media personality, who was accused in 1994 of murdering his wife and her lover in Los Angeles. In the course of the trial details emerged of his history of violence against his wife, including a recording of her call to the police emergency phone number.

McLaughlin (1998) argues that the trial created the space in the media for a serious discussion of the nature of domestic violence. However, the media chose to frame the story in terms of the personal problems of the couple and in terms of the violence being a series of isolated incidents in the woman's life. This prevented them looking at the widespread and persistent nature of violence against women. She argues that the legal experts who offered commentary on CNN diluted the significance of the evidence of domestic violence 'by treating the trial as a sporting event or by trivializing the most damaging evidence' (McLaughlin, 1998:87).

A male domain? These kinds of selectivity and bias have been explained in terms of the gendered nature of media organisations. Though it is accepted that there have been increases in the numbers of female journalists in recent years, it remains the case that the majority of senior executives and decision-makers in media organisations are men. Tunstall (1996), for example, puts the figure as high as 80 per cent. It has also been observed that the working culture of the media, and particularly that of newsrooms, is predominantly masculine. Female journalists are subject to two kinds of pressure. One is to work within the gendered definition of news, which distinguishes between 'hard' news and 'soft' news: 'hard' news is about politics, economics, and government and is more suitably reported on by men; 'soft' news is about lifestyles, fashion, and shopping and is therefore the 'natural' province of women.

The other pressure is to adopt masculinised forms of reporting. The day-to day working culture of newsrooms is predominantly male with an emphasis on the aggressive and strong elements of male camaraderie, where male standards predominate. Kitzinger (1998:198) has observed the way in which the gut feelings of male journalists are treated as 'professional instinct', while those of female journalists are treated as 'subjective' and 'biased'. This puts female journalists under considerable pressure to adopt male styles of self-presentation and male styles of writing in an attempt to be seen to be as tough as the men. The pressure on female journalists is, as it were, to 'go male' and to become 'one of the boys'.

Nobody's world: the view from post-modernism

The triumph of the image. The final view is associated with a diverse range of post-modernist writers, including Gianni Vattimo and Jean Baudrillard. According to them the media cannot provide a coherent image of the world, whether of a radical, conservative, or sexist nature. The proliferation of sources of information and the speed of its transmission has undermined the capacity of the media to present a stable framing of the world. It has also diminished the ability of audiences to develop a consistent understanding of the nature of social and political reality.

They claim that the distinction between reality and its representation in the media, which is central to many of the arguments that we have considered in this chapter, is no longer a tenable one. They argue that it is pointless to search for hidden 'truths' or 'reality' behind media representations or beneath the realm of images and appearances. The primary existence of key events, such as wars and elections, is now on television. As a result there is no 'real' to which to compare them; the images themselves have become the reality. In this sense, then, the media do not represent reality: they are reality. Media images, as Fiske and Glynn (1995: 506, 507) put it, 'produce a more urgent reality than events themselves'. These images, they argue, have 'become our primary reality'.

An avalanche of information.   Alongside this change has been the huge increase in the amount of information reaching us through the media. This has created a situation of 'multi-perspectivism' in which the media now give voice to all kinds of groups and all points of view. Vattimo (1992:5–6), for example, talks about the 'giddy proliferation of communication as more and more sub-cultures have their say', and about the way in which 'minorities of every kind take to the microphones'.

This bombardment of information might be assumed to have positive consequences in terms of the increase in the store of public knowledge and comprehension of the world; but, according to post-modern theorists, it has the opposite effect. It fragments and impairs the capacity of the media to be the carriers of coherent meaning. The speed of information technology means that communication has become a series of short snippets, each disconnected from the one before it. As Kellner (1995:60) puts it, 'the media devour information and exterminate meaning', producing a culture of discrete and disconnected images without any underlying coherence.

The other effect is that the very diversity of images undermines the ability of people to comprehend them. The amount of information and the speed of its transmission creates what Vattimo (1992:17) calls a world of 'simultaneity', in which the capacity of viewers to construct coherent views of the nature of social reality from media coverage is undermined. Moreover, the compression of time and the obsession with the presentation of the immediate and the new in the media means that audiences do not have the time or the knowledge to construct over-arching schemes for the interpretation of events. Just as they are about to comprehend and assimilate the meaning of one event and to understand its significance, they are bombarded with news about a 'newer' and more 'vital' one. Consequently, viewers experience the world as a fragmented, disjointed, and meaningless place.

Furthermore, according to post-modernists, the mode through which audiences experience the media is being slowly but fundamentally altered. Under the avalanche of images it is moving from the level of rational understanding to one in which instant sensual stimulation is predominant. As Harms and Dickens (1996:211) put it, 'the constant experience of juxtaposed images from diverse contexts weakens their symbolic meaning, leading individuals to respond on a more sensual level'. In practical terms this means, for example, that audiences may often be more preoccupied with the demeanour of newsreaders than with the content of what they are reading.

Post-modernists and the media: a summary.   Post-modernists argue that the news lacks coherence and that audiences are unable to form coherent images of the world from watching it. They regard the current state of the media as a part of what appear to be irreversible cultural changes brought about by the decline of modernity and its replacement by post-modernity. Ignatieff (quoted in Morley, 1996:61) has characterised this new culture as an 'amnesiac culture' and as a 'three minute culture'. In this sense the incoherence of news is simply part of the cultural experience of post-modernism.

Assessing the arguments

What we have done so far is to outline the range of perspectives that claim to account for the nature of selection and framing in the media. The question we must now ask is, which of these perspectives is most adequate to capture the nature of media coverage? In this section we look at some of the problems that arise in trying to make a choice between them.

Framing and the dominant ideology

There are a number of problems with the argument that media framing is consistent with the interests of the dominant class or power group in society. These range from the issues created by evidence of the increasingly strained relationships between powerful groups and the media, through to the question of the flexible manner in which the powerful are conceptualised. However, the issue that will be focused on here is the apparent ability of the model to neutralise most kinds of contrary evidence. We can see this if we consider how the model deals with two separate objections that have been made to it.

A power elite: but where?   Simon Cottle (1993:107–33) looked at the groups and individuals that are covered in environmental stories on British television news. He found that they included environmental pressure groups, individual citizens, the representatives of local and central government, and scientists and experts. These groups, he argued, are much too diverse to be regarded as a power elite and are unlikely 'to produce closure around a dominant viewpoint, but rather reflect...the organized expressions of vying social, political, economic and cultural interests' (Cottle, 1993:120). This leads him to question the extent to which the media can usefully be seen as supporting the powerful when, as is typically the case, powerful elites do not have a unity or a common purpose to defend.

The answer from the proponents of the theory is that such a formulation misconstrues the nature of the ruling or dominant class. At any particular point there is no single unified ruling class, and hence there is no single ruling class ideology for the media to present. The ruling class is a coalition or alliance of powerful groups, and the ideology that reflects its interests will be as diverse as those interests are themselves (Hall, 1977). Research such as Cottle's simply illustrates this diversity rather than fundamentally challenging the theory. What the composition of the ruling class does is to set limits to the range of interpretations that will be found in the media, and these limits will be as wide or as narrow as the composition and the interests of that class. Thus what appears to be a significant objection to the theory can be transformed into one that it can incorporate.

Ideological independence or recuperation?   The same issue arises when we consider the research of David Murphy (1991) on media coverage of the Stalker affair in Britain and Daniel Hallin's (1987) on the US media coverage of Central America. Their work deals with what Bennett and Lawrence (1995:20) have called 'moments of ideological independence on the part of the media', and as such might appear to offer a significant challenge to the view that the media routinely favour dominant interests; yet here again the notion of limits can be deployed to accommodate or undercut the implications of these kinds of research results.

John Stalker was a senior English police officer assigned to investigate a series of controversial killings by the British Army in Northern Ireland in 1982. At a crucial point, as he was preparing to obtain secret police tapes of the killings and to interview the head of the Northern Ireland police force, he was suddenly withdrawn from the investigation. The official explanation was that he was associated with a businessman who had connections in the criminal underworld. However, the media, as Murphy (1991) documents, never accepted this.

Instead it uncovered a sequence of events which revealed that the British Army had acted outside the law and, effectively speaking, operated a shoot-to-kill policy. It showed that the Freemasons, a secret brotherhood, had considerable influence over the decisions made by the English police. It also implicated the then British Prime Minister, Margaret Thatcher, and her Tory government in an attempt to cover up the killing of innocent civilians by the state. The *Daily Express* newspaper, for example, a strong supporter of the Thatcher government, was among the first to discuss the possibility that the state had been involved in the murder of its citizens.

Hallin (1987) compared media coverage of American involvement in Central America in the 1980s with the way in which its participation in the war in Vietnam in the 1960s had been covered. He found differences in the frameworks through which both wars were reported. The taken-for-granted assumptions in the coverage of the Vietnam War had been those of the Cold War, and involved the unquestioning acceptance by the media of the official view that the Soviet Union posed a genuine threat to the USA's interests, whether in Vietnam or elsewhere in the world. This was still the official assumption about Central America in the 1980s, but here it was treated by the media as a political assertion of the US administration and not as a self-evident truth. This was part of the marked change in the attitudes of journalists to the statements of political authority figures, which was most evident in an increased scepticism about their pronouncements and in the use of the term 'propaganda' to characterise the views not just of the 'enemy' but also of the US administration.

A sceptical media.   These examples appear to offer a direct rebut-
tal to the model of the dominant ideology. These stories, and the
manner in which they were framed by the media, 'must', as
Murphy (1991:263) argues, 'constitute a challenge' to arguments
about the dominant ideology. However, the model is sufficiently
flexible to accommodate both of them. Again, supporters of the
dominant ideology argument deploy the notion of limits. They
argue that this sort of coverage appears to represent a critique of
the powerful but, on closer inspection, their critical stance is circumscribed and limited.

Thus the coverage of the Stalker affair showed a media that was
sceptical about the state's account of its actions, but there were
clear limits to this scepticism. It did not extend to their coverage of
a similar event that occurred at around the same time, the killing
by the British secret service of unarmed Irish Republican Army
(IRA) activists in controversial circumstances in Gibraltar (see
Miller, 1994). It also did not extend, as Murphy himself recognises,
to accepting the IRA or the nationalist account of the events in
Northern Ireland that Stalker was sent to investigate. Thus while
many newspapers wrote editorials criticising the government for
the way in which it handled the Stalker affair, none wrote supporting the IRA's position or policies.

Similarly, Hallin himself rescues the dominant ideology by arguing that what was going on was not the freeing of the media
from the perspectives of the powerful but a redefinition of the
limits within which they could operate. The Cold War ideology
was displaced but its replacement did not, he argues, constitute a
significant challenge to the status quo. It did not, for example, lead
to more favourable coverage of groups in the USA who opposed
the war in Central America. Elite critics, such as politicians and
churchmen, were given coverage that was 'respectful but limited'
(Hallin, 1987:19), while the coverage of less 'respectable' but more
radical opposition was non-existent. The coverage of radical
groups in Central America was equally conservative, especially
of guerrilla groups who believed in the need to use violence to
achieve political change and social justice. The media were, as
Hallin (1987:19) puts it, 'equally unsupportive of any attempt to
challenge established authorities whether at home or abroad'.

Neutralising criticism.   In these ways the argument about a dominant ideology combines notions of ideological dominance and
limited critique in a manner that, effectively speaking, neutralises

all potential criticisms. Any examples of where the media either failed to present, or failed to defend, the interests of the dominant class can be accommodated in two ways: the first is through the contention that, by the nature of their composition, the powerful do not necessarily have a single point of view, and hence discordant views can slip into the media; the second is that the media are allowed to be critical or sceptical as long as they remain within certain limits. Thus the concept of 'critique within limits' protects the dominant ideology argument from decisive criticism.

But what are the ideological limits?　　To avoid this it is necessary to indicate the ideological limits within which the media operates or by which they are constrained. Gitlin (1980:271) is one of the few to have addressed this issue. He has specified what he believes these limits are in the USA. The media cannot, he argues, call into question:

> the legitimacy of private control of commodity production; the legitimacy of the national security State; the legitimacy of technocratic experts; the right and ability of authorized agencies to manage conflict and make the necessary reforms; the legitimacy of the social order secured and defined by the dominant elites; and the value of individualism as the measure of social existence.

If news coverage remains within these limits then the validity of the argument about the dominant ideology is established. If, on the other hand, it goes outside them then the argument is invalid.

This is a significant advance but it is one which in turn raises its own problems. The most obvious one is that the media regularly transgresses many of these limits. As Ericson (1994:234) puts it, 'the state and its institutions are constantly faced with threats to its legitimacy from the media's revelations of its system failures'. The capacity of 'authorized agencies' to manage social problems is regularly challenged: for example, in media questioning of the capacity of the police to deal with corruption within their own ranks or the ability of public institutions to reform themselves. Similarly, the 'legitimacy of technocratic experts' also comes under scrutiny in the media, as, for example, on food safely issues and on foot and mouth disease. But equally, on many occasions, the media do not transgress them.

So is it reasonable to ask how many transgressions are necessary to constitute a decisive challenge to the theory, or is this the kind of sterile cul-de-sac that this approach leads to? Does it lead to a misplaced quantification that reduces media power to an issue of how often the preferences of the powerful prevail in media coverage? This question is probably ultimately unanswerable, as there will always be extra occasions to take into account and extra examples of media coverage to consider.

The media as a half-open door

Similar kinds of issues arise when we consider the second argument about media framing. It meets our intuitive sense of the variety of media material and of the critical attitude that the media adopts towards the powerful generally, but especially towards politicians. It claims that there is contest in the media both for coverage and for control of the interpretations of events. These contests occur within certain limits but alternative voices have access, get media space and can influence the ways in which issues are framed. However, difficulties arise when we try to interpret the significance of the empirical examples that are used to support the argument.

Beating the powerful.   James Curran (1990), for example, has argued that broadcasting organisations in particular may be relatively open to oppositional perspectives. He bases this conclusion on a study of British media's coverage of the Tory government's decision to abolish the Greater London Council (GLC) in 1983. The GLC, he suggests, won the media contest. It was able to frame its case in terms of consensual values such as the importance of local democracy and the need for local participation in political decisions that had local consequences, both of which were presented in the media as being under attack from the government.

Deacon and Golding (1991) have also questioned the ability of the powerful to shape media coverage. The example they use is the failure of the Tory government in Britain in the late 1980s to generate popular support for a new form of taxation, the Community Charge. The government introduced the new tax and launched a major public relations campaign to sell it to the electorate. They were unsuccessful in getting their point of view across, and the consistency of public opposition and hostility forced them to drop the tax. The terms in which the issue was presented in the media, including those media traditionally supportive of the Tory party, were overwhelmingly unfavourable to the government's case. Opinion polls showed that people were primarily dependent on the media for their information about the tax and so, Deacon and Golding conclude, it is reasonable to assume that the terms of media coverage were an important element in the government's failure.

A leaky system. These examples suggest that the media do not inevitably frame events and issues in terms that are favourable to the dominant culture and the dominant power elite: in certain circumstances the media are more open than many critics would suggest. However, it is possible to over-state the significance of the support they offer for a model of limited pluralism and the extent to which they challenge models of ideological dominance. The limited pluralism argument points us to issues such as the circumstances under which the media challenge dominant elites and how often they do so. But it has not, as yet, systematically explored these issues.

The failure to do so means that examples of more pluralist media coverage can easily be transformed into examples that support the thesis of a dominant ideology. After all, while Deacon and Golding (1991:310) found that aspects of the government's case for a new tax were challenged in the media, they also found that there were clear limits to the media critique. It did not extend to a questioning, for example, of the threats that would be posed to civil liberties through the disenfranchisement of those who failed to pay the tax, and the possibilities its administration opened for abuses of personal privacy and of the judicial process. The media's difficulties with the tax were simply with the means being used rather than the ends being pursued.

In this sense the model of limited pluralism shares many of the dilemmas of the model of a dominant ideology. They both acknowledge the openness of the media to alternative and oppositional points of view and they both argue that there are limits to this openness. They both have (as yet) failed to specify what the limits to this openness are. In the absence of this level of specificity it remains somewhat unclear as to how precisely the two models differ.

Television as a liberal weapon of ideological warfare.   Assessing the argument that the perspectives of the media are drawn predominantly from a liberal or radical agenda raises the same problems that we have identified in previous sections. There are examples of research that supports the argument and research that questions it. However, the current balance of evidence does not encourage us to endorse the argument.

The claims by Ranney (1983) and others that the media are on the side of state involvement in the economy are increasingly dated. The predominant framing of news about economic change and development, in both the USA and Britain, is in terms of the inevitability of globalisation and of what are perceived as its inseparable allies, free trade and unrestrained markets. These, the framing goes, are features that must be accommodated to and not ones that can be resisted. This can be seen in media coverage of those who protest against the process of globalisation at the various meetings of world leaders, whether these are in Seattle, Genoa or Quebec, and at the somewhat more private meetings of world experts and opinion makers. News framings stress the violence of the protesters to the exclusion of any concern for the arguments that are being offered or for the criticisms that the protesters are making about the globalisation process. Increasingly the media have become cheerleaders for the new global economic and business order (Nichols and McChesney, 2000).

However, it is doubtful if the media could ever have been characterised as anti-business. Routine economic news in the media has always largely been news about business, and the health of the economy is routinely and unquestioningly equated with the state of the stock exchange. If the exchanges are doing well, this is a sign of an economy in good health. If they are doing badly, then so too is the economy. This, as Croteau and Hoynes (1997:174) point out, ignores the fact that what is good for business is not necessarily good for everyone else. An increase in a corporation's profitability and a consequent increase in its stock price may reflect, for example, the market's evaluation of its lay-off of labour. In this sense it is also relevant to note that no major newspaper or television station devotes either a section of a newspaper or an entire programme to labour, yet they all do for the world of business. This is hardly the behaviour of an institution that is seriously anti-business.

The media have also successfully overcome whatever reluctance they had about supporting military action by Western governments. Their role as largely uncritical supporters of military actions against Iraq since 1991 and their unqualified support for the Western bombing of Serbia in 1999 have been well documented (see Soderbund, Wagenburg and Pemberton, 1994; Vincent, 2000). The objections of journalists to military action was, according to right-wing critics, rooted in their participation in, and identification with, the counter-culture of the 1960s. This was blamed for producing the kind of media coverage that contributed to the American defeat in the Vietnam War. However, as Daniel Hallin (1984) has shown, the source for the coverage of the Vietnam War was not the counter-culture but the views of the political elite. When they believed that victory in the war was possible this was mirrored in media coverage; however, when they began to doubt this, the notion that the war might not be winnable gained support and coverage in the media. The tone of reporting on the war only changed when the attitudes of the political elite changed. In much the same way their positive attitudes to contemporary military actions may reflect the changed attitudes of political elites, particularly liberal ones, to Western military action (see, for example, Ignatieff, 1998).

Assessing the feminist argument

The assessment of the feminist argument about media framing is limited by the lack of a substantial body of research on women's involvement in news and current affairs (see van Zoonen, 1994:65). However, there are three points that the available research allows us to consider: one relates specifically to the issue of the reporting of crimes against women and the other two are more general, relating to the dynamics by which, it is argued, a gendered media is produced.

Crime reporting. The analysis of media coverage of crimes against women suggested that there is an over-emphasis on crimes of violence and a tendency to frame these crimes in terms of individual pathology rather than in more structural terms that would emphasise the oppression of women in a patriarchal society. However, it can be argued that these selectivities and framings are not unique to the reporting of violence against women but may in fact be typical of the reporting of crime in general. Research suggests that media reporting over-represents violent crime whatever the gender of the victim. It also suggests that there is a tendency in such reporting to ignore the contribution of structural factors and to emphasise aspects of individual pathology.

Humphries (1981:205), for example, found that the media coverage of crime in the USA ignored 'the socio-political circumstances surrounding the events'. Chibnall (1975) noted the ways in which notions of individual pathology shaped media coverage of crime in Britain. Finally, Muncie (1984:20) showed how the media ignore 'any social context relevant to criminal activity' in their reporting on juvenile crime. Thus overall it can be argued that the kind of coverage that crimes against women receive is not due to a gendered approach to media reporting but to an 'events' orientation, in which the media focus is on specific events, and to an individualistic ideology in which events can be explained as the actions of discrete individuals rather than in terms of abstract social processes.

Sexism or market forces?   The second point relates to the argument that the gendered nature of news can be explained in terms of the male dominance of the news media. Marjorie Ferguson (1990) has questioned the belief that more women in media organisations will increase the access of women to the media and alter the manner in which they have been represented. She argues that having more women in high-status management jobs does not have a trickle-down effect and does not undermine the 'cultural hegemony of male dominance' (Ferguson, 1990:225). She bases this on the failure of women editors to alter the sexist content of British tabloid newspapers. The reason, she claims, is that the success of an editor is judged by circulation rather than 'by standing up for sisterhood' (Ferguson, 1990:225). Indeed, as Tunstall (1996) suggests, female editors of tabloid newspapers share an important characteristic with male ones: they are sacked as suddenly and as regularly as male editors are.

The new (female) journalism.   Some critics have argued that recent changes in news invalidate much of the criticisms of feminists. One of the most significant of these has been the increase in the number of female journalists and, in particular, the increase in the number of female newsreaders. This latter position was traditionally seen as a male bastion.

The role of newsreaders is to establish the authority of the programmes in which they appear and to guarantee the truth of what they are saying. A series of ritualised conventions has emerged through which this authoritativeness can be dramatised (Root, 1986:79–94). This includes the sole right to direct an uninterrupted address to the camera, a moderate and neutral tone of voice, a conservative mode of dress, and the appearance of emotional neutrality. A head of grey hair does not go astray either. This authority is consolidated by drawing on the halo effect of other forms of authority and status in society. Newsreaders have been predominantly middle class, white and male. The notion of a female newsreader had been unthinkable for many years. In 1971 an executive with the BBC questioned whether anyone would believe it if a woman newsreader announced the outbreak of war (Root, 1986).

The fact that increasingly women have become newsreaders or anchorpersons for news bulletins could be used to indicate that the link between gender and authority has been broken. This trend began in local news programmes in the USA but is now an accepted feature of the news bulletins of most major media organisations. As van Zoonen (1991:221) says, 'the appearance of female newsreaders . . . . indicates that power, authority and expertise are no longer features exclusively reserved for men'.

She has extended this argument to suggest that to an increasing extent the gender of news personnel is unimportant to the nature of news (van Zoonen, 1994). She argues that male values in journalism are based on the fetishism of facts, the use of sources that are overwhelmingly male, and on the cultivation of detachment as the appropriate attitude to the events being reported. Female journalists claim to have a different attitude to news. They have more respect for readers and viewers, and are more interested in the 'human' side of stories. In addition they have a commitment to compassion and are not afraid to show their emotions. These features have traditionally been seen as feminine values, and as such have relegated female journalists to 'soft' news stories.

However, she argues that news journalism is changing. New forms of news are emerging, driven by market consideration and commercial pressures (see McManus, 1992). These emphasise 'human interest' rather than social significance, emotional investment rather than detached neutrality, the needs and desires of audiences rather than the objective importance of events, and entertainment rather than edification. The growth of this kind of consumer-orientated news is an attempt to broaden the appeal of news and, in the phrase of a news editor interviewed by van Zoonen (1998:40), to 'people-ise the news'. News personnel are increasingly under pressure to adopt informal and intimate modes of address with audiences.

The emergence of this kind of journalism is opening up new opportunities for women as female journalists have always favoured, and claimed to practise, 'a more human and involved approach to news' (van Zoonen, 1998:45). It also provides new opportunities for female values to have an impact on media coverage. The watershed for the emergence of this kind of news was the media coverage of the death in a car crash of Princess Diana, a semi-detached member of the British royal family, in Paris in 1997. The outpouring of national grief was matched by the abandonment of detached news coverage, and women reporters played an important part in the coverage.

Equality or stupidity?   These changes can be presented as a triumph for equality, but some critics do not accept this; they see them as part of the devaluation of the public sphere and of what might be termed the 'dumbing down' of news. For them the invasion of intimate and personalised modes of address is a symptom of the decline of the notion of news as analytical reporting of the events of the world and its replacement by news as a form of entertainment. As Neil Postman (1986:103) puts it, this is news 'as a stylized dramatic performance whose content has been staged largely to entertain'. Franklin (1997:5) has termed news converted into entertainment 'Newszak', which reduces 'crucial events into a cosy chat show' (Simpson, quoted in Franklin, 1997:5).

It has also been argued that the entry of women is restricted to those who meet certain standards of dress, age and appearance. So while women have entered the traditional male bastion of television journalism, traditional issues of sexism have not disappeared. MacDonald (1995:49–50) has shown how, for example, women's appearance is a factor in their acceptability as newsreaders and programme presenters. One presenter on British television was forced out of her job in 1993 after she was the subject of negative media criticism. This was not directed at her competence or authoritativeness, but at her inadequate dress sense and her reluctance to show her legs.

A conclusion?   It is clear that the feminist perspective on media framing is incisive and relevant. It is also clear that this perspective has had an impact on the media in terms of employment patterns and media content. However, an overall assessment of this perspective is limited by shortcomings within the perspective itself. We can see this if we ask what a medium that gave a higher value to 'women's discourse' would look like. This immediately raises the questions of what such 'women's discourse' is and how can it be identified. As MacDonald (1995) points out, the term has a different meaning for different groups of women. It has one for feminists, another for women who are anti-feminist and yet another for those women to whom feminist debates are of little relevance. Hence there are no agreed standards through which such a discourse can be unequivocally identified, and so there are no clear standards to measure the degree of movement to a non-gendered media.

There are similar difficulties in the area of the employment of women in the media. For some, the movement towards more equality in employment patterns and in remuneration is to be welcomed and encouraged. For others, it is not enough. They argue that in addition 'there needs to be more women with a politicized understanding of the ways in which women's subordination is currently reproduced, and with the will to change it' (Arthurs, 1994:100). If it is necessary to make a distinction between women in terms of the nature of their political commitment, then it suggests that there may be substantial numbers of women who do not share fully the views of feminists. They do not experience the media as gendered and do not share the antipathy of many feminists to media content.

Assessing post-modernism

The assessment of the post-modernism view on the media poses a set of problems that we do not encounter with the other perspectives. The principal one is that it involves bringing criteria to bear on the theory that it does not recognise and accept. The notion that some arguments may be more 'real' or 'true' than others is one that is problematic for most post-modernist theorists. They reject the notion that there is 'a realm of verifiable public truths' (Morley, 1996:283) against which claims to truth can be judged. All such claims are relative, and none is more accurate or more authoritative than any other. Hence the form of assessment to which this chapter aspires is one to which post-modernists would be unsympathetic.

It is also necessary to distinguish between two separate strands of the post-modernist argument. The first says that the media are unable to provide a coherent view of the world; this will be addressed in this section. The second says that audiences are unable to make sense of the world that is presented to them in the media and particularly on television. This issue relates to how audiences deal with and respond to media material, and is dealt with in Chapter 7.

We also have to contend with the lack of research in the area. Though post-modern theorists give considerable status to the role of the media, they offer few detailed empirical analyses in support of their claims. We can, however, gain some critical distance from their arguments by looking at the attention that they give to the notion of spectacle in the modern media. For them events are spectacularised in their mode of presentation in the media and, in the process, they are emptied of meaning. They become no more than their surfaces, all noise, bright lights, rock music and fancy camera work, signifying nothing. This is generalised into the argument that the format of media messages is more important than their content, because it is the mode of presentation and not the content that has an effect on audiences.

Are media spectacles meaningless?   However, it is possible to argue that, although the media may employ the mode of spectacle, this does not automatically deprive the events being covered of meaning or render them incoherent. Take the example of the media coverage of the US Senate hearings on Clarence Thomas in 1991. These have been presented within a post-modern framework as a media spectacle and as a virtual event (see Hart, 1994; Robinson and Powell, 1996). The relevant background was that Thomas, a black Republican lawyer, was nominated to the Supreme Court by the then President, George Bush. He was to replace Thurgood Marshall, who was retiring. Marshall had been the first black judge in the Supreme Court and had been a noted defender of civil rights. One of the main issues at the confirmation hearings was the accusation of sexual harassment made by a black woman, Anita Hill, who had worked with Thomas.

The confirmation hearings had all of the qualities that attract media attention and that encourage spectacular modes of presentation. They had melodrama, sex, race and personal confrontation. Ultimately, however, like all media spectacles, Hart (1994) argues, they changed little of substance: they were simply part of the way in which politics in a post-modern era is reduced to another branch of the media entertainment industry.

Yet, for all the trappings of media spectacle, at the heart of the matter there was a competition between two opposing frames or interpretations. These contested for media dominance and, through that, for access to and control of how the public defined and responded to the issue. One frame drew on a gender-based agenda that reflected the concerns of women about harassment in the work place. This framed Hill as victim and Thomas as sexual predator. The other frame drew on concerns about the power of feminism and liberalism. This saw Thomas as a victim of racism and Hill as a front for those objecting to the appointment of a conservative to the Supreme Court. In the end, Robinson and Powell (1996) conclude, the conservative frame won the contest and achieved media dominance. If we attend only to the spectacle of the events, we might miss this important point.

In this way, the arguments of post-modernists sensitise us to issues of media presentation and to the effects that these may have on how events are represented and how they are understood. But in the process it may give too much attention to the formats and technologies of the media and, as a result, neglect the issue of media content. As Harms and Dickens (1996:220) argue: 'communication involves more than just format. The content and the interests behind it are no less important elements in the communication process.'

Conclusion

In this chapter we have reviewed the range of perspectives that exist on framing in the media. We have also looked at the range of criticisms that can be made of them. It would appear from this that there are few unambiguous conclusions on the central question of whose frames predominate in the media. It is also apparent that this question cannot necessarily be fruitfully and decisively answered by empirical research. As we have seen, examples of media coverage that support particular arguments can all too easily be countered by references to cases that do not.

These concerns have been reflected in a recent turn in media research. While remaining within the general view that 'news coverage typically supports established institutions' (Rogers and Dearing, 1988:558), it argues that there are discursive openings and opportunities in the media through which new events and new perspectives on events can get into the media agenda. Hackett (1991:281) has argued that the media 'is not a level playing field, but sometimes it is possible, even playing uphill, to score points, to win a match, and perhaps occasionally even to redefine the rules of the game'. The key question then becomes, under what circumstances does the media provide an arena in which or through which existing frames can be challenged? How, and under what circumstances, do what Bennett, Gressett and Halton (1985) call 'media representational systems' change to accommodate new stories and new issues? This issue, along with others, is addressed in the next chapter.

CHAPTER 4

The Production of Media Messages: Who Sets the Media Agenda?

Introduction

In the previous two chapters we have focused on the ways in which the world is represented to us in the news media. We outlined and examined the various theories that attempt to characterise and explain the nature of these representations. In this chapter we alter the focus somewhat to look at the mechanisms through which media content acquires its particular character. We do this by looking at the social forces that impinge on, and influence, how the news media operate.

News organisations must accommodate to, and take account of, the range of elements that make up the environment in which they operate. As a result media content is the outcome of a complex process of production in which social, political and economic factors interact to produce a particular and distinctive end product. In this chapter we outline the most significant of these factors and we detail their influence on the nature of media messages.

We focus on five of these: the power and influence of media sources, the politics of media personnel, the relationship between ownership and control, the influence of the audience, and the effect of organisational routines on media output.

The sources of media stories

Information is the raw material with which news organisations work. It is put through a series of bureaucratic and technical processes and through these it is transformed into news. However, the importance of information presents journalists and news personnel with a problem. They are seldom direct witnesses to the events on which they report, which means that they have to rely on others to tell them what happened and how it should be interpreted. Those on whom they rely are referred to as 'news sources', and their importance raises a series of questions for the sociology of the mass media.

What is a news source?

The term 'news source' can, as Blumler and Gurevitch (1986) point out, be an ambiguous one. Generally it is used to refer to individuals and organisations that either directly or indirectly influence or shape the news. However, empirical research tends to work with more limited definitions, such as those who appear on (or who get quoted in) news stories, or those to whom a reporter 'explicitly attributes information' (Hallin, Mankoff and Weddie, 1993:753). This produces a workable definition for research purposes, but it loses the important way in which sources can influence stories through the selective and well-timed leak, through the off-record briefing, and through a range of other methods of information control that do not necessarily require them to be openly identified.

Who are the sources?

Working with the more limited definition, research suggests that there is a heavy reliance on the powerful for news. Government officials and institutional sources – such as professional organisations, pressure groups, business associations and 'experts' – predominate as the sources of media stories. Hallin, Mankoff and Weddie (1993), for example, found that 1 per cent of sources made up 25 per cent of those cited in stories about national security in the USA. The most prominent were 'rethreaded administration officials' (Reese, Grant and Danielian, 1994).

There is further concentration within this category. National or federal government officials predominate over local or state officials, and within the national or federal government those in the most senior positions (such as the President or the Prime Minister) are the most important sources of news. Similarly, within the institutional sources, business and corporate people predominate. The pivotal role that news gives to those in centres of power is heightened by the prominence with which they are placed in new stories. Government sources, for example, tend to appear higher up in newspaper stories, or earlier in television news items than non-government ones.

By contrast ordinary people, private individuals, or what Gans (1979) calls 'unknowns' seldom feature as sources for the news, and only then in restrictive circumstances. They appear as 'epitomizing cases' when they are used to put a human face on statistics, as in the use of individual unemployed people to illustrate the effects of unemployment. They feature in the role of passive victims in the coverage of crime or of disasters and accidents, or else they are highlighted when they participate in 'odd' or 'deviant' activities (such as residents' protests, or queuing all night for the opening of the spring sales or to purchase tickets for rock concerts).

Why do they depend on such sources?

Why do journalists rely on such a limited range of sources for news, given their alleged fear of manipulation by powerful groups? According to David Murphy (1991), it is because such sources solve a number of production and newsgathering problems; most notably, they solve the problem of verification because stories originating with official sources are by definition 'reliable'. If a news editor challenges a journalist on a story, the fact that the source is a powerful individual or organisation in society establishes it as legitimate and as newsworthy. The information that such sources provide is also by definition 'significant' because it comes from significant and important individuals and institutions.

The predominance of official sources is also, according to W. L. Bennett (1996), the means through which the media can present itself as discharging its political responsibility. The underlying assumption is that in representative democracies, power has been delegated to public officials. Getting the 'official reaction' allows the media to claim that it is meeting its responsibility of making such elites accountable to citizens. Reporting on them is, in effect, a way of appearing to keep power under scrutiny.

Does dependence equal control?

This pattern of media sourcing can be interpreted in a less benign fashion. It provokes the question of whether powerful news sources control the content of the media: Sigal (1986:33), for example, contends that they do. 'By adhering to routine channels of newsgathering', he argues, journalists 'leave much of the task of news selection to its sources'. W. L. Bennett (1996) has developed this argument with his notion of the 'indexing hypothesis'. He argues that journalists 'index' the range of their coverage so that it is reflective of the range of views of political and social elites, rather than those of the general population. The indexing rule reflects, according to Lawrence (1996:438), 'a journalistic orienta- tion towards power and politics that cedes to officials the responsi- bility for setting the political and news agendas'.

Hall (1982) has elaborated on this. He argues that certain groups in society are recognised by the media as accredited sources, and as such they have privileged access to (and greater claims on) media coverage. Their access comes from their institutional power, their representative status, or their claims to expert know- ledge. This means that they meet journalistic criteria of credibility and authoritativeness and so are able to act as what Hall calls 'primary definers'. They can define what the issues in society are and, equally importantly, they can define the manner in which they are presented as issues.

This does not mean that the media function merely as a propa- ganda weapon for the powerful or that alternative voices are absent; but such voices are at a significant disadvantage in gaining media access. The privileged access of governmental and corpor- ate elites limits the kind of issues in the news to ones initiated by them. The narrow range of the sources used restricts the range of perspectives and viewpoints that are considered to be relevant to the debates provoked by news stories. In order to get into the media, those who represent alternative viewpoints 'must respond in terms pre-established by the primary definers and privileged definitions' (Hall, 1982:62). Thus they seldom initiate stories, and merely respond to those initiated by the powerful.

Challenging the dominance view

These views have been challenged. Philip Schlesinger (1990), for example, has argued that the media's use of sources is more diverse than is suggested by people such as Bennett and Hall. There are two reasons for this.

The first is that Hall works with the implicit assumption that powerful elites and governments speak with a single unified voice. The reality is that they are often divided in their interests and in what they are seeking to achieve through media coverage. Divergences are not unknown between government departments and state agencies, between governments and corporate elites, or between different sections of the corporate elite. In these circumstances, which group do the media turn to as the primary definer?

The second is that Hall fails to consider the issue of changes in the structure of access to the media. Do those groups who had the right of access in the 1970s still have it, or have they been joined or displaced by new ones? Hall's argument, according to Schlesinger (1990:67), 'tacitly assumes the permanent presence of certain forces in the power structure'. As such it cannot explain the declining access to the media, for example, of the trade unions in Britain and the USA, and the growing access of environmental pressure groups such as Greenpeace.

On this basis, Schlesinger argues that control of the media agenda is not routinely guaranteed to the powerful but it is something for which they must compete. They have a number of advantages in this struggle, particularly material and symbolic ones. The range of resources they can call on is greater than those available to alternative voices, but it does not automatically mean that they are assured of a favourable outcome.

Accessing the media: coming in from the cold

This debate has lead on to a consideration of the circumstances in which events 'can slip the nets of official containment' (W. L. Bennett, 1996:379), and alternative groups or those outside the political mainstream can become key sources for the media. P. Patterson (1988) argues that routine reporting only privileges the accounts of powerful groups if they play by the rules and provide information on which journalists can build stories and meet their organisation's requirements for news. If they do not, journalists will look elsewhere. This can produce stories that question official versions of events and can lead to alternative groups acquiring media legitimacy.

Molotch and Lester (1974) have argued that the lack of preparedness of the powerful for accidents such as oil spills, explosions at nuclear power plants and the leaking of damaging confidential information means they are unable to control media coverage. These kinds of event give journalists licence to escape from 'the bounds of cultural consensus' (W. L. Bennett, 1996:379–80). In these situations, groups who promote alternative perspectives get the kind of access to the media that is normally not possible for them. A nuclear accident, for example, allows conservation, environmental and citizen groups on to the media agenda to challenge the prevailing ideology of nuclear power.

In the process particular incidents can, according to Bennett and Lawrence (1995), acquire iconic status. The beating of a black man, Rodney King, by white police officers in March 1991 in Los Angeles, for example, became an icon that symbolised the continued existence of racism as a social problem. It gave journalists licence to report on issues that do not normally feature in routine media coverage, such as racial discrimination in the justice system. It also allowed them to bring in a range of voices that would not normally be heard in the media.

Similarly the dramatic and unexpected explosion at a nuclear plant in the Ukraine in 1985 meant that the name 'Chernobyl' became an icon for the high risks of nuclear power. It legitimated media concern with its dangers and gave media space to its critics. In this way a dramatic or unexpected item or issue that becomes a news icon can transform 'the cultural scripts that (are) applied to the problem' (Bennett and Lawrence, 1995:37).

There are also openings created in the media when official sources are slow to respond to new issues. The rise of Greenpeace to its status as a legitimate and authoritative source in the coverage of environmental issues was helped in no small measure by the failure of government sources to respond to press coverage of particular incidents (Hansen, 1993). Anderson (1993) has shown how such an opening allowed Greenpeace to get coverage in the British media, and particularly in the tabloid press, for incidents such as the deaths of seals in the North Sea in 1988, and for its view that the source of the problem was industrial pollution.

Alternative sources can also gain access to the media when there are divisions and disagreements within political elite groups. Miller and Reilly (1995) argue that scares over salmonella and 'Mad Cow Disease' in the late 1980s and 1990s revealed divisions between two government departments in Britain. The two involved, Health and

Agriculture, had different concerns (one for public health, and the other for the farming industry). They offered contradictory advice to the public and attacked each other in media briefings. This allowed alternative experts and radical pressure groups to take the initiative and get their views on to the news agenda.

The price of being a media source

These kinds of circumstance offer openings for alternative voices and issues to gain access to the media, but they are not entirely unproblematic for those involved. If the media identify particular groups as legitimate sources of news, they are offered potential access to large audiences but, in return, they have to conform to certain organisational specifications. They must, for example, have a clear and hierarchical leadership structure with clearly identifiable spokespeople, thus satisfying the journalistic practice of only quoting those who appear to be in authority or who appear to clearly represent the movement. If a movement has a decentralised structure and no official spokespeople, then the media will in effect appoint them (Sigal, 1986; see also Gitlin, 1980).

This can create tensions and dissent within such organisations. The fear is that their spokespeople will become too media-friendly and will 'sell out' (Miller, 1998). Similarly the cost of media access may be control over the issues that the organisation can pursue. Barker-Plummer (1995) found that older members of the Women's Movement in the USA cultivated journalists and offered information subsidies by pointing out stories they might be interested in and through staging events they would be able to cover. The benefits of this policy were that they became key sources for journalists and key figures in building the media agenda on women's issues. The costs included a reticence over issues that they felt journalists might have difficulty covering, such as those surrounding female sexuality and its discontents.

Concluding considerations on media sources

The research discussed here suggests that powerful groups are central sources of news and, while they do not automatically control the ways in which issues are defined in society, they have considerable influence on the process. Alternative voices get in but under limited sets of circumstances and with certain clear limitations of the kinds of alternative voices that are listened to.

The reliance on a limited set of sources has clear consequences for media coverage. It produces substantial agreement among the media on what the major stories and issues are, and increasingly leads to a significant degree of convergence on a small number of big stories. This has been accompanied by limitations on the range of interpretations of the stories that make it into the public domain.

The politics of media personnel: a liberal power elite?

A second argument about the influences on media content directs attention to the role of the political and social values of those who work in media organisations. In the USA, for example, it has been argued that media personnel are generally more liberal or left wing than their audiences, and as a result the material that they produce is biased by these political commitments. This has led to them being characterised as the 'new power elite' (Lichter, Rothman and Lichter, 1986). Their liberalism is reflected in an antagonism to multi-national corporations, a suspicion and cynicism about government and state authority, and a contempt for all kinds of religious and spiritual values. At a concrete level this identification with liberal values and with liberal politicians explains the length of time it took for stories of the infidelities of Bill Clinton to become major news. Others paradoxically explain the media's extensive focus on the then president's sex life as an indication that the liberal media elite had turned puritan, and indeed somewhat hypocritical, in its attitudes to extra-marital sex (Gitlin, 1998).

In Britain the argument had been that media personnel had similar social and educational backgrounds to people that they were reporting about, and this produced a conservative and pro-establishment complexion to their output (see Miliband, 1973). This has been replaced by the claim from prominent conservative politicians and commentators that a liberal elite now controls many leading British institutions, including education and the media.

How liberal are the liberals?

Assessing this approach requires us to deal with two broad issues. The first is, what precisely are the value commitments of journalists? This issue is difficult to resolve in any conclusive fashion due largely to the reluctance of media personnel to respond to researchers. However, David Croteau (1999) found, in a survey of Washington-based journalists, that they are committed to a highly qualified and nuanced version of liberalism. They are liberal on social rather than economic issues. Few journalists had left-wing views on economic matters, and there was little evidence of any antipathy to capitalism as an economic system. The tendency was for the journalists to identify themselves as centrist rather than right or left. This was confirmed in a comparative study of journalists in Great Britain, Germany, Italy, Sweden and the USA. This found that the majority placed themselves close to the mid-point in the political attitude scale (Patterson and Donsbach, 1996:458).

Keeping their politics in check?

The second issue is the degree to which the personal ideological orientations of journalists can influence the content of the media. It is true that, like most people, journalists hold particular political values and it is also true that (in certain circumstances) these have some influence on their work; but there are a number of limitations or constraints on the extent of the influence. One is the general employment situation for journalists. Bourdieu (1998:71), for example, argues that while a small number of journalists can act as small-time capitalists, selling their work to the highest bidder, others are much less secure. 'We are witnessing', he says, 'the growth of a vast journalistic sub-proletariat, forced into a kind of self-censorship by an increasingly precarious job situation'. While the extent to which this is true may vary from country to country, the increasing reliance on free-lance workers and the success of proprietors in Britain in taming union power are clear sources of control on individual expression among media personnel.

Another is the ideological orientation of the media organisation for which they work. It is generally accepted that national newspapers in most countries are identified with particular political and ideological positions. These ordinarily range from the liberal to the right, with few representing either a near or a far left position. If the political orientation of journalists fits that of the newspapers for which they work, then there is no conflict: they can give their ideology full rein. If it does not, there might be problems.

Broadcast and television organisations are, by contrast, less easily ideologically categorised. They tend in general to orient themselves to the political middle ground. In some countries they are required to do so by law, while in others the economic imperative to reach the largest possible audience is the driving force. In such systems the realities of work in these organisations mean that there is less scope for the political views of journalists to find a direct outlet.

Patterson and Donsbach (1996) found that, in the USA at least, there was no clear relationship between the political views of journalists and those of the organisations for which they worked, but they had few problems working in organisations with ideologies to which they were opposed at a personal level. Sigelman's (1973) study of two ideologically contrasting newspapers found that journalists did not have any major difficulty in fulfilling editorial assignments as long as they had some autonomy in shaping the way in which the final story was produced (that is, as long as their professional expertise as journalists was respected).

Media personnel have a range of professional and organisational commitments that take precedence over their personal politics. The predominant professional commitment is to an ideology of objectivity. According to Tuchman (1978), this requires journalists to present both sides of a story, to get quotes from experts, to obscure their own input into the story, to disguise their authorial voice, and to avoid what would be considered explicit editorialising. As a number of surveys shows, the role of objective disseminators of information is an important part of the self-image of journalists. 'Once they are in the business', Patterson and Donsbach (1996:466) tell us, 'their partisan beliefs are clearly secondary to a professional orientation'.

Overall, then, the capacity of the personal political preferences of individual journalists to influence what they produce is limited by the realities of their employment situation, by the ideology of the organisation for which they work, and by the structural requirements of their role as professional workers. Workers in the media have, as Epstein (1974:xiv) puts it, to modify 'their own personal values in accordance with the requisites of the organisation' and, one might add, the profession, in which they work.

Ownership and control

Introduction

The third factor is ownership. The contention here is that those who own the media control its content. As Golding and Murdock (1991:15) put it, 'different ways of financing and organising cultural production have traceable consequences for the range of discourses and representations in the public domain'.

In assessing this argument it is useful to look first at the ways in which media systems are owned and financed, and then to examine the effects this might have on their content. Broadly speaking, the media systems in particular countries can be owned in three ways: by the state, by privately-owned corporations, or by a mixture of public and private ownership. With the collapse of Soviet communism, state ownership of the media has become less significant, though it still remains an important feature of countries such as China and Cuba. However, for the purposes of this chapter we will focus on the other two forms of ownership, beginning with private ownership.

Patterns of private ownership: more media, fewer owners?

In those countries where the media are almost exclusively privately owned, there is general agreement that such ownership is becoming more strikingly concentrated in a limited number of companies. This increased concentration is referred to as 'conglomeration', and conglomerates come in two forms (see Murdock, 1982). One is 'general conglomerates', where media companies become part of corporations whose major interests lie in areas outside the media, such as banking, real estate or financial services; the other is 'communication conglomerates', which are formed when existing media companies widen or deepen their ownership in the media industry (Carveth, 1992).

This deepening of ownership can be done in three ways. One is to buy into or merge with other media companies that serve the same market (a process known as 'horizontal concentration'). This happens when, for example, a television network buys into cable television. The other two are forms of 'vertical concentration'. The first is where corporations that make and distribute programming buy into, or are taken over by, ones that manufacture the hardware used to show media products (such as televisions, video recorders and computers). The other is where corporations, which are established in one area of the communications industry, buy companies in other sectors of the business, thus creating what are called 'synergies' or cross-media empires. The merger of America-on-Line and Time-Warner in 2000 is the latest of these. It is the largest merger in business history to date, and brings together media companies as diverse as CNN, Netscape, Warner Brothers and Time Magazine.

Such synergies offer considerable advantages to their owners. They can use their presence in a number of media markets to sell their products more effectively (Golding and Murdock, 1991). They can offer advertisers access to a full range of media. This reduces the number of agencies with whom advertisers have to work and gives synergies a larger share of advertising revenue. In this way they allow for a full realisation of 'the cross-over potential of media products'. The scale of their control also extends the impact of any restrictions that advertisers place on media content. Their owners have unprecedented control over the production, retailing and dissemination of the material they produce. For these reasons synergies are the most significant development in the contemporary communications industry.

Patterns of private ownership: more countries, fewer owners?

The other major trend in media ownership is the transnationalisation or globalisation of media ownership. Media conglomerates are increasingly expanding beyond national boundaries and now operate in all parts of the world. According to McChesney (1998:12–13) the global market has two tiers. The first consists of around ten media conglomerates, including Disney, Time-Warner, News Corporation, Sony and General Electric. With sales of between $10 billion and $25 billion in 1997, they are among largest companies in the world and are mainly American owned. There is a second tier of around 40 companies, with sales revenues ranging from $1 billion to $5 billion. These are primarily owned in Europe and North America, with a few in Asia and Latin America. In effect, around 50 corporations dominate the global media market.

The consequences of private ownership: do owners control?

The media generally treat these trends and changes as primarily economic in nature; however, they raise a number of questions for the sociology of the mass media. Does private ownership on this scale mean that there is a conflict between the role of the media 'as a key resource for citizenship and its economic base in private ownership' (Murdock, 1990:1)? Or, alternatively, is it the case that this particular pattern of ownership is the guarantor of a free press and an open media?

The political economy perspective most clearly articulates the view that the system of ownership is central to understanding of media content and, through that, of media power. It argues that private ownership on this scale leads to a media that is limited in scope and diversity. The model is a broad one and there are a number of variants within it. These differ in their specification of the mechanisms through which ownership is translated into control.

The manufacture of consent: the work of Herman and Chomsky

One example is the 'propaganda model' proposed by Herman and Chomsky (1988: see also Herman, 1998). They argue that the mass media in the USA is a transmission belt for the ideas and ideologies of the powerful, a group that they see as including governmental and corporate elites. Control operates by means of a series of filters through which information has to pass to acquire the status of news. These include an industry in which there is concentrated ownership, which is dependent on advertising for its profits, and which is dependent on political and corporate sources for information. These normally guarantee that only 'suitable' stories and opinions survive but, if they prove insufficient, direct political pressure is applied to keep the media in line. This takes the form of direct intervention by owners and politicians or harassment by right-wing policy groups (such as Accuracy in the Media or the American Enterprise Institute).

Chomsky (2001) cites the work of Project Censored in support of his argument. This is a US-based organisation that each year selects the top 25 news stories which have been censored by news organisations, generally in response to political and corporate pressure. The top censored story in 2001 was about the attempts of multi-national corporations such as Monsanto and Bechtel to gain control of world water supply systems, and to charge the full cost for its supply. This has implications for the capacity of poor countries to afford the cost of the most basic resource. Despite its importance, the issue never made it to the national press, though it did get coverage in some small left-of-centre publications.

The view from Britain: Peter Golding and Graham Murdock

The work of Golding and Murdock (1991 and 1996) is another example. They reject any simple determinism, arguing that it is not possible, for the most part, to read particular examples of media production as direct reflections of the interests of owners. Although 'corporations dominate the cultural landscape' (Golding and Murdock, 1996:16), the manner is which this translates into cultural control is not as direct and undeviating as Herman and Chomsky would have it.

They argue that in the present structure of media ownership, the direct exercise of proprietorial power for ideological or business reasons can occur. This has been a constant feature of the history of the media industry (see Bagdikian, 1993). It began at the turn of the twentieth century with press barons such as the Harmsworths in Britain and William Randolph Hearst in the USA, and continues at the turn of the twenty-first with media moguls such as Silvio Berlusconi in Italy and Rupert Murdoch (nominally an Australian, but with global media interests). Berlusconi has used the three major television channels that he owns in Italy as personal campaigning tools for a series of successful bids to be Premier of the country. Similarly, Murdoch uses his media in pursuit of his business ends with some relentlessness. It has led him to control News Corporation's coverage of China in a bid to get his satellite television stations into this huge and potentially lucrative market.

For most owners, however, their media organisations are simply another part of an industrial or commercial empire. They set financial targets in the same way as they do in other parts of their business empires, and employ staff who will see these are achieved. If the chosen personnel fail to achieve the desired financial goals, then they are replaced. This means that the ideological substance and stance of the organisation is a matter of indifference to its owners (as long, that is, as it produces the required level of profit).

Golding and Murdock (1991) argue that those who own media organisations have a degree of discretion around the policies they pursue and the operating targets that they set, but there are clear structural limits to this. Media organisations operate in a capitalist environment, and this imposes the imperative to make a profit. 'No matter who controls the corporations', Murdock (1982:135) tells us, 'profit maximisation remains the basic structural imperative around which the capitalist economy revolves'.

Advertisers: the power behind the throne

It is at this point that advertising becomes important. According to McManus (1992), advertising contributes most of the revenue and income of newspapers and network television in the USA, so advertising must be attracted if profit targets are to be realised. This places news organisations under pressure to 'deliver' the kind of audience that advertisers want to reach, and to create an environment in which advertising messages will be seen in the most sympathetic light. In effect, then, news becomes a commodity and a resource that is used to attract the audiences, who are in turn sold to advertisers to produce profits for media organisations.

The commodification of news

This process has a number of implications for the nature of news. News organisations may be forced to avoid controversial and challenging issues either because of the risk of alienating and upsetting particular sections of the audience, or because it is too expensive to cover, particularly when compared to the cost of routine and predictable news items. This leads to a concentration on issues that are assumed to outrage and energise audiences (for example, the extensive and exaggerated coverage of violent crime).

The news will also tend to ignore issues that are of relevance to those sections of the audience that are of little interest to advertisers. They may wish to reach the largest possible audience, but it must be one in which there is significant representation of certain minority groups, such as the rich and those who have either high levels of disposable income or considerable power over corporate spending. Advertisers, as McManus (1992) puts it, do not pay for news quality but for the audience 'quality'. News will reflect their concerns, rather than those of other groups such as the poor or the elderly.

Finally, advertisers want to attract an audience that is paying attention to what is on the media, otherwise their messages may pass unnoticed (McManus, 1992:790). This has led to pressure to present news in an entertaining fashion to hold the attention of viewers and, if possible, to increase their number. As not all events and issues can be made entertaining, only those that can will become news. This creates a preference in the media for 'human interest' stories over more conventional political and economic ones.

Back to Murdock and Golding

In this way, according to Golding and Murdock (1991), owners have power to shape the media but their power is circumscribed by the need to make a profit and this indirectly creates a situation in which large advertisers act in effect as a licensing authority. Their decisions on where to spend their advertising budgets are an indirect but significant influence on the content of the media. This influence, and the path through which it becomes significant, is likely to become more prominent as the ownership of media outlets becomes more concentrated and as the pressure to make profits through the sale of advertising increases.

Defending the Corporation

These kinds of claims have not gone unchallenged. According to Bagdikian (1993), the ownership of the media by large corporations has been defended on a number of grounds. The main one is that their size and the extent of their market dominance enables them to resist pressures from governments and other interests, such as advertisers, to restrict or limit the information they make available.

Similarly, the role and alleged power of synergies has also been questioned (see McAnany and Wilkinson, 1992). In theory synergies possess the potential for market dominance and power; in reality, this is seldom realised. The level of debt incurred in creating a synergy, and the consequent interest payments on the required borrowings, can be enormous. Owners are often forced to sell off sections of their operations in order to survive, thus reducing the level of synergism. It is also difficult to get the range of different companies that go into the creation of a synergy to work together. Personnel come with different experience, different expertise, and different marketing and creative abilities and, as Turow puts it (1992:689), 'just because it worked for Disney does not mean it will work for everyone'.

Those who come at the issue from a cultural studies perspective accept that economic power is important to the understanding of the media, but reject the central place that political economy assigns to it. They argue that while economic factors may exert some influence on what gets into the public domain, this is increasingly a minor one. Grossberg (1995:75), for example, argues that while it is true that 'not all meanings circulate equally along the same paths... there is little that is commercially unthinkable'. They also argue that such factors do not influence how audiences interpret and respond to media material. For most media sociologists, however, it remains the case that, as Bourdieu (1998:39) puts it, an explanation of the media that did not take account of the concentration of ownership 'would obviously (be) inadequate but an explanation based solely on it would be just as inadequate'.

Public service broadcasting: the basic principles

So far we have examined the private form of media ownership; we turn now to the system of public ownership. This form of ownership has been promoted on the grounds that as a public resource, a national media system should have four features (see Negrine, 1998; Hellman, 1999). It should be available to all in a society, irrespective of wealth or location; it should cater for all of the interests and tastes in society; it should provide citizens with the information and education that they need to contribute to enlightened public debate and for informed democratic participation; and finally, it should create what Scannell (1989:143) called a 'common universe of discourse' in a society. It should create a sense of community and togetherness and, through that, contribute to social cohesion.

These ideals can best be realised through an ownership structure with financial independence from the state and from commercial organisations, which can be achieved in a number of ways.
The most typical system, found in many Western democracies, is
where the national broadcaster is financed by the imposition of a
licence fee, supplemented where necessary by advertising revenue. Under this system it exists alongside privately-owned
media organisations financed entirely by advertising revenue,
but subject to state controls on programme content and ownership
ambitions.

The end of public service broadcasting?

Whether these ideals were ever fully realised by public service
broadcasting services is a matter of some dispute. Golding and
Murdock (1996:16), for example, say that the independence of the
BBC from government interference was 'always fragile', but there
is agreement that the ideals underlying such services are now
under pressure. An initial justification for public service broadcasting was the scarcity of channels. However, the digital revolution has undermined this argument as channel capacity is now
potentially infinite. The pressure applied to public finances in
many countries in the 1980s and 1990s produced a turn against
state monopolies and a trend in favour of markets. In this climate
of deregulation governments relaxed the state monopoly, and
allowed commercial broadcasters to set up or extend their competition with public service organisations. Finally, the speed of social
change in many countries has made the notion of national identity
somewhat problematic, and so difficult for public service organisations to serve.

These changes have had, according to Murdock (1982), particular consequences for public service broadcasting. Large commercial conglomerates now dominate the media market in most
countries and they set the terms of competition in the market
place. Their ability to compete for labour and talent can, for
example, set the level of production costs for state broadcasters
and restrict or undermine their capacity to produce quality
programming. Also, the ideological turn against the state has
meant that public service broadcasters are under pressure to maintain a certain proportion of their audience in order to justify their
licence fee.

The response of public service broadcasters has been to renego-
tiate the balance between their informational, cultural and economic roles. They continue to claim that the cultural role is
unique to them and they continue to honour it after a fashion. At
the same time, they take what Syvertsen (quoted in Hellman,
1999:125) says are 'compromising steps towards popular genres
in order to protect their share of viewing'. They begin to offer
comparable products to compete successfully with commercial
stations. This is reflected in a 'lightening' in their schedules and
a trend towards lowest common denominator programming.
Under this strategy programmes of a cultural, educational or
political nature are increasingly diverted to off-peak and secondary viewing hours. This has been characterised as a 'dumbing
down' in their output.

However, Hellman and Sauri (1994) caution against large-scale
generalisation and argue that the consequences for public broadcasting vary depending on the particular society that is examined.
They claim that the effects of the changes in the broadcasting environment have been more complex. There has been some convergence
but this has been in the direction of a more extended public service
orientation. Commercial organisations may be motivated by the
pursuit of profit, but they are also constrained by the desire for
public and political legitimacy. As a result they have retained or
expanded informative or cultural programming to achieve this
legitimacy and to be identified in the public mind as serious broadcasters. This issue is dealt with again in the conclusion.

The power of the audience: giving the public what it wants

The notion that the audience is important in influencing the production of media messages comes from two sources: the first is
that media organisations need to attract an audience, and to do
this they must cater to its needs; the second (and more complex)
source is in the nature of social communication. Successful communication requires us to have some idea about the people with
whom we are communicating. To be sure that they will understand us we must adapt our style of communication to fit the
mental image we have of them. Applied to mass communication
this means, according to Hagen (1999), that the image media
organisations 'have of the audience is decisive for the message
they produce'.

Ignoring the audience and writing for themselves?

So what images do media personnel have of their audience? The available research indicates that, for the most part, journalists know little about their audiences or about their knowledge of current affairs (see Ettema and Whitney, 1994). This is surprising given that audience research would seem to be an obvious source of such information. Yet a number of studies, such as that by Gans (1979:230), found that journalists pay little attention to audience research and that it plays a 'marginal role' in news production.

The sense they have of their audience is constructed from a number of narrow and disparate elements. One is the response of family, friends and neighbours, or from chance meetings that they have at parties or in the street. In addition, according to Ettema and Whitney (1994) and others, the 'audience' to which news personnel are primarily oriented is made up of their immediate superiors and fellow journalists. Hagen (1999) says that they are most responsive to their professional group, and that 'exceeds any image they have of the general public'.

They also feel that being required to meet the demands and wishes of their audience in some kind of mechanical fashion is a threat to their professional autonomy, and that feedback from the audience is a source of extra stress and, as such, one that could be done without. They see their job as communicating to an audience of citizens (that is, responsible people who wish to be kept well informed about relevant public and political issues). This image shapes their selection of stories and their mode of presentation of material. They believe that journalists rather than audiences know the news that needs to be told and that it is their job to tell it, a viewpoint characterised by Bondeberg (quoted in Hagen, 1999:138) as 'school-teacher television'.

The growth of market-driven journalism

However the question arises as to whether this style of working 'for themselves' (Gans, 1979:230) has survived recent changes in the media industry, particularly those detailed in the section on ownership. Commercial considerations have become more central to news divisions and they have been infiltrated by notions of cost-cutting and profit generation. This has created pressures to maintain or enlarge the audience for news bulletins. Audience research has, as a result, become more important. The pressure has grown to give audiences what they 'want' rather than what news personnel feel they 'need'. News production is, according to this argument, increasingly driven not so much by the needs of citizens for information but by the desire of media organisations to meet peoples' wants and appetites as consumers.

The use of news consultants has been central to this process. News organisations hire them, particularly at a local level in the USA, to recommend ways to get more viewers. According to Postman and Powers (1992), the consultants draw up a profile of the kind of viewers that a media outlet should have. They then check the organisation's personnel and news output to see if these are attractive to such viewers. If not, they suggest changes. They have, for example, revised news formats, including the length of news stories. They have set limits to the number of stories per newscast, and they have emphasised the need to make visual material central to every story. Their concept of ideal news is 'technically uniform, visually sophisticated, easy to understand, fast paced, people oriented stories that are produced in a minimum of time' (Bantz, McCorkle and Baade, 1997:273). If possible these should be about crime, scandal, celebrities, or the bizarre and unusual. They have also promoted the 'family concept' of newsreaders. This is where the news is presented by a male and a female newsreader, both good-looking in a conventional sense, and generally around the same age, though it is acceptable for the man to be older.

Summary

From this it would seem that the influence of audiences on news content is changing. It is moving from one in which audiences were seen as a group to inform and educate about political and social affairs, to one in which increasingly the audience is seen as a commodity to create and as a group to entertain. The dumbing down of news content is the means through which this is achieved.

Organisational features

Introduction

The fifth factor that shapes media content is the nature of the organisations that produce it. It is argued that news organisations develop particular strategies to deal with the environment in which they operate, and these working arrangements have implications for the nature of what they produce. The strategies have evolved to meet three requirements of the news-gathering process: the need to produce reliable and accurate news, the need to generate information that will attract and retain the attention of an audience, and the need to select stories that can be processed economically, efficiently and routinely.

The problem for news organisations is that they deal with raw material that is presumed to be unexpected and unpredictable. The news is that which is about to happen, and so it should not be foreseeable in advance. Yet, like all large organisations, news-gathering ones cannot operate with this level of unpredictability: they must try to introduce an element of certainty into their production processes. But how, Tuchman (1978) asks, 'can an organisation routinise the processing of unexpected events?'

The answer is that news organisations have developed a series of rules and routines to solve the problem. The routine procedures allow them to allocate the resources of the organisation in a manner that ensures a regular output is produced. The rules enable news personnel to decide which events are news and which are not, and they give guidance on how to present the selected events as news. We begin by considering the procedures.

Working the beat

The development of the system of 'news beats' (Fishman, 1980) or 'news nets' (Tuchman, 1978) solves the problem of resource allocation. It involves the routine assignment of reporters and recording crews to locations that have been predefined as the kinds of places in which newsworthy events occur, and hence as places from which a regular supply of news stories will be guaranteed. As Tuchman (1978:21) puts it, 'news media place reporters at legitimated institutions where stories . . . may be expected to be found'.

The courts, the national parliament and the press conferences of powerful interest groups and political parties are cases in point. These locations can always be relied upon for a story even when nothing of great significance happens at them. Fishman (1980:34), in his study of a Californian newspaper, found that 'when both the city editor and the reporter agreed that nothing was happening, the reporter was still responsible for writing something about the beat'. In this sense 'the beat defines the world of possible news' (Fishman, 1980:16).

The news cycle

The second routine of significance for news organisations is their production cycle. All organisations have a schedule or cycle within which they produce their output. For news organisations, Palmer (1998:387) tells us, 'publication occurs at pre-scheduled intervals which are largely independent of what happens in the outside world'. For most media, particularly newspapers but also television and radio, the basic interval is a 24-hour one. Production is organised around this constraint and reporting works within its most visible manifestation, 'the deadline'. As a result news is a perishable commodity with a 24-hour lifespan. By the next edition or news bulletin, as Dunwoody and Griffin (1993) have pointed out, yesterday's news is 'old' and assumed by the media to be of little interest to their audience.

This means that events that happen within the production cycle of media organisations and on which information can be gathered within the deadline have a higher chance of becoming news than events that do not. Galtung and Ruge (1973:63) argue that the frequency of an event is 'the time span needed for an event to unfold itself and acquire meaning'; hence, 'the more similar the frequency of an event is to the frequency of the news medium, the more probable that it will be recorded as news'. A murder or a military coup happens at a specific point in time on a particular day, and so will be reported as news. A court case or a famine unfold over time and do not fit easily into the production cycle of the media, so they do not become news as easily. This has been called 'an events orientation' and produces a definition of news as events, rather than as the social processes that produce events.

News values

However, large numbers of events occur within the production cycle of the media but this is not sufficient for them to become news. They must in addition become 'visible as potential news stories' (Hall, 1973:18). They must be recognised and identified as newsworthy. Media personnel have developed an informal set of rules or guidelines that assist in the identification process which are referred to as 'news values'. According to Barrat (1986:95), they provide 'the news worker with essential guidelines to the selection, construction and presentation of the world in news'. They are passed on in the socialisation process in news organisations, and journalists with them are characterised as having a 'nose' for news.

Different writers have given different lists of what these values are (see, for example, Gans, 1979; Barrat, 1986; Palmer, 1998), but there is some agreement that the following are important. They may not in themselves be sufficient to turn an event into a news story, but they increase its chances of being recognised as such. An event must be either *dramatic* or capable of being presented in dramatic terms if it is to become news. The media are, therefore, attracted to events that are, in their terms, unexpected, and hence have a novelty or 'newness' value.

If there are events that the media feel should be covered for other reasons, the dramatic imperative can lead to an inflation of language in an attempt to instil drama into them. Thus routine disagreements between political figures can become 'open conflict', a new item ceases to be a 'surprise' and becomes a 'shock', and warm days become 'scorchers'.

It also helps if the meaning of an event is clear and can be presented in relatively *unambiguous* terms. This meets the demand that news stories should be easily understood by the widest possible readership. This can be achieved by presenting accounts of situations that have heroes and villains, some suspense and conflict, and some resolution (Barkin, 1984). This deflects attention away from more uncertain areas, such as speculation about motives, intention or meaning. As a result the events surrounding, say, a political demonstration or an outbreak of violence are more dramatic and less ambiguous than the causes of it, and so more likely to be reported.

This explains the attractions of the *negative* or 'bad news' to the media. News workers are not attracted to bad news out of a sense of personal perversity; negative events are simply more compatible with news values than positive ones. They are more likely to happen within the rhythms of the production cycle of the media. They are generally unexpected, so lend themselves to being related in dramatic terms. Their meaning is likely to be clear and there is likely to be consensus in society about them (not many people are, for example, in favour of plane crashes or violent crime).

It helps also if there is *elite involvement* in the event. The actions of elites and of elite nations are believed by news workers to be of more consequence and so are more likely to be covered as news. Thus, like the US President or the Queen of England, we all have birthdays. Theirs are more likely to be treated as newsworthy than ours. *Cultural and geographic proximity* are also important. Those events which happens in places near to us in a geographic sense, or which happen in places or to people with whom we have some form of cultural identification, are more likely to become news. One British or American soldier killed in Macedonia is, for example, a news story in the West. The death of a Macedonian soldier may not be.

If events and issues can be presented in *personalised* terms as the actions of individuals then they have a greater chance of becoming news. As a result conflicts, complex events and political positions come to be represented in the media through the personalities that are involved in them. People are used, Sigal (1986:14) suggests, to 'symbolize the impersonal in the news' and as 'surrogates for institutions'. This, he argues, can turn into anthropomorphism. The media can present people as if they were not simply representative of political positions, governments, and entire countries but their embodiment. The use of Margaret Thatcher's name to represent a political ideology is a case in point.

There is also the question of *context*. In order to communicate quickly and efficiently about events and issues, news workers must place them in a context that makes them comprehensible and meaningful to the audience. The contexts that are used regularly are those that are assumed to be common-sense cultural beliefs (see Kitzinger and Reilly, 1997). This means that events and issues that fit into existing contexts, or for which there are readily available frameworks, are more likely to become news than events that do not have these qualities (Galtung and Ruge, 1973:68).

Kitzinger (2000) shows how certain events become the context for the reporting of other ones. They become a media template or rhetorical shorthand, the simple mention of which contextualises, explains and justifies the presentation of an event as news. The example she uses is the events surrounding the inquiry into claims of child abuse in Cleveland in the north of England. 'Cleveland' became the 'dominant analogy' (Kitzinger, 2000:75) or template to symbolise inappropriate bureaucratic and professional interference in the lives of ordinary people. The use of this phrase in relation to a new item immediately provides the context through which audiences can 'understand' the story with the minimum effort. Such templates are also difficult to dislodge. Subsequent investigations showed that the professionals were largely correct in the actions that they took in Cleveland, but the images the initial analogy evokes have been more difficult to displace.

Finally there is a series of rules and conventions that apply to news selection in particular media. It is, for example, a television convention that filmed action is more interesting than someone talking to the camera. Similarly, it is believed that good visuals are what only television can offer and so they are considered an essential element of television news. This is referred to as the *visual imperative*. This means that an event that generates good pictures has a better chance of being covered on television news bulletins than one that does not. The issue of 'Mad Cow Disease', for example, was helped on to the media agenda by the availability of good visuals, most notably the pictures of Daisy 'the staggering cow' (see Kitzinger and Reilly, 1997).

Organisational factors and their consequences: favouring the favoured

It has been argued that these rules and routines give privileged access and coverage to powerful institutions and groups in society. The use of 'news nets' reinforces the notion that the locations of powerful people and organisations are the places where important and newsworthy events happen. Equally, it disadvantages groups whose activities are not covered in a routine way by a 'news net' (Sigal, 1986:25). Community organisations and grassroots movements are not, for example, normally part of a 'news net' and so do not have comparable access to the media.

Knowledge about the production cycles of the media can, according to Schudson (1986:81), be used by the powerful to gain advantageous access to the media. Politicians are aware of the deadlines of the various media, and structure their activities in line with them. Their press conferences and photo opportunities are strategically planned to facilitate easy coverage by the media. Boorstein (1962:22) has described these as 'pseudo events', with no significance other than being organised purely to gain media coverage.

News values also operate to favour the powerful. Personalisation is, according to Hall (1973:183), 'the isolation of the person from his relevant social and institutional context, or the constitution of a personal subject as exclusively the motor force of history'. This deflects attention away from a concern with the contribution of wider social forces to particular events and as such, according to Edelman (1988), acts as a form of protection for established institutions. The question of context is also problematic. It may be necessary to locate events in particular contexts to make them comprehensible to the audience, but the problem is the kinds of contexts that are used. These are justified by reference to the collective common-sense of a society. Ericson, Baranek and Chan (1987:62), however, claim that they are based on 'limited assumptions and a limited range of solutions' which 'take on the character of inevitability'. In this sense they represent a narrow and partial view of what the social consensus is.

Opening the closed shop

However, while these factors may place certain groups at an advantage, their operation does not produce total closure in the media. There are a number of ways in which less powerful groups can use them to get new issues and perspectives into the media.

Knowledge of media routines. Powerful groups can maximise their exposure in the media by tailoring their activities to suit media deadlines, but it is also open to oppositional groups and new movements to do the same. Greenpeace members, for example, have been able to use their knowledge of media values and routines to attract media coverage (see Hansen, 1993). They have the resources to stage dramatic and colourful events and to supply the media with free or relatively cheap video footage of them at a time when many media organisations are suffering cutbacks in their news collection budgets.

There is a further dimension to this. Altheide and Rasmussen (1976) show that getting a sufficient supply of news is a problem for news organisations. Their relationship with dominant sources guarantees a steady supply of news, but there will be times when they may be unable to provide enough. Oppositional groups can use this knowledge to force their concerns into the news. It is significant in that respect that the famine in Ethiopia in 1984

became news as a result of 'issue entrepreneurship' by development agencies (Cracknell, 1993). They were successful because
August is traditionally regarded as a slow time for news. Most of
the major routine suppliers of news (such as governments, state
agencies and powerful interest groups) are on holiday.

Using cultural contexts and news values.   These also provide opportunities for opening the media agenda. If an issue or event can be
formulated in terms of prevailing news values, or 'made to activate
existing chains of cultural meaning' (Hansen, 1993:453), then its
chances of getting on to the media agenda are significantly increased. Bosso (1989:168) has shown how aid agencies were able to
use the visual imperative – in this case, the provision of 'good
pictures of people dying' – to turn a famine into a major news
story. Beckett (1996:59) has shown how what she describes as the
'coalition of claims-makers' (child-care professionals, parents and
feminists) was able to use 'the culturally salient image of the "child
victim" to attract the attention of the media journalists and bring
sexual violence against children on to the media agenda'. Moreover,
they were able to dominate how the media framed the issue for a
number of years. Similarly, the environmental movement has been
able to use the cultural theme of the importance of unspoiled nature
to highlight the issue of industrial pollution and to force it on to the
media agenda as an issue that merits coverage.

The rise of investigative journalism.   A change in journalistic practices has also been responsible for opening up the media agenda.
This is the rise of investigative journalism, which has now become
institutionalised with considerable media space devoted to the
investigation of scandals and to the uncovering of the illegal
activities of the powerful. In Britain the traditional deference of
the media, and particularly of public television, has become diluted, and journalistic attitudes to the powerful are now more
adversarial than was previously the case. As Sabato (1991:3) says
about the USA, 'more and more the news media seem...more
bent on killing kings than on making them'.

Closing the open shop: rules and routines fight back

Limits of Media Routines.   The creative use of news values and
media routines can open the media to new issues and new voices,

but the extent of the openings should not be over-stated. It has been found that the groups which promote new issues often lose control of them when they get on to the media agenda. This is particularly the case when they enter what Strodheff, Hawkins and Schoenfeld (1992) describe as the third stage in the life of a new media issue: that of routinisation. Linne (1993), for example, found in her analysis of the coverage of Greenpeace in Denmark that activists can draw attention to an issue but, when the story was established in the media, government officials and others regained control of it. Hansen (1993) also found this in Britain, where increased coverage of the activities of conventional politicians on environmental issues was accompanied by a decline in media coverage of the activities of Greenpeace. As he puts it, 'the news-making initiative has increasingly been seized by the government and the forum of formal politics' (Hansen, 1993:160).

The limits to new values and cultural contexts.   Similarly, the use of dramatic or staged events to get media coverage is only successful in the long term if those involved succeed in moving beyond getting coverage for their issues and in becoming legitimate sources that are consulted as a matter of routine by the media. This can be difficult to achieve as there is often a conflict between the tactics that command media attention and those that establish media legitimacy. New groups may have to stage dramatic or confrontational events to break through the media attention barrier, but the use of these tactics carries specific risks that the cultural resonance they provoke may be a negative one.

The American Indians, for example, have used confrontational tactics to gain media attention for their grievances since the 1960s (see Baylor, 1996). But they found that the bulk of the coverage was devoted to their militancy and not to other aspects of their claim, such as its basis in civil rights and past treaty violations. As Baylor puts it (1996:245), 'the issue of militancy overshadows any presentation of the real grievances and issues behind Indian protest'. This is also a problem that anti-globalisation protesters now face.

The use of cultural assumptions to gain media coverage can also have unpredictable consequences. This comes, according to Gamson and Modigliani (1987), from the nature of cultures. Most cultural themes and values are ambivalent and multi-dimensional. When a cultural theme is used to secure media coverage it inevitably, though not immediately, provokes the use of its cultural counter-part or 'counter-theme'. The use of the image of the child as victim has a counter-image in the culture. This is the child as liar, as impressionable, and as unreliable. Opposition groups activated this and broke the media consensus on child sex abuse. Beckett (1996) found that while the frame of 'collective denial' dominated early media coverage of the child abuse issues in the USA, 'false accusations' and 'false memories' have become the contexts through which more recent coverage has been organised and framed.

Suitable cases for investigation?   Investigative journalism has been responsible for uncovering major abuses by powerful groups, but it has been argued that this kind of journalism is in danger of losing its focus. This is reflected in a change in the kinds of subjects that are now considered worthy of investigation. Sabato (1991), for example, claims that the resources of the media are increasingly being devoted to the investigation of rumours about private lives of politicians. Once they start the issue is pursued 'intensely, often excessively, and sometimes uncontrollably' (Sabato, 1991:6). Investigative journalism now 'magnifies, over-scrutinizes and relentlessly pursues rumours or gossip about the relatively minor personal failings of political and public figures and in the process gets caught up in an over-reaction of its own making'. He characterises this kind of journalism as a 'feeding frenzy', similar to the feasting of sharks when they turn on a wounded or bleeding prey.

The media pursuit of the Clinton–Lewinsky affair was an example of such a frenzy. Enormous media resources were devoted to it, while more serious scandals such as those surrounding the collapse of a major bank with political connections, the Savings and Loan Bank, or the US bombing of factories in the Sudan were largely ignored (see Hitchens, 1999). This is having a very direct impact in the growing hostility of the public to the press and in a decline in their expressed level of confidence in the media as a social institution. In this sense, Sabato (1991) argues, the ultimate victim of the feeding frenzies has been the media itself.

Summary

In this section we have considered how organisational and professional routines and practices shape how events and issues become news. These tend to favour the powerful in that they allow them more control over the content of news. Other groups can, however, use a knowledge of these routines and practices to get access for alternative accounts and interpretations, but this is a constant and often uneven struggle.

Conclusion

In this chapter we have looked at the social mechanisms that influence and shape what the media produce. Overall the argument is that being 'news' is not some intrinsic quality that certain events in the world possess. We have suggested instead that media processes intervene significantly and decisively between the occurrence of events or issues and their recognition and presentation as news. Like all forms of raw material, some events and issues are accepted by news organisations whilst others are rejected. The survivors enter a production process and emerge at the other end as items in a news bulletin or as stories in a newspaper. It is in this sense that sociologists refer to the 'manufacture' or the 'making' of news (see Cohen and Young, 1981).

CHAPTER 5

Changing Media Agendas, Widening Public Access?

Introduction

In previous chapters we looked at the question of whose frames dominate the media agenda and at how this kind of dominance is secured. In this chapter we consider the argument that new kinds of media programming and new forms of communication technology can widen access and participation in the media and, as it were, let the 'public back in'. The new programming is represented by the rise of talk television and of what can loosely be termed 'reality television'. The new media technology is the Internet. We will consider each of these in turn. The central concern is the extent to which they succeed in allowing more democratic access to information flows and processes of opinion formation in society.

Talk television

The public sphere as a problem

The argument that talk television represents an opening of access to the media takes at least two forms. They share the assumption that the mass media constitute the public sphere in modern societies and that this sphere is in difficulty. For Carpignano and his colleagues (1990:35) there is 'a crisis in the legitimacy of the news as a social institution in its role of dissemination and interpretation of events'. The news media are no longer accepted by significant sectors of the public as providing authoritative accounts and interpretations of current affairs in society. Journalists are increasingly seen as spokespeople for the powerful, something which is

reflected in the difficulties in distinguishing between their interpretations and those of powerful political and social elites. The
views of particular sections of the population, most notably those
of working-class men, are effectively excluded from the media.

For Shattuc (1997) the crisis is related to the distinction between
the public and the private spheres. The public sphere is seen as the
arena of rational public debate. As such it is a masculine domain,
concerned largely with 'men's' issues. The private sphere, by contrast, is the arena of the domestic and the emotional, and hence
largely concerned with 'women's' issues. The public sphere is more
socially valued because it is where 'important' issues of news and
current affairs are discussed. This results in the exclusion of the
concerns of citizens of the private sphere, namely women.

The exclusion of the experiences and perspectives of these
groups – and of others such as ethnic minorities (see Leurdijk,
1997) – is deepened by the degree to which authoritativeness for
the media has become increasingly anchored in information rather
than experience. It is encapsulated in the notion of the expert and
the media regularly counterpose the 'opinions' of ordinary people
against the 'truth' of experts. These are generally male, and their
claim to authority rests on the extent of their knowledge of events
rather than their experience of them. Thus economists are the
experts on unemployment and not those who experience it. Criminologists are the authorities on crime and not crime victims. As
Carpignano and his colleagues (1990:36) put it, 'the knowledge of
events acquired through the consumption of information prevail[s] over the narration of experience'.

Talk television as the solution

These writers have promoted the idea that talk shows represent a
solution to problems of the public sphere. They provide a means
through which the public, and particularly previously excluded
groups, can express their views and intervene in (and shape) public
consciousness and public debate. They allow a wider range of
issues and individuals on to the public agenda and create new
criteria for the validation of what passes as social knowledge.
Talk shows are, Shattuc (1997) suggests, 'the newest incarnation
of the public sphere'. Jerry Springer, one of the most prominent talk
show hosts, put it more colourfully: 'They are', he claimed, 'the
only forum on TV where everyday people can be part of the show'.

Restoring ordinary talk

Talk shows also restore ordinary conversation to its place at the centre of public debate. It had been displaced by the controlled and manufactured communication strategies perfected by the public relations industry and adopted by politicians in their appearances on the media. Contributors to the shows speak with all the inconsistency, incoherence and eloquence of ordinary talk and conversation, and it is on this basis that audiences can identify with them. They speak the same kind of language.

The truth of experience

This is paralleled by the restoration of lived experience as the guarantor of truth. Carpignano and his colleagues (1990:36) argue that on the shows 'the authority of the expert is displaced by the authority of a narrative informed by lived experience'. The test of the authenticity and the truth of what is being advocated is the degree to which it is drawn from and reflects people's direct experiences of the world.

Down with experts

For Livingstone and Lunt (1994), the confrontation between 'experts' and 'ordinary' people is one of the strengths of the shows. They provide a space in the media where the perspectives of experts and ordinary people can come together and confront each other. In the process the kinds of explanations experts offer may not go down well and their status can be challenged. They may not be able to match the anger, enthusiasm or sense of righteousness that the experiences of ordinary people can generate. As a result, experts have been attacked and shouted down on the shows. They have also been thrown off them (Himmelstein, 1994), and even, on occasion, listened to with some respect (Leurdijk, 1997).

Self-disclosure

The reliance on direct personal experience is intensified by the level and nature of the self-disclosure that such shows appear to promote and on which they thrive. Greenberg and his colleagues (1997) analysed eleven top talk shows in the USA in 1995. They found that personal disclosures were common, with an average of 16 per hour-long show. They were most typically about forms of private sexual behaviour, ranging from the mundane to the bizarre.

The level of self-disclosure has been dismissed as prompted by the offer of money, or as a reflection of the exhibitionism that contemporary culture appears to value and reward. However, the reality is more complex. Joyner Priest and Dominick (1994) argue that self-disclosure is linked to the issue of access. Participation in the shows gives marginalised groups the opportunity to contest their deviant status. It is, for example, one of the few places in media culture where people whose sexual orientations are regarded as deviant can 'speak on our own terms or hear others speaking for themselves' (J. Gamson, 1995:45).

This kind of self-disclosure can be dangerous. By appearing on the shows participants publicise their deviant status on a scale that could expose them to further discrimination, particularly within their own communities. Joyner Priest and Dominick (1994) found that participants in shows in the USA are well aware of these risks but feel they are worth taking because of the opportunities that the shows offer to educate a nation-wide, and potentially a world-wide, audience. As one respondent put it, 'we're pushing the boundaries of society a little bit so that the next individual who comes along doesn't have as much hassle' (Joyner Priest and Dominick, 1994:86).

This objective influenced their mode of self-presentation on the shows. They contested their deviant status by emphasising the degree to which their activities were compatible with the social values of love, personal choice, and civil and human rights. It is unclear if this kind of activism promotes acceptance by audiences or if it frightens them into rejection and conservatism. However, those who self-disclosed did report that their experience on the talk shows had been personally empowering (Joyner Priest and Dominick, 1994).

Bring on the politicians

The access offered by talk shows has also attracted politicians in the USA and Europe. The format of the shows allows them to speak over the heads of the media, as it were, and to gain direct access to the public. Research indicates that they also enter into the 'spirit' of the shows. Schutz (1997) found that politicians used the formats of the shows to self-disclose, to talk about their marital and family relationships, their friendships, their values and their religious faith. Research also indicates that, particularly in the early phases of political campaigns, their appearances on talk shows have a significant and positive influence on voter percep-tions and attitudes (Pfau and Eveland, 1996).

Audiences and class prejudice

There is some evidence from viewing patterns that the shows are successful in reaching groups that are disenfranchised in the media. Women are more likely to watch day-time talk shows than men, the unemployed are more likely to watch than the employed, and retired people constitute an important part of the viewing audience. Overall, the lower one's social class, the more likely one is to watch the shows (Livingstone and Lunt, 1994: 46–9).

Indeed, according to Masciarotte (1991), these characteristics of the audiences explain much of the criticism of the shows, and in particular middle-class discomfort with them. They are a reflection of social prejudices about the seriousness of women's talk and the mode of speech of working-class people. Middle-class people often find such people difficult to understand and hard to take seriously. However, she argues that politics includes the right to speak in one's own voice and the right to assert ones identity. Within this definition talk television is, she says, a 'political forum'.

Talk television: the case against

Critics have been less positive about the contribution of talk tele-vision. Page and Tannenbaum (1996:51), for example, suggest that the degree to which the shows constitute the basis for 'an entirely happy story of democratic triumph' is open to question.

They argue that while the shows may in the past have provided a forum for the debates about excluded and suppressed issues, this is no longer the case. They have become more extreme in their search for suitable subjects and more sensational in their mode of presenting the issues. Abt and Mustazza (1997) characterise this as a movement from rational debate to freak show. They refer to the shows as 'toxic' and as the new pornography. The episode of the *Jerry Springer Show*, 'I Married a Horse' (which dealt with bestiality), is a case in point.

Critics also argue that nominally these shows are open to ordinary people, but being ordinary is not sufficient to be a guest; other characteristics are required. Those with more extreme opinions and a more extreme manner of expressing them are more likely to get on the shows. Similarly, those who are willing to disclose deviant behaviour, particularly of a bizarre sexual nature, are more likely to be acceptable. In addition, guests must be capable of providing what Grindstaff (1998) has called 'the money shot'. This is the 'moment of raw emotion from angry denunciation to tearful confession, the visible display of anger or sorrow or joy or remorse that makes daytime talk simultaneously trashy and compelling'.

The failure of people to live up to these standards has meant that many of the shows are now stage-managed. If 'ordinary people' do not exist then the producers of the shows have to invent them. This is reflected in the revelations about the use of actors to play roles that are intended to titillate or antagonise the audience and the viewers. As a result the shows are unlikely to end with the emergence of a humane and sensible consensus on an issue but with a fight, and on occasion with a murder. This occurred in the USA after an episode of the *Jenny Jones Show* in 1995 and the *Jerry Springer Show* in 2000. Oprah Winfrey, one of the originals of the talk show format, claimed that it is simply a matter of time before the killings happen on the shows themselves (*Observer*, 4 March 1999).

Critics also dispute claims that these shows have brought a range of suppressed or excluded topics into the public sphere. They argue that the range of topics on the shows is narrow. Greenberg and his colleagues (1997) found that the leading topics were family issues such as parent–child themes, marital relationships, dating and sexual activity. By contrast there was little evidence that more conventionally political issues, such as racism and poverty, were being discussed, though this may be a cultural characteristic of American television. In Great Britain these topics were frequently highlighted (see Livingstone and Lunt, 1994), and Leurdijk (1997) argues that such themes are also common in Dutch talk shows, where in general such shows are more serious and less sensational than their American counter-parts.

The reasons for the narrow agenda in the USA relate to the commercial context within which the programmes are produced.

They are primarily intended to make a profit rather than provide a public forum. Within this context overtly political topics have to be avoided. They risk alienating sectors of the audience and (perhaps more significantly) sections of the advertising industry, thus exposing the producers and television networks to an unacceptable risk of financial loss. In this way the door of access is opened and closed by the hand of commerce.

Commercial considerations may also influence, however indirectly, the kinds of solution that the shows offer to the problems that they discuss. There are a number of separate arguments here. One relates to the way in which the shows misuse the therapeutic model and offer 'soundbite pop psychology to address serious pathologies' (Abt and Mustazza, 1997:16). This argument questions the status of many of those described in the programmes as experts, and points to the degree to which they provide audiences with 'platitude camouflaged as profundity' (Himmelstein, 1994:339).

It has also been argued that while the shows try to create a therapeutic environment, this is not done for therapeutic purposes. They do not intend to cure people but to encourage them to tell, 'ever more titillating stories in the competitive quest for profit' (Himmelstein, 1994:362). These revelations are intended to arouse viewers and audiences and to produce the kind of heated confrontations and controversies on which the ratings for the shows depend. As such, talk shows commandeer a therapeutic discourse but do not do so for genuinely therapeutic reasons.

Critics have also raised the issue of whether a therapeutic discourse, even if it is used correctly, is appropriate for many of the issues that the shows discuss. The shows locate problems at the level of the individual and at the level of the individual's personal experience. They also promote a self-help logic which implies that solutions can be found at the same level. But, as Joyner Priest and Dominick (1994:77) put it, 'positioning problems at the level of the individuals elides the political and social forces that underpin the topics'.

Thus, for example, on the rare occasions when racism is discussed its solution is shown to lie at the level of individuals dealing with their prejudices and not at the level of collective mobilisation or organised political action. Cloud (1998:3) argues that this form of discourse 'offers consolation rather than compensation, individual adaptation rather than social change' and, as such, it is a political strategy for the containment and deflection of political and social discontent. Social conflicts that can be explained through narratives of individual psychological dysfunctions do not require large-scale social change to resolve them. In this way the therapeutic discourse of talk television is a conservative and conserving force that poses no threat to existing power structures.

Finally there is the question of the uses made of the participants. Talk shows such as *Ricki Lake* and *Jerry Springer* now routinely end with the 'final thoughts' of the presenters. They use this to affirm and restate the values that participants in the shows violate. The Springer show on bestiality, for example, ended with the host's observations of the need for a return of straightforward romantic love. In this way participants are used as a device for a ritual cleansing of the moral order and as a means through which the validity of the existing social order can be reproduced. The typical participants are from inner-city tenements and trailer parks. To take, as Ehrenreich (1995) puts it, 'lives bent out of shape by poverty and hold them up as entertaining exhibits' is 'class exploitation, pure and simple'.

Conclusion

In this section we have looked at the argument that talk television opens the public sphere to excluded groups, excluded issues and excluded ways of talking about life experiences. We looked also at claims that, while this may have been the case in the past, it is no longer true. The shows are now based on sensationalism, exploitation, and the misuse of therapeutic modes of interpretation. They have moved from fora for the excluded to morality plays for the middle class.

Reality television: the (more) real thing?

Real people, real lives

The second kind of new television programme format is 'reality' or 'actuality' television. The kind of programmes encompassed by the term include *Video Diaries, Caught in the Act, America's Most Wanted, Video Nation, You've Been Framed, Hard Copy* and *Inside Edition*. What they have in common is an emphasis on what Kilborn (1994) calls, 'the vibrancy and spontaneity of real-life events'. They base their appeal on offering direct access to the 'reality' of events, unmediated by the apparatus of professional media organisations or by the machinations of media personnel. Embedded in the programmes is the notion that, in Bondebjerg's (1996:37) phrase, there is 'a deeper, authentic dimension of reality', and the programmes provide access to it.

The domestication of technology: the rise of the camcorder

They have been made possible by technological developments. The main one has been the development of the camcorder and its promotion as an item of domestic technology. This, it is claimed, has empowered viewers because it allows them to record the events that they regard as significant in their lives and which are often not recognized as such by professional broadcasters. In addition, the camcorder is also used almost routinely now by organisations such as the police and the emergency services to record their own activities for internal purposes. These recordings can then be made available for inclusion in 'reality shows'.

Cultural nuances

The shows originated in the USA but they have become part of the staple programming resources of most European television stations. The European versions have been modified to reflect the cultural nuances and priorities of the host culture. Thus, as Kilborn (1994) shows, the typical American shows, which focus on crime and deviance, have been unsuccessful in France. The ones that worked focused on love, sex and family relationships, two of which, at least, are assumed to be typical cultural interests of the French. Similarly the kind of reality television produced by an organisation such as the BBC reflects its concern with public service broadcasting and with 'the principle of extended public access' (Kilborn, 1998:216).

The democracy of video

However, this form of programming is represented as more than merely a change in television formats; it also carries with it a series of claims that it is changing the nature of the relationship between audience and broadcasters. The availability of the technology, combined with the willingness of broadcasting companies to use the material, has produced a situation characterised by some as representing 'the democracy of video'. A less conspicuous version is the claim that these programmes represent new forms of democratic involvement in the media. Thus the argument is that reality television marks a major modification or democratisation of media power.

The new public sphere

The claims made for reality television are similar to those made for talk shows. They are seen as opening up the public sphere to a wider range of voices and to a wider range of material. The official voice is no longer the one through which the experiences of, for example, natural disasters or crimes are represented. Reconstructions of these events now use the personal testimony of those involved and this testimony is the means through which the legitimacy of a version of events is validated or held to be 'true'. In many cases, the accounts of victims and officials are given equal status.

As a result, the confessional, the intimate and the self-revealing have become accepted ways through which ordinary people can represent themselves and their experiences and concerns on the media. In effect, reality television adds a more personal voice to the public forum. It represents 'the creation of a new mixed public sphere where common knowledge and everyday knowledge play a much larger role' (Bondebjerg, 1996:29).

Critical voices

The issue of exploitation. The criticisms that have been levelled at reality television mirror those aimed at talk shows. Critics argue that, appearances to the contrary, issues of control and access have not gone away. It is suggested that many of the shows exploit those who provide the actual footage. This may be shown in a context that they would not have wished or with which they might not agree. It has also been suggested that people do not fully appreciate the implications of exposing their personal lives and personal problems to a national television audience (Kilborn, 1998:206). Bradford (1993) claims that some of the producers of the shows routinely mislead participants, particularly where the re-enactment of violent crime is concerned. They gain the confidence of witnesses and victims by assuring them that there will be no sensational scenes, but these pledges are not honoured in the finished products.

The control of access.   There also issues of access, and these relate to the process through which people and events are chosen for such programmes. A programme such as *Video Diaries* (broadcast by the BBC) is, in many ways, the epitome of the virtues of reality television. It consists of a series of films made by ordinary people, who have complete control over what is filmed and over the editing process. As such, the process seems to be as democratic as you can get; yet it may not be so benign. The BBC retains control over which 'ordinary' people it selects and so the 'diarists are operating much more to the broadcaster's agenda than they might imagine' (Kilborn, 1998:206).

Hidden biases.   There may also be hidden biases in the selection and presentation of the crimes and the personal problems on which the programmes have such a high dependence. It is argued that these depictions are uncritical, stereotyped and presented as individual dramas, without any reference to the general context within which the stories are embedded and through which they could be understood. Personal narrative is at the core of the programmes, and this means that the socio-political angle to the stories is suppressed.

Although the programmes claim to present crime in new and different ways, their depictions are every bit as stereotyped as those in crime reporting and television crime fiction. There is an over-representation of violent crime and of crimes that have been solved by the police (Oliver, 1994). Corporate and political crimes and their victims are never covered. Criminals are male and are more likely to be Black or Hispanic. They are shown as out of control and as selecting their victims on the basis of random whim, yet the victims turn out to be mainly women and children. In this way, Cavender and Bondmaupin (1993) argue, the programmes present the world as an unsafe and dangerous place in which anyone can be a crime victim. Thus they increase the fear of crime and justify the high levels of surveillance of public places.

One of the strengths of the programmes is the way in which they treat ordinary people as important. However, Bondebjerg (1996) argues that most programmes highlight situations in which ordinary people are victims of extraordinary rather than ordinary circumstances and events. These generally involve victimisation by random forces of nature such as floods, freak weather and earthquakes, or by accidents such as road, rail or air accidents. What tends to be common to these depictions is that people are presented as victims of situations over which they have no control and on which they can only report as passive observers, rather than active participants.

Sexual and class bias also permeate many of the shows. Bradford (1993) argues that the American shows, at least, tend to avoid stories about gays, people of colour, or about women who are judged by the producers to be unattractive. There is also, she claims, misogyny at work in the way in which female sexuality is dealt with. Women are presented as either madonnas or whores. Expressions of sexual desire by women are punished, whereas the shows celebrate the sexual appetites of men and present them as normal. This has opened them to the claim that 'male restorationism' is part of their agenda.

The claims about class bias draw their impetus from the fact that the stories that the shows deal with are mainly about lower-class people and about narrowly circumscribed aspects of their lives and their behaviour. When they are not dealing with their involvement in crime, the focus is on the eccentricities and oddities of their behaviour and the attitude adopted towards them is one of condescending indulgence. In a manner similar to that in talk television, they become participants in freak shows. Middle- and upper-class people are seldom seen in programmes about alien abduction, and generally speaking they were not the last people to see 'Bigfoot'.

Invasion of privacy?   The growing use of hidden cameras and of footage obtained without the subjects' consent raises ethical problems. These can be extended to include putting people into situations that are potentially embarrassing or compromising and then filming their responses. In this way, Bradford (1993) claims, the shows are 'messing with people's lives'. She gives an example of the filming of a man and a woman making love in a car in an area of a city that had become a 'lovers' lane'. The couple were unaware they were being filmed, and he was later charged with public indecency. After the video sequence was shown on national television for the second time in a month, he shot himself. Bradford acknowledges that this is an extreme example, but claims that it is simply an extension of the damage that the shows do to people's lives.

A nation of voyeurs.   The final criticism of the shows is that they encourage narcissism in their participants and a voyeurism in their viewers. All areas of social life are now considered suitable for transformation into television entertainment, and many of the programmes have set new standards in personal self-exposure. This trend has been amplified by the techniques of many of the programme makers. Through interviewing strategies of feigned or real demonstrations of empathy, they can get participants to cry and then zoom in to capture the moment. In the business this is called, according to Bradford (1993), 'passing the onion'.

This in turn transforms viewers into voyeurs. They become spectators at exhibitions of human discomfort, personal pain and intimate self-revelation. They get involved in what Corner (1995:6) calls, 'the vicarious witnessing of highly particularized misfortune and distress'. The failure of the programmes to provide context or perspective for this kind of material forces viewers to resort to simplified models of response and of judgement. Thus we either 'love' or 'hate', 'pity' or 'patronise' the participants and categorise them into fairly crude groupings such as 'good' or 'bad', 'nice' or 'nasty'. In this way the programmes are designed to engage our emotions rather than to promote a more balanced and emphatic understanding of other people's lives.

Conclusion

In this section, we examined arguments about the contribution of reality television to widening the level of democratic access to and involvement in the media. Has it been successful at this? There is no simple answer. The extent of increased access depends very much on the nature of the reality programmes involved and, to some extent, the broadcasting tradition of the country in which they originate. Thus, broadly speaking, those produced in the USA and for commercial networks tend to be more vulnerable to criticisms of bias, sexism and exploitation. But the pressures on those operating within a public service broadcasting tradition to move towards this model are significant and difficult to resist. One of the central appeals of these kinds of programmes is that they can be cheap to produce, and all types of broadcasting organisation are currently susceptible to this kind of pressure.

However, there are two more evident and less disputable changes brought about by this kind of programming. The first has been its effects on more conventional television documentaries, particularly those with informational aspirations. These have been forced to incorporate the techniques of 'reality television' into their production. There is now a more democratic selection of issues and voices, an increased reliance on the techniques of reconstruction, an increasing emphasis on the emotive and the emotional, and the incorporation of the narrative drive of fictional television into the presentation and pacing of the programmes. The second change has been the enlargement of what Kilborn (1994:436) calls 'the grandiose sense of entitlement of television', which suggests that no area of social life can be immune from the reach of television camera and that all areas of life are suitable for exploitation as television entertainment.

The latest developments in reality television confirm this. These are programmes whose producers create situations into which ordinary people are placed and where their every response is captured by cameras. *Big Brother* and *Survivor* are important examples. How long will it be before the participants on such shows have sexual intercourse in the full knowledge that this will be transmitted live on television?

The new media: caught in the web or freed by it?

The second way in which control over access to channels of information may be reduced is through the use of what are called new media and through the communicative possibilities that these offer. These are the various forms of computed mediated communication, most notably the Internet and its various manifestations such as web pages, bulletin boards, news and discussion groups, and e-mail.

The case for the new media

It is claimed that these forms of communication have a number of advantages over the more traditional mass media. For ease of presentation we can reduce these to two broad ones, the democratising of access and the democratising of content.

Democratising access

Access to the Internet is, potentially at least, open to all in society. It only requires a computer and some relatively modest technology to be able to open a website, download relevant information, and contribute to online discussions and debates. This can be achieved without leaving one's home and is, or so it is claimed, relatively inexpensive. As a result the Net offers a cheap and universal means through which people can share information, contribute to political discussion and interact with individuals, groups and institutions on a local, national and international level.

Universality of access is increased by the way in which the technology offers its users the capacity to remain anonymous. They can adopt new names and titles online, and they can use re-mailers to make their communication untraceable. While some would see this as dangerous in the scope that it offers for defamation and false information, others see it as offering possibilities for full and open participation and disclosure. Grossman (1997), for example, argues that 'the reason for using anonymizing services varies: discussing personal histories of child abuse or addiction, selling technical information in contexts where your company might object to its name being revealed, or fear of the political regime in which you live'. This means that the Net is the ideal technology for free and democratic communication.

The democracy of content

The second advantage is that the Net is capable of carrying an unlimited amount of information. Newspapers and television are constrained by limitations of time and space, but the Net is not. It has been estimated that at any given time there are over 80 million web pages on the Net (Huberman and Lukose, 1997). This means that the technology can create a more open public sphere in which citizens have access to a wider range of information and interpretation than the conventional media provide.

This, in turn, should lead to a more informed population and more accountable and accessible political institutions. This can happen in three ways.

Access to information.   The first is the capacity of the Net to act as a means to provide and disseminate information. It can offer access to all kinds of political documents, whether these are the policy statements of political and business groups, official government documents and discussion papers, lists of government regulations, or simply application forms for state services. All of these are available in paper format, but the Net offers a level of access that such resources are not always perceived as having.

This access is not confined to traditionally powerful individuals and organisations; it is available to all kinds of political and community movements, whether these are local citizen groups, neo-fascist movements, loosely structured collectivities of anarchists, or sophisticated progressive environmental organisations. They can use the Net to publicise their policies and activities and as a means through which radical and challenging information and news items can be circulated. Peace and human rights organisations, for example, came together during the Gulf War in 1991 to offer an alternative news service, called Peacenet. The site continues to be available (www.igc.org/igc/peacenet). Those who use it say that it is unique because it brings together an extensive range of radical publications and provides access to the kind of political perspectives and views which are not normally found in the media (Sachs, 1995).

The technology can also be used by activists to connect with other groups through the various forms of computer networking that the Net makes possible (see Friedland, 1997). It has been calculated that more than 130 communities in the USA have created electronic fora on the Internet. This has allowed them to disseminate routine community information but also to circulate information on, for example, the potential dangers and safety records of industries moving into their areas (Campaign Web Review, November 1998) and on the dangers posed by potential new residents (such as released sex offenders).

Hunger and homeless advocacy groups have also formed electronic communication networks to share information and advice on campaigning. The Civic Practices Network in the USA carries news stories of attempts by communities to rebuild civic life, and it also provides training manuals for prospective communities to use for organisational purposes. According to Friedland (1997:206) it has more case studies on civic and community-based approaches to environmental issues in the USA than the online server of the Environmental Protection Agency. He argues that it is useful to think of such groups as using the Net to create 'social capital' networks. Over the years these groups have accumulated knowledge and experience in organisation, mobilisation and problem-solving. Access to the net allows them to share this 'capital' with other like-minded groups, and in this way increase their collective effectiveness.

Reconnecting to politics.   The second way in which the Net can contribute to political and social life is through the facilitation of communication and debate between individual citizens and between citizens and politicians. Carey (1989) argues that the key to successful communication is interactivity. The capacity to contribute and respond to public debate and discussions turns participants from passive consumers to active citizens. Net technology offers this capacity. It provides the basis for a huge number of politician and social discussion groups, including electronic town hall meetings through which citizens can express their views to politicians and receive their responses.

These uses have led enthusiasts to suggest that we are witnessing a rebirth of civic activism and political participation. Sakkas (1993), for example, says that political discussion groups on the Net are a new way to get people 'reconnected to their government'. The existence of the Net means that people who have not previously been involved in political matters can use computer terminals in public buildings to participate in public discussion and influence decision-making. Wittig and Schmitz (1996) have, for example, shown how homeless people in a major American city were able to use a municipal electronic network to lobby the authorities to establish a centre for them.

Similarly Jesse Ventura, a Reform Party candidate, became Governor of Minnesota in 1998. He came from outside the political spectrum and from behind in the opinion polls to defeat prominent Democratic and Republican Party candidates. His victory has been attributed to the skill with which his campaign team used the new technology. His website was used to mobilise volunteers, raise campaign funds, organise rallies, counter misinformation or criticisms circulated by either the media or other candidates, and encourage new voters. The 'new voters' group was a key factor in his victory.

Electronic town halls.   The third use that is being promoted and championed is the capacity that the Net offers for the creation of direct democracy. Current forms of democracy are based on the irregular participation of citizens in the political process through elections. The new technology, by contrast, allows politicians to consult more regularly with their electorate, through electronically facilitated samplings of viewer attitudes, opinions and choices. As Barnett (1997:206) puts it, 'referenda immediately become more practicable and more desirable'. This has the potential to lead to forms of political decision-making that more clearly reflect the preferences of citizens.

Overall, Buie (1999) argues, the Net is facilitating 'a new era in participatory democracy'. Central to this is what he calls the 'five minute activist'. This is the person who 'can log on, catch up on the issues he or she believes in, offer an opinion or advice, volunteer, and make a financial pledge'. Such activism is only possible because of the new communications technology.

The realities of electronic communication

These are the advantages and the potentialities that electronic communication has to offer, but the key question is the extent to which these potentialities are being realised in practice. It is an important issue as there is a tendency to over-state the changes that new forms of technology – such as the Net – are likely to produce. Turkle (1996:56), for example, has spoken about the 'over-heated language that currently surrounds discussion of computer mediated communication'. This is not helped by the absence of a body of systematic social research on the Internet. Nonetheless, we can point to a series of issues that must be addressed in any systematic evaluation of its impact.

Access: open to all?

The first is that of access; however, the exact number of users of the Net is difficult to determine. According to the Internet Domain Survey of January 2000, over 72 million computers are linked to the Net. This represents almost a doubling of the number that was found in a similar survey 18 months previously. This rate of growth is impressive, but other estimates suggest that the number with access to the Net may be over-stated. In most countries it constitutes a small proportion of the population. Some surveys of net users in the country that is often considered the most connected in the world, the USA, say that they make up about 20 per cent of the adult population. Others put it as low as 11 per cent of the population aged 16 and over (survey reported in Tedesco, Miller and Spiker, 1998).

There are also questions about the social characteristics of users. The results of a range of surveys show that regular users of the Net are college-educated (if not also college employed), with above average income. They are also more likely to be white, male and living in the rich and industrialised West, and probably in the USA (figures in Nakhaie and Pike, 1998; Tedesco, Miller and Spiker, 1998; Hedley, 1999). This would suggest that Castell's (1996) characterisation of Internet users as a 'metropolitan elite' is accurate. Internet use remains, he claims (1996:359), 'the domain of an educated segment of the population of the most advanced societies'.

For some proponents of the Net these results are not surprising and they do not consider them as an insurmountable obstacle to the spread of the technology. They simply reflect the fact that the early adapters of most new forms of technology have been from the higher social strata. From there, they argue, the technology will diffuse through the national and world population in much the same way as television and video recorders did. While critics may accept this as an accurate trajectory of past technologies, there are a number of significant obstacles to the universal adaptation of this one.

The first is that the technology is presented as relatively inexpensive, but there are hidden and not so hidden costs. These include costs of routine maintenance, the experiences of many users with machines that 'crash', and the constant updating of software by manufacturers, which in turn requires more expensive and more powerful computer hardware. The quantity of information that users encounter and that they must trawl through in order to find what they want may also discourage infrequent users of the Net. Winston (1998:335) has written about the 'clutter and absurdity of most information the engines have to search'. The slow speed of connection may also be a discouragement. He has argued, with some over-statement, that 'California needed to be asleep if any chance of reasonable access were to be achieved' (Winston, 1998:325). These kinds of costs by their nature impose a social growth ceiling on the spread of the technology.

A second obstacle is that the working language of the Net is, effectively speaking, English. When this is combined with the distribution of computers it ensures that the most prominent debates on the Net are about US politics and, as Shields (1996:2) puts it, 'non-American viewpoints are regarded as abnormal'. A third obstacle, which also contributes to the gender differences, is the phenomenon of 'flaming'. This refers to the level of insults and personal attacks that are a feature of Net discussion groups. These are facilitated by the lack of any control over access and the difficulties that this poses for the development and enforcement of standards of courtesy, or what is called 'Netiquette'. Sakkas (1993) argues that this discourages people from participating in many of these groups.

A final obstacle is that levels of technological literacy in the USA (and, if there, presumably also in other countries as well) are fairly low and this discourages access and use (Hacker, 1996). Using the technology requires relatively high levels of linguistic, textual and word processing capacities, and these are dependent on a certain level of educational achievement. Moreover, people with high levels of education are more likely to encounter computers and to work directly on them in their work place than are those who are less educated. Educational and occupational capital, to adopt a phrase from Stubbs (1998:2.12), converts into what he terms 'computer cultural capital' and this, as he remarks, is 'no less exclusionary than other forms of cultural capital'.

The digital divide

This raises the possibilities of new forms of stratification in society, represented by notions such as 'a digital divide' or 'an information aristocracy', or by the terms 'information rich' and 'information poor' (see Schiller, 1983). Access to and use of such technologies, it is claimed, mirrors the current social divisions in most societies and between rich and poor societies. To the extent that access is a valued form of social and cultural capital, it deepens the nature of such divisions. As Webster (1995:91) puts it, if new information technology is 'being born into a class society, it is marked by existing inequalities and may indeed exacerbate them'.

In this respect Castells (1996:363, 364) argues that the impact of the Internet will be 'the reinforcement of the culturally dominant social networks', the intensification of 'pre-existing social patterns' and the increase in 'the social cohesion of the cosmopolitan elite'. Increasingly, he argues, we live in a world in which there is 'shrinking room for the computer illiterate, for consumptionless groups, and for under communicated territories' (Castells, 1996:25). The ultimate deprivation will be exclusion from, or

inability to participate in, the global networks created by information technology.

It is the existence of these global networks that lead him to
characterise modern society as a Network society. This is one
where new information and communication technologies (and
the global connectedness that they have facilitated) are the infra-
structural and economic backbone. These technologies have enabled, most notably, the emergence of a global financial market
that allows for fast movements of capital, instant global value
searching by investors, and, related to that, the 'geographic redis-
tribution of investment so that, while economies suffer, most
global investments do not' (Castells, 2001:60). This pattern
of global and rapidly mobile investment has created a pattern of
what he calls 'Info-Growth', from which the usual suspects have
benefited. These are the economies of Western Europe, Asia, and
principally that of the USA.

However, the price of this growth is that a substantial body of
people is excluded from its benefits. Many of these live in countries, such as those on the African continent, that do not have the
kind of technological infrastructure and investment opportunities
that are attractive to the global investor. Others live in technologic-
ally advanced societies but do not have the skills or the education
to participate in the information economy and in information
networks. Information technology, in this sense, amplifies inequal-
ity and exclusion. In this new kind of network society, 'the critical
mass of disposable people', as Castells (2001:66) puts it 'expands
significantly'.

The Typical User: Citizen or Netizen?

A second claim about the Net is the potential that it offers to open
up new sources of political information, to attract new people into
the world of politics and to lead to a rebirth of political enthusi-
asms and political interests. Again the research would suggest that
these aims are not being achieved.

Time-saving for the committed?

What it shows is that, for example, while political and campaigning groups may wish to use the new technologies to reach new
people, most of their communication in fact targets and reaches

their pre-existing audience. As Barnett (1997:210) argues, most of the e-mail messages sent by groups such as Amnesty International contain information and promotional material that would previously have gone by mail. Thus much of the use of the Internet by political groups represents the substitution of one form of communication for another and cheaper one.

It was also claimed that the Net would attract politically alienated individuals into the political process (Sachs, 1995:97), but again there is no strong evidence that the Internet is attracting new users to its political and social information sites. The demand for political information from the Net is high, but this demand is coming mainly from those who are already politically involved and not from those marginal to the political world (Hacker, 1996). They are already serious consumers of political information, but they now getting from the Net the kind of political and social information that they previously got through more conventional media. As Barnett (1997:213) puts it, the new media may be little more 'than a form of technological time-saving for the politically active or the politically interested'.

Trading insults or information?

The Net offers the capacity for citizens to talk directly to other citizens without a media or state gatekeeper. This can be done through political discussion groups and chatrooms, which proliferate on the Net. But is there any evidence that these are more open, more democratic or more deliberative than those found in the conventional media or, for that matter, in the local bar? Again the research is limited, but it does suggest that the quality of contributions and debate can be of questionable value.

Franke (1996), for example, found that most contributions to online discussions were either too brief or too bizarre to count as serious dialogue. Most were assertions of partisan views and were generally sarcastic in tone. Stubbs (1998) looked at e-mail conferences on the Net about the wars in Yugoslavia in the early 1990s. He found that important information was been posted on the state of politics and on human rights abuses in the region, but, in general, most exchanges consisted of statements and counter-statements, together with 'mutual name-calling' and 'the widespread use of crude nationalist invective'. They contained very little real argument 'beyond the repetitious assertion of the "truth" ' (Stubbs, 1998:

5.4–5.5). Even discussion groups that claim some success, such as that managed by Sakkas (1993) on the 1992 presidential election in the USA, suffered from personal attacks and the posting of excessively frequent, long or irrelevant messages. The volume of messages became so great that it imperilled the value of the discussion group.

Making power accountable?

Other critics have focused on the capacity that the Net offers for holding power accountable. The capacity that the Net offers to send e-mail messages to world political figures, such as the American president (*president@whitehouse.gov*), has been promoted as a significant extension of democratic accountability and democratic dialogue. However, it has been pointed out that this is not interactive. 'Getting a form letter stating that the president is glad to hear from you' is not necessarily a demonstration of a democratic exchange (Hacker, 1996:227) unless there is some evidence that the priorities and policies of politicians are changed by the interaction. For the most part, politicians use figures on the number of e-mail messages they receive as an endorsement of their policies rather than as a reason to change them. 'There is', says Schudson (1992:43), 'the possibility that new forms of political communication will become a mere palliative, if there is no real chance government will act to remedy the problems the talk is about'.

There are also questions about the value of electronic referenda. Ostensibly these are interactive, but in practice most simply require the user to make a selection from a limited set of options and then press a button to register a choice. This leaves them open to abuse and creates what Schudson (1992) calls 'the potential for manipulated public opinion'. They can only tell us what a narrow and unrepresentative group of the public think about a limited range of policy issues. This means that the use of electronic public meetings as the legitimation for political action may be seriously misleading.

Even playing field?

The degree to which news groups can be used to contest effectively with powerful interest groups can also be questioned. The fate of a discussion group (alt.religion.scientology) set up by former members and critics of the Church of Scientology is a case in point. The group attracted both critics and believers, but soon it became a battlefield. Scientology as a religion is built around what Peckham (1998) describes as a system of stratified revelation. New members have to go through (and pay for) a series of stages of disclosure, with each one representing a deeper level of knowledge of, and a deeper commitment to, the religion. Critics disrupted this process by posting entire segments of the more advanced texts on their website.

The Church responded in two ways (Peckham, 1998; see also Grossman, 1997). One was to use the law against its critics, a strategy that was justified by the Church on the grounds of copyright infringements; the other was to post large numbers of positive messages to the anti-scientology news group, a process known in the technical parlance of web technology as a 'vertical spam'. According to Grossman (1997), 'from the end of May to the end of July 1996 an estimated 20,000 messages consisting of brief quotations from Scientology promotional material were posted to *alt.religion.scientology*'. This strategy undermined the capacity of critics to keep up with and respond to all the positive messages. It also ensured that 'the comparatively small number of critical posts could be lost in the sea of information' (Peckham, 1998).

At a more sinister level, critics claimed that supporters of Scientology resorted to deceit. They were alleged to have forged messages to give the impression they were coming from other people and so discredit critics. They were also alleged to have forged instructions to Web servers to block postings coming from particular critics or, more seriously, to try to close the newsgroup altogether. All of this suggests that the combined strategies of powerful groups such as the Church of Scientology require a considerable level of energy, computer expertise, access to the legal system, and sheer doggedness on the part of its critics if newsgroups containing critical material are to survive.

Issues of accuracy and interactivity

The Net has been promoted as an information provider and as a new means of accessing information. However while one of its strengths is that there is no formal filter or censor to restrict the kind of information that is available, equally there is no mechanism to guarantee the accuracy and completeness of that information. Anyone with access to a server can create a Web page and post information to it. So how reliable and trustworthy is the information on the Web?

It is important to recognise that information on the Net may be unreliable and inaccurate. According to Kramarae (1998:110), many people have commented on the difficulty of sorting out 'real from unreal, authenticated from rumoured'. The Drudge Report (www.drudgereport.com) is one of the more influential websites. It was responsible for the 'first true Internet driven story in the history of American journalism' (Sutherland, 1998), the story of Bill Clinton's affair with Monica Lewinsky. Yet Drudge himself acknowledges that 20 per cent of what he puts out is inaccurate. As Sutherland (1998) remarks, 'any newspaper with this level of inaccuracy would be destroyed by libel suits'.

It is also important to recognise a distinction between maintaining a web page and providing comprehensive information. Many powerful interest groups and powerful state agencies maintain web pages, but this does not mean that they have become unreservedly forthcoming in the information that they provide. The USA's Central Intelligence Agency is a case in point. It has a web page, but it is not necessarily the place to go to find out if they are spying on you.

Connell and Galasinski (1996) argue that their pages present the organisation as a disciplined and legitimate service provider whose task is to prepare accurate information for the American president. As such it claims to act in accordance with the domestic law of the USA. Some people would not regard this as a comprehensive account of their activities. Moreover, while their site does give information on some of their more questionable activities, this can be easily overlooked. The documents on the history of the organisation for 1961, for example, give equal status to moving office and invading Cuba.

Similarly, but at a somewhat different level, there is the issue of how comprehensive and how interactive many governmental websites are. Musso and her colleagues have shown, for example, that while many municipalities in California provided websites, these 'were rather superficial with regard to substance' (Musso, Weare and Hale, 2000:10). They provided information about business, tourism and the services offered by the municipality, but few provided the kind of information that might encourage and promote political participation. They provided vertical links to state and city officials, but did not provide horizontal ones to citizen or community groups. Most sites, in fact, could be characterised as electronic phone books, 'merely repeating information commonly available in the government pages of most directories' (Musso, Weare and Hale, 2000:12).

The same problem applies to the conventional media. Schultz (2000) found that while many of these, most notably newspapers, now offer 'talk-back' facilities as, for example, in the provision of e-mail addresses for journalists, for the most part the journalists do not read their mail or respond to it. Moreover, few of the journalists at the *New York Times* who responded to his survey had ever looked at the paper's online fora for readers' views and story suggestions. The reasons they gave included lack of time, the misuse of the system by public relations organisations and activist groups, and the amount of hate mail that they receive. This means, as Schultz (2000:212) puts it, that these websites offer 'interactivity without substance'.

Issues of access: the bad and the ugly?

The content of the Net is also regarded as problematic in other ways. There is concern over its use to promote and distribute pornography, the capacity that it offers for deviant groups such as child abusers to circulate information on appropriate victims, and the extent to which it offers a platform for hate groups such as White Supremacists and neo-Nazi networks (Graber, 1996).

The issue of sex and pornography is one that has most animated discussion about the Net. The most popular topic for news groups and websites is sex and, as Baym (1998:39) indicates, the spread of sex-related discussion groups and sites has outpaced all others. The content of such sites can include information on where prostitution is available on a world-wide basis, the transmission of live sex shows, the sale of women as brides, and the live transmission of the sexual abuse of children. Only the revenue from the sale of computer products and travel tickets on the Net has, according to Hughes (www.womanspace.ca), exceeded that from sale of pornography.

Control and regulation

This has raised the issue of the control and regulation of the Net. One of the attractions of computer-mediated communication, for its supporters, is the extent to which it appears to be free of commercial interference and beyond political control. According to

Purdy (1998), *Wired Magazine*, the online bible for what he calls 'the shock troopers of the information economy', expresses a clear ideology of libertarianism. It sees the role of government in the development of the Internet as minimal, and best characterised 'as staying out of the way'. They were pleased when the attempts of the US government to regulate the Net were declared unconstitutional by the Supreme Court in 1997. This has not stopped the government from trying more recently to ban sites that contain information or links to sites about illegal drugs such as methamphetamine. These attempts are made more difficult in the USA where the First Amendment guarantees free speech. It remains to be seen how successful attempts to regulate the Net will be in societies without these kinds of constitutional guarantee. Peckham (1998), however, argues that this sort of regulatory legislation is unenforceable and more or less ignored by those who provide web pages.

The surveillance society?

The final issue raised in debates about the Net is that of surveillance. One of the advantages of electronic communication is that it allows us to keep an eye on powerful political and commercial organisations. A more sinister formulation is that the technology allows them to keep an eye on us.

One version of this argument points to the way in which many service providers, such as America-on-Line, sell lists of subscribers to other companies. These can then be targeted with specific commercial and promotional material. This is facilitated by the presence on many computers of pieces of software called 'cookies', which take note of the sites that are visited and compute from this a profile of the user's interests, consumption patterns and other social and demographic information. This information has obvious uses for commercial concerns.

As such it could be argued that this is relatively harmless, as long as the user is aware it is going on. It is also something that can be disabled with a relatively low level of computer expertise (see *www.cookies.com*). For others it is an invasion of privacy and is open to more sinister uses, such as the collation of such information by law enforcement institutions, private security firms, and state intelligence organisations. As Marx (1995) puts it, 'there are skid marks all over the [information] highway. Electronic trails create unprecedented possibilities for knowing where a person is, whom they are communicating with and what is being expressed and what information they are accessing'.

Conclusion

In this section we have considered arguments about the degree to which computer-mediated forms of communication solve problems of access to and participation in the public sphere. On one hand, there are those who argue that these will increase the access to information, consultation and decision-making in the political process. The more enthusiastic see this as a means of constructing a genuinely participative democracy (Coleman, 1999). On the other hand, there are those who see it as being captured by dominant commercial interests and turned into a technology for the generation of profit. In the process, users of the Net will be transformed from citizens into consumers.

In this way the Net, as Vincent Mosco (2000) has pointed out, is currently caught between these two models for future development. One is based on the ability to pay, and possibly with restrictions on the provision of certain kinds of information. Here control will be in the hands of large corporations such as America-on-Line, who will operate their systems for commercial gain. The other is a more open, democratic and participative model. This is currently present in community networks, dependent on public support and based on access through terminals in public libraries, schools and post offices.

He argues that the trend towards the commercialisation of the web is becoming the dominant one, and this can be seen in a number of areas. These include its increasing promotion as a channel for advertising, the attempts to extend copyright and content charges, its development as a platform for e-shopping, and the attempts to capitalise on its potential as a means to deliver home entertainment. Governments have facilitated these through, for example, holding off on the application of sales taxes to web shopping. This model of development will create a new form of exclusivity based on ability to pay, and it could in effect transform a resource with the potential to become a new public sphere into an old-fashioned private domain. The Information Superhighway will, in effect, become a toll road.

There are some obstacles, however, as governments are also impeding its full commercialisation. Their desire to use the web as an instrument for the surveillance of citizens conflicts with the desire of commercial interests to develop secure encryption software to allow consumers to feel happy using the Net as a shopping mall. In this sense it is the conflict of interests between business and the state, rather than between commercial and public uses of the Net, that may determine its future direction.

CHAPTER 6

Innocent Entertainment? The Sociological Study of Television Fiction

Introduction

We have looked in previous chapters at how media power can be examined in relation to factual material, such as the media's coverage of politics, crime and mental illness. In this chapter we extend this to look at how issues, events, people and social values are represented in fiction on television.

The study of fictional material is important for a number of reasons, the first being the extent of its presence in the media. On any given day, up to 90 per cent of the material on television can be classified as fiction. Such material also has correspondingly significant shares of the audience. 'The simple fact is', as Morley (1999:200) puts it, 'most people watch fiction on television most of the time'.

The second is that fictional material may have a greater potential to influence us. This is primarily and paradoxically because we least expect it to. Audiences consider entertainment and persuasion to be distinct and separate processes, so they watch fictional material in a less constrained and more relaxed manner. It is low on the 'moral hierarchy' of television programmes (Alasuutari, 1992) and so is unworthy of concentrated attention. This means that it may have much greater ability to be influential simply because audiences are not prepared to accept that it can. Hence it has to be given serious attention in any examination of the power of the media.

How to study television fiction: (1) the search for recurrent patterns

A number of approaches have been developed in media sociology for the study of fictional material on television. The first involves the search for what are termed, 'recurrent presentational patterns'. This approach asks if there are recurrent themes or patterns identifiable in the presentation of issues, events and people across the range of fictional material in the mass media. It draws on a range of research methods that we outline here. Our presentation will be confined to the study of gender and race.

Counting heads

Typically this approach utilises content analysis. This involves the counting of specific features of media content and the construction of tables that show the frequency with which these features occur. These can then be compared to statistics on the occurrence of that particular feature in the 'real' world. Applied to the study of gender, it has found that typically women are under-represented in media fiction.

Lichter, Rothman and Lichter's (1986) analysis of the characters in prime-time television between 1955 and 1986 in the USA is a representative example. It concluded that women are not present in such programmes to the same degree as men. When they are there, they are presented as less educated and shown to hold low-status jobs in which they do not exercise power or authority. They are more likely to be shown in their roles in the home and in the family, and only rarely in the workplace. They also tend to be younger than male characters. There are few older women in prime-time television. Finally, they have distinctive physical features, being usually tall, thin and attractive in a conventional sense.

As might be expected, the results for men are largely the opposite. Fejes (1992) has summarised the findings. These show that male characters are more numerous than female ones, they tend to be older and employed in high-status jobs (particularly those traditionally defined as male, such as medicine, law and politics). Their marital status is less likely to be highlighted than that of women. There is also no necessary connection between their physical characteristics and their attractiveness as characters. To a greater extent than is true for women, fat men can be fun (Fejes, 1992).

Other studies suggest that female characters tend to be concentrated in certain kinds of programme, including domestic dramas, soap operas and situation comedies. Indeed soap opera is the only programme type where the numbers of women characters approached equality with the number of male ones. The under-representation is most marked in children's programmes (see Durkin, 1985, for relevant references). According to one study, only 9 per cent of the cartoon characters were female.

Counting characters: the notion of stereotyping

The counting does not stop at what might be termed the categorical level. It also allows the consideration of the frequency with which male and female characters are shown with particular qualities and capabilities. In this way it mobilises the concept of stereotyping: that is, where particular qualities are disproportionately associated with particular kinds of characters so that they come to represent the universe of these characters' capacities and become a shorthand through which they can be symbolised.

Greenberg's work (1975) is an example. He took three aspects of behaviour and looked to see if they were disproportionately associated with male or female characters. He took the giving and getting of instructions, and asked who gives orders to whom in fictional television. He looked at the characters that are shown as needing support, and asked in what kinds of circumstances are they shown as needing help and what kind of help do they need? Finally, he asked which characters are shown as making plans and whose plans are successful? He then applied these categories to three years of fictional television, 1975 to 1977, in the USA.

He found that men gave more orders than women and, most crucially, orders that originate with men were acted upon more frequently than those that originate with women. Men also tend to get their orders from other men, whereas women tend to get their orders equally from men and women. Male characters mainly needed support in situations where they were threatened with physical danger. Female characters needed support in situations where they had personal and emotional problems with which they could not cope. These included the loss of lovers and husbands. He found that while men were shown as needing physical support, they were significantly less likely to ask for it. Women, by contrast, were shown as needing emotional support. They asked for it and received it, generally from men. Finally, men dominated plan-making: they made more plans that women and were more successful in bringing them to a conclusion.

This association of the physical and rational with men and the emotional and domestic with women has been confirmed by other studies (for a summary, see Fejes, 1992). These show that men are disproportionately shown driving, participating in sports, using firearms, conducting business on the telephone, and smoking and drinking. Women are disproportionately shown preparing and serving food, and doing housework. Men are shown as assertive, aggressive and independent. The women who are shown with these qualities tend to be villains. For the most part women are shown as peaceful, warm, passive and dependent.

From content to ideology

These analyses of gender representations are based on content analysis. However, while this has particular strengths it may not be the most appropriate methodology through which changes in such representations can be charted and tracked. It has been criticised on the grounds that those items or issues that occur most frequently in the media may not necessarily be the most significant (Burgelin, 1972). The ratio of male to female characters may, for example, remain unchanged over time, but this may be less important than qualitative changes in how these characters are portrayed. The precise number of female characters may be less relevant if those who are there are presented as assertive and self-confident. Content analysis can miss out on this sort of change.

The tradition of ideological critique or discursive readings has evolved to meet this problem. It adopts a qualitative approach to the study of media texts by trying to get beyond the concern with the manifest or obvious content of programmes in order to explore the latent or underlying meaning. It looks at how images, scenes, characters, narratives and story lines in television fiction are used to construct or represent particular discourses or ideologies. They are used to carry particular messages, representations or readings of the social world. The aim of this kind of analysis is to uncover what these messages or readings are. As such, it has illuminated a number of themes in the representation of gender.

The backlash against the single woman

According to a number of writers, an emerging theme in popular culture in the late 1980s and early 1990s was the backlash against what Elizabeth Traube (1990:2) called the 'imagined threat of female power'. The focus of a number of successful films of the period, including *Presumed Innocent*, *Jagged Edge* and, most significantly of all, *Fatal Attraction*, was on the demonisation of the single, independent career-minded woman. The underlying theme was that the intrusion of ambitious single women into male areas of society brings with it the risk of violence. The women are most likely to be its victims, but it is a violence that they are responsible for provoking.

In *Fatal Attraction*, a cool, efficient, professional single woman has a one-night stand with the male character, played by Michael Douglas. The experience is undermining. She cannot live with his rejection and pursues both him and his family. In the process the film makes an explicit connection between the professional woman and witchcraft. The medieval test for a witch was immersion in water: if the woman drowned she was not a witch; if she survived she was and so was burned to death. It was a hard test for an accused woman to pass. At the end of the film the single woman is drowned in a bath. Satisfied with a job well done, Douglas turns his back on her. She rises out of the water with a knife to kill him. Douglas's wife then shoots her. The film finishes with a soft focus shot of a photograph of the family, now restored to its oneness. In the end, the point of *Fatal Attraction* is, Faludi (1992:152) claims, that 'the best single woman is a dead one'.

The same theme is present in the television series *Cagney and Lacey*. This show was seen as breaking through the gender barriers that surrounded crime dramas, yet many feminists had difficulties with it. Their concerns were based on an analysis of how the characters of the two women change and the differences that emerge in the attitude of the programme to their respective but different lifestyles. At the beginning of the series these were treated as equally legitimate, but Alcock and Robson (1990) argue that as the series developed there was a growing contrast between Lacey's sense of completeness as a stable, family-loving woman and the disintegration and humiliation of the independent single woman, Cagney, into alcoholism.

The re-emergence of action man

Coinciding with, and undoubtedly related to, the denigration of the single independent woman has been what Jeffords (1989) has referred to as 'the remasculinization of the male'. This can be seen most clearly in the revival in the late 1980s and early 1990s of action adventures such as the series of *Rambo*, *Die Hard* and *Lethal Weapon* films, at the centre of which is 'the display of raw masculinity' (Kellner, 1995:66).

Male bonding was a central dynamic in them. Typically two male characters were pitched together and, while initially unsympathetic and resistant to each other, they develop a close friendship based on mutual support and mutual protection in situations of violence and physical danger. The bond was often inter-racial, although Tasker (1993:44) argues that roles were not equal. The task of the black man was to 'marvel at the hero's achievements and to support him through difficult situations' and to operate as a 'supportive, sometimes almost fatherly, figure'.

Female characters, and what are perceived as female characteristics, were also highlighted as signs of weakness. Negotiation and non-aggression were, according to Jeffords (1989), presented as creating and compounding problems that subsequently require demonstrations of male power to resolve. Displays of feminine qualities, such as emotional frailty, by male characters were subsequently expunged by a display of 'hypermasculinity' (Fuchs, 1993). The Mel Gibson character in the *Lethal Weapon* series was, for example, depicted in the first film as weeping and as entertaining suicidal thoughts after his wife is killed. He achieves the relevant catharsis through an extended and impassioned involvement in shooting and killing.

This remasculinisation has been explained as a response in the USA to defeat in the Vietnam War, and more generally as a response to the crisis produced for men by the advance of the women's movement on a global level. As such it can be interpreted as the restatement of traditional masculinity, suitably modified to meet and dominate the new ideological climate. Others have argued that the excessive nature of these demonstrations of male power is not an indication of triumph, but of deep insecurity. The inflated muscularity of Sylvester Stallone or Nicholas Cage is not the quiet re-assumption of power and authority by men but a plaintive cry and plea to be noticed and, if possible, taken seriously.

Coming to terms with gender transformations

It would, however, be wrong to leave it at that. Gauntlett (1995:112) has argued forcefully that the one of the problems with many analyses of the media portrayal of gender relations is that they are out of date by the time they are published. The themes of backlash and remasculinisation do not take sufficient account of more recent and significant changes that have implications for our understanding of gender representation.

The new man

The analysis of recent changes in the portrayals of men is less developed than that of women; none the less, a number of changes have been important. The violent male hero identified in the remasculinisation thesis is fast becoming an anachronism. The revival has run its course, and recent films starring Sylvester Stallone or Arnold Schwarzenegger have been unsuccessful. By contrast, action films with a more sensitive and younger male hero, such as *The Matrix* (starring Keanu Reeves), have captured the imagination and interest of audiences. Mel Gibson, famed for his tough guy roles, has been the quickest of the oldies to spot the trend. His latest action heroes have been of a more sensitive variety, as in *Braveheart*, and he has parodied the macho type in *What Women Want*.

These changes can also be observed in television where macho characters can still be found, but their use of (and relationship to) violence is no longer an unproblematic one. As Gauntlett (1995) has pointed out, one of the main characters in the American crime drama *NYPD Blue*, Andy Sipowicz, is shown in many ways as the traditional hardline male cop. He has no hesitation in roughing up suspects, and this is justified in the programmes by the kinds of people against whom the violence is used: drug dealers and child abusers are typical examples of the 'scumbags' that merit violent treatment. But he is also shown as suffering for its use. The approval of his colleagues is often reluctant and in some cases withheld and, at a personal level, his macho manner is shown 'as increasingly inappropriate, ineffective and a lifestyle dead-end' (Gauntlett, 1995:113). His inability to deal in a routine way with the gay secretary in the detectives' unit is also presented as a problem, but the problem belongs to Sipowicz and not the secretary.

This kind of masculinity is also challenged in *The Sopranos*. At one level this is a standard gangster family drama, a version of *The Godfather* set in the suburbs of New York; but there is one clear difference. The lead character, Tony Soprano, is a violent and dangerous man to whom the use of violence should be second nature. To some extent it is, but he finds its use a deeply disturbing experience. It infiltrates his dreams and he is forced to discuss it with his female psychiatrist. The fact that he sees one is an indication of an ambivalence about masculinity. In a somewhat similar vein the British crime series *Cracker* shows its hero as possessing particular and unique skills in interpreting and understanding the behaviour of a range of psychopaths, but he is incapable of managing his own addiction to gambling and of forming loving relationships. James Bond would certainly not have approved.

Indeed it is hard to imagine Sipowicz, Cracker or Bond being welcome or at ease in the company of the most popular television detective in Britain in the 1990s, Inspector Morse. He is the opposite of the traditional male and masculine detective. 'Unlike other detectives', Thomas tells us, 'emotion and intuition rather than intellect and deduction' are his trademark. He also has a deep distaste for violence, dramatised in his inability to look at the bodies of murder victims. Moreover he is the ideal lover for women, 'always more involved than the women in question, and not afraid to admit it' (quoted in van Zoonen and Meijer, 1998:30).

Coward (2000) has argued that less limited representations of men can also be found in the television series *Superman*. The film and the comic book versions of this character demonstrated his heroism through acts of endurance, courage and strength, all of which had the simple and laudable aim of saving the world. Such male heroism does not come off too well in the latest television series. It is 'presented as an absurd residual neurosis provoking ambivalent feelings and unwanted backward-looking structures of desire in both men and women' (Coward, 2000:103). The new Superman is gentle, emotional and often confused.

'Reconstructed males' also feature in comedies such as *Home Improvements*. Here the main character, Tim, gives free flow to his assertive brand of masculinity on his television show, but it is challenged and deemed unacceptable in the conduct of his private life and in his relationship with his wife (McEachern, 1994). She resists his attempts to assert male authority in the home. He learns from this and subsequently uses his show to promote the case for better communication and less dominating behaviour by men.

Changing women

Undoubtedly there have been significant changes in the portrayals of women. These include *The X-Files* where the rational scientist is a woman, Scully, and the emotional, instinctive character, Mulder, is a man. He *feels* extra-terrestrials exist, while in the early series at least she *knows* they do not. She is presented as independent, assertive and single, but this is not accompanied by any denigration of her as a woman. As Parks (1996:123) argues, she 'reiterates the dominant norms of heterosexual femininity' – she wears tailored suits, plenty of make up, and clearly tends to her hair – and so 'is culturally intelligible as a woman'. She is also not compromised or domesticated through a sentimentalised relationship with family. McLean (2000:260) shows that while her family is important to her, there is 'little emotional affect in her relationship to its members'; 'her family obviously bores her, and she them'. The key relationship in the show is that with Mulder, but it is not a compromising one. The relationship is close and trusting but strictly platonic (except occasionally in dreams).

Similarly Smart (2000:48) has pointed to the presence of what she calls 'post-feminist' woman in the characterisation of Kathryn Janeway as captain of the starship Enterprise in the long-running and popular Star Trek series, *Voyager*. Many of these episodes revolve around her powers of leadership – it is 'tough, and the crew have to obey' – and her ability to take difficult decisions. Like the 'legendary Captain Kirk', she 'bends the rules constantly, takes enormous risks, and always wins' (Smart, 2000:48). These qualities are complemented by her status as a distinguished scientist and technologist. This portrayal of her an 'an honorary man' does not compromise her femininity. She has no shortage of traditional feminine gear (what Smart terms 'frilly frocks'), and she manages her hair appropriately for the occasion: it is up for business and down for pleasure.

Two other programmes present women in ways that are, to a greater or lesser degree, departures from conventional representations. The American comedy *Roseanne* created the space in which unruly and fun-loving women and mothers could be central characters in television comedy (Kirkham and Skeggs, 2000). Two such women featured in the British show, *Absolutely Fabulous*. They were very much 1980s people. One was a public relations executive and the other, her best friend, a fashion editor. They were shown as personifying the materialism and selfishness of the decade in which greed was good. However, they also had attachments to the ethos of the late 1960s and 1970s, particularly in the shape of serious interest in the consumption of drink and drugs. The comedy revolved around this conundrum. The demands of conventional femininity for morally and socially appropriate behaviour clashed in comic ways with their desire to be either stoned or drunk.

The series, as Kirkham and Skeggs (2000) show, was structured around a series of themes including the critique of materialism and the positive presentation of the concerns of feminism. The women were shown as resolutely amoral in the pursuit of immediate pleasure. Anything that diverted from either shopping or drinking, such as maternal responsibilities for the well-being of children, was a pointless distraction. In this sense it challenged the traditional stigmatisation of women's pursuit of pleasure and attraction to hedonistic behaviour. Friendships between women were presented in a positive light, and the principal women characters were shown as pursuing and constantly asserting their own independence.

The second series, *Beverly Hills 90210*, has, at one level, little in common with either *Roseanne* or *Absolutely Fabulous*. It is in many ways a standard-issue American high-school teenage drama in which the pursuit of romance has a higher priority than the achievement of educational excellence. The female characters are rarely single and seldom without boyfriends. In addition, as Rokler (1999:77) shows, they meet 'rigid American beauty standards'. They are unusually thin, dress in the latest fashions, wear a lot of make-up, and are highly sexualised. 'This sexualisation' is, she argues (Rockler, 1999:77), 'presented as a natural everyday part of these women's lives'.

The ideology of consumption is presented in much the same way. Direct product placement, in which major brands had their products highlighted – either through being used by the characters or else commented on by them – became routine parts of the shows (see Wasko, 1994). As such it seems an unlikely place for positive representations of women, yet Rockler argues that despite these constraints the women are presented in positive ways. They are shown as intelligent and as doing well in school, as successful at running businesses while still students, and at standing up to macho boyfriends. One female character, presented as highly sexualised, is shown as ending a relationship with a boyfriend because he is violent and abusive to her.

Absolutely feminist

So to different degrees and to different extents these accounts suggest that there have been positive transformations in the images of women and men in the media. These changes can be accounted for in a number of ways. One is as showing the sensitivity of programme makers to the changes in gender relationships in the wider society and as attempts to compensate for the years of negative stereotyping of women.

This does not necessarily represent a complete triumph for new images or indicate the demise of more traditional ones. 'Baywatch Babes' can still be found on television, although increasingly this is through being parodied in comedy shows. What it does reflect is a growing diversification of media images of gender. Moreover, it suggests that media representations are dynamic rather than frozen, and it directs our attention to the forces that drive the dynamism.

Changing in order to remain the same?

However, the changes have also been interpreted in a somewhat different fashion, as attempts at 'ideological recuperation' (Stabile, 1995). This is the process through which changes in gender relations are acknowledged but framed in ways that reinterpret male dominance and female subordination in a manner more appropriate to the contemporary situation. Thus it is accepted that these programmes highlight and dramatise contemporary tensions and contradictions in the construction of gender roles, but it is argued that these are ultimately resolved in favour of the status quo. Programmes involving the 'new man' have been described as offering 'a new, improved, modernized version of hegemonic masculinity' (Craig, 1996:69). Similarly, many of the programmes that highlight the new independent and assertive woman do so in ways that ultimately undermine her. These are changes, but within very clear limits.

McEachern (1994), for example, argues that the apparent progressiveness of a programme such as *Home Improvements* conceals the reinstatement of conservative masculinity (see also Craig, 1996). The central male character presents himself as equally responsible for the domestic sphere but it is his wife who cleans the house and feeds the family. 'Women and femininity', she says (McEachern, 1994:16), 'remain associated with home care and child raising'.

Kirkham and Skeggs (2000) see the comedy in *Absolutely Fabulous* as double-edged. The critique of materialism and the class system only works 'if the objects used in making the critique are not still seen as desirable by those not privileged enough to abandon them' (Kirkham and Skeggs, 2000:317). Making fun of the obsession of many women with fashion may not come across that way to people who can still only aspire to, but never reach, that level of clothes consumption. If audiences are made up of people who are socially excluded from the possibilities that the programme satirises and belittles then it may reproduce the 'very desires and longings it mocks and works against'.

Finally Rockler (1999) argues that while *Beverly Hills 90210* gives space to positive aspects of feminism, it tends typically to undercut them. For example, it presents those who cry 'date rape' as lying, and individual feminists as people who argue that women should be independent of men but then steal your boyfriend.

Black or white television?

The media representation of race has, according to some at least, followed the same trajectory as the representation of gender. Racial minorities have moved from media absence to media presence, and the issue of their representation has moved from questions of quantity to concerns about quality. This is similar to the way in which the analysis of gender began in content analysis and increasingly finds itself in ideological analysis. The media have moved from a situation in which racist images and stereotypes were commonplace to one in which their absence or presence is a matter of considerable dispute.

As Croteau and Hoynes (1997:140) show, blacks were either absent or confined to the roles of entertainers or servants in the early days of Hollywood. This continued in the early days of television when there were few (if any) dramatic roles for blacks. This began to change in the 1960s. Surveys from then until the late 1980s showed that while blacks constituted about 11 per cent of the population in the USA, they made up somewhere between 6 per cent and 9 per cent of television characters. By 1992 their proportion had reached 12 per cent of the population and 11 per cent of television characters. At this level there has been a gradual movement towards more proportionate representation.

Moreover within this movement there have been many fictional programmes that have dealt with and challenged white racism (Gauntlett, 1995). British soap operas, such as *Eastenders* and *Brookside*, have taken on the issue and increasingly it figures in programmes such as *NYPD Blue* where Andy Sipowicz has been presented as struggling with racist attitudes (in addition, that is, to his homophobia). It surfaces in his attitude to his immediate and black superior, Lieutenant Fancy, and his suspicions that crimes involving black people may not be dealt with by the book. These always prove unfounded.

The programme that was seen by many as pivotal in the arrival of positive black representation was *The Cosby Show*. This was one of the most successful comedies ever produced in the USA, and it gained a world-wide audience. It saw itself in political terms as correcting past representations of black people and of the black experience. This was achieved through the depiction of a black upper-middle-class family with a normal home life, with parents as competent and successful professional workers, with children committed to educational achievement and the family as a whole committed to upward social mobility. Moreover its success opened a space in which a range of black programmes became possible. These included *A Different World, Family Matters, Moesha*, and the *Fresh Prince of Bel-Air*. The *Fresh Prince*, in particular, argues that 'all people should be true to their origins and not try to imitate others' (Merelman, 1995:202).

Others, however, saw this movement in ideologically recuperative terms; that is, it represented an accommodation with the black presence and experience in the USA but it did so through portraying them in the same terms as the white families of television, as happy families with happy problems. The price was the neglect of key and defining aspects of the black experience, such as racism, violence and poverty (Jhally and Lewis, 1992). Moreover, if the notion is that the show enabled more representations of the black experiences and that it was a 'transitional point', then what did it enable and what was it transitional to?

Some argue that what it has allowed or reflected is the routine incorporation of black characters into television shows in Britain and the USA. They are there as doctors in medical dramas such as *ER* and *Casualty*, as police officers in *The Bill, Prime Suspect* and *The Knock*, and as characters rather than objects of fun in a range of situation comedies. Indeed, in some shows it is the racism of the white characters that is mocked, as in the British situation comedy

One Foot in the Grave. They also have achieved the ultimate parity of esteem through being present, occasionally at least, as fellow gangsters in *The Sopranos*.

Other critics argue that the transition has been to more of the same. They argue that the spin-off programmes remain very much within the same territory. They celebrate blackness but it remains very much an affluent and unrepresentative form of it. The issue of racism is touched in many of the new shows but the touch is light. The problem is presented as one of misunderstanding and mistrust, and of prejudiced whites who simply have not had sufficient contact with black people.

A schizophrenic media? Merelman on race

Merelman (1995) suggests that the situation may be somewhat more complex. This becomes apparent if we step beyond the question of depictions of race in the fictional programming and include broadcast journalism in the equation. This 'mainly emphasises the problems of the black underclass', through 'a seemingly endless parade of broken families, drug users, violent young males, teenage gangs, pregnant unmarried mothers, the poor and the welfare dependent' Merelman (1995:200).

Wilson and Gutierrez (1995) expand on this by suggesting that there are five phases in the reporting of race. The first is the *exclusionary* phase, in which blacks were simply left out of the news. When they did begin to get media coverage – in the *threatening issue* phase – they were represented as a danger to social order. The third phase is the *confrontational* one. Here the media look 'with white man's eyes' at the moves by blacks to improve their political and social situation. This resulted in a focus on civil unrest and street riots. The result was reporting that 'was skewed towards the preconceived biases and attitudes of 'white-middle class America' (Wilson and Gutierrez, 1995:156). This meant that events such as the 1992 Los Angeles riots were presented as a conflict between black and white, whereas they were motivated by class rather than racial concerns.

The fourth phase is the *stereotypical selection* one, when reporting covers racial issues in a way that confirms prejudices about racial minorities. It is 'designed to neutralise white apprehension of people of colour while accommodating their presence' (Wilson and Gutierrez, 1995:156). In this phase the bulk of stories emphasise the involvement of blacks in crime, drugs, promiscuity and general laziness, thus reassuring white audiences that most blacks are still in their place. There are stories on black successes but these are framed in ways that portray successful blacks as posing no threat to white dominance. The fifth phase is the *multi-racial* one, in which prejudice and racism have been removed from news coverage. This does not require that all news about blacks be good news: it simply requires that they are present in the same range of news as whites. This phase is, they argue, 'still largely a vision'.

Blacks in the news: the British experience

Ross (1998) argues that this kind of coverage is largely the case in the British context also. There has been a decrease in the more blatantly racist reporting of the 1980s, but its underlying assumptions of the 'black-as-threat', the 'black-as-problem', and the 'black-as-criminal' still structure the selection and framing of news stories about race. These are mainly about immigration, crime, violence or conflict generally. The more 'positive' stories tend to be about millionaires, entertainers or sports stars whose lives and experiences are beyond those of most black people. In this sense, she concludes, 'stereotypical reportage is the norm rather than the exception' (Ross, 1998:230).

The missing lives

Thus Merelman (1995:201) argues that the media representation of blacks can best be characterised as schizophrenic. There are more positive but still limited images available in fictional television, but a continued predominance of negative stereotypes in news and current affairs. The significance of this is that it ignores a third black way of life. This middle way 'is neither "entertaining", as pictured in television sit-coms, nor "lawless" as pictured in news programs'. It is the lives and experiences of 'the hardworking blacks of modest means'.

Back to numbers?

These examples show how the strengths of ideological analysis lie in a capacity to study individual series and programmes and to derive insights into representations of gender and race that are not possible with content analysis. But when we ask whether such representations have changed, and how significant the changes are, the limitations of a qualitative approach become apparent (see Lewis, 1997). It is skilful at identifying how gender and race are constructed in particular films and television series, but less successful at telling us how widespread such constructions are in popular culture and society generally. This has opened it to the suggestion that it is merely 'speculative criticism' (Sumner, 1979).

How to study television fiction: (2) in search of universal structures

The second way of looking at television fiction draws on the work of a number of writers, most notably Todorov (see the account in Fiske, 1987). He analysed folk tales and argued that while the details may change from story to story, there is a common and consistent structure underlying these differences. Most stories begin with a 'state of equilibrium', which is either shown or implied. This equilibrium is 'disrupted' by events or individuals and there is a 'fight against the disruption'. The story concludes with 'a resolution in another, preferably enhanced or more stable state of equilibrium' (Fiske, 1987:139).

This model has the potential to direct attention to questions of sociological significance, but sociologists have not used it very much in their analysis of television fiction. It can lead us to ask what, for example, is the social nature of the equilibrium with which programmes open? Is there a consistent pattern to the types of norms that are violated and the kinds of people who disrupt the equilibrium? Is there a consistency to the sort of people and the kinds of action that correct the disruption? How is conflict resolved, and is there a consistency in the methods through which resolution is achieved? How does the new equilibrium compare to the old one? The search for answers to these questions can reveal important dimensions of fictional dramas.

This perspective can, for example, usefully be applied in studying violence in the media. It encourages us to look at the framework of relationships and attitudes within which violence is presented. Gerbner (1992) has identified the consistency with which violence in television fiction is both the source of problems and the solution to them. The use of violence by villains disrupts the moral order, and moral resolution or purification requires them to be wounded or killed. The use of violence by good characters becomes the means through which moral equilibrium is restored.

How to study television fiction: (3) genre analysis

The third method of studying television fiction is genre analysis. This also derives from literary criticism but it has been developed and applied to television. The term refers to the type or category to which a programme belongs. Thus 'action films', 'situation comedies' and 'soap operas' are particular categories and different genres of programmes. They differ in the set of themes that they deal with, in the format that they follow, and in the pacing of action and activity in the story line. They also follow different but predictable sets of rules and conventions.

Audiences know the characteristics of particular genres. They are attracted to programmes because they belong to a particular genre and they expect to find the rules and conventions followed by the programme makers. There is the expectation that certain themes are appropriate in action films that are not appropriate in soap operas. Similarly certain kinds of language (particularly swearing) are acceptable in action films but not in soap operas.

From family to friends

The advantages of the concept are that it enables us to put some structure on the range and variety of programmes on television. Changes in genres also allow us to study how a society is developing and changing. Situation comedies are, for example, a standard genre set around families and the minor misunderstandings and difficulties of everyday life. But while the family format and the mundane nature of the action remain the same, the unit that passes as a 'family' has changed. In the 1950s and 1960s they were set very clearly around the traditional family and the domestic sphere. In the 1970s the setting changed to the work environment, as in the *Mary Tyler Moore Show* where the 'family' was made up of work colleagues. Coming up to the present, we have the 'family' as a group of twenty-somethings sharing an apartment building. The intimacy of the home is replaced and reproduced through the intimacy and warmth of *Friends*.

Difficulties with genres: the debate about soap operas

However, it has been argued that while the concept of genre may
be useful it is not a particularly powerful tool for the sociological
analysis of the media. The reasons for this include difficulties in
applying the concept, the question of whether genres are recognised and used by audiences, and the breakdown of genres as
reflected, for example, in the increasing importation of elements of
soap operas into police dramas and vice versa.

The difficulties in applying the concept can be illustrated through
the consideration of soap operas. It has been argued that this is a
female genre. Brunsdon (1983), for example, claims that the narrative of soap operas assumes that the audience is female. This is clear
in the personal emphasis in the story lines and in the tensions and
climaxes, which are built around people's conduct of their personal
relationships. The understanding of the programmes requires 'a
viewer competent [with] the rules of romance, marriage and family
life' (Brunsdon, 1983:80), and in our society these are assumed to be
female skills.

Brunsdon (1985) goes on to argue that the attractions of soaps
for women lie in their conventions and genre formulae. They
offer ritualised and reassuring pleasures of 'familiarity and regularity' (Brunsdon, 1985:86). The problems they deal with are ones
with which women can identify, and the solutions they propose
are very much within traditional norms of happiness and hetero-
sexuality. This is no surprise to women as they know the rules
of the genre and so expect such resolutions. But, within these
limitations, they provide a means through which women can be
become involved and explore problems and stories that touch
their lives. As such these features of soap operas have, according
to Liladhor (2000), liberating potential for women. They offer
positive images of women and of their competencies, and so
provide them with the material to consider and create new models
of femininity.

However, Livingstone and Liebes (1995) suggest that their liberating potential is over-stated. The underlying and repetitive
message is the centrality of the personal and domestic sphere for
women, their emotional dependence on men, their unreliability
around children and the competitive nature of their relationships
with other women. Through the vehicle of romance, men, they
claim (Livingstone and Liebes, 1995:171), 'dominate the whole
scheme of things, even if their roles in the narrative are secondary'.

From texts to viewers

The argument from genre characteristics identifies soap opera as a female genre and provides a means through which the pleasures that it offers can be theorised and understood. The problem is that this central point is not borne out by audience research. Wober (1984:68) claims that in Britain at least audience figures show that soap operas are not as popular as they are claimed to be, their audiences are not as loyal as is supposed and, in particular, women do not watch with the regularity that is claimed for them. They may have the same size audience over a period of time, but it is not one of constant and consistent viewers; the mode is intermittent, with viewers moving in and out of the audience (Wober, 1984:68). The research has also suggested that the audience may not be as female dominated as it is made out to be. Morley (1986) found that significant numbers of men watch soap operas, but because of the female image of the programmes they are less likely to admit to it.

How to study television fiction: (4) values and the culture industry

These ways of analysing television fiction offer considerable and useful insights in the mass media, but it can be argued that the sociological study of this area needs to be more broadly conceived and treated as an extension of the study of social culture. Culture, according to Geertz (1973), is the 'ensemble of stories we tell ourselves about ourselves'. Television is the means through which stories are circulated in the modern world. Programmes tell certain stories and enact certain values. The important questions are whose stories are told, and whose values are highlighted, dramatised and affirmed?

There are three broad perspectives on this issue. The first one, associated with the Frankfurt School, argues that the products of mass culture constantly emphasise and affirm conventional values. The second, associated with writers such as Douglas Kellner, argues that there is space in television fiction for dissenting voices and for limited critique of the existing system. The third perspective is associated with Newcomb and Hirsh (2000) and it argues that television, in the USA at least, can be conceptualised as a cultural forum in which all significant values and attitudes are given a presence and a voice.

One-dimensional television: the Frankfurt School and mass culture

The work of Horkheimer and Adorno (see, in particular, 1977) stresses the banality, emptiness and false promise of mass culture. They believe that art has the potential to contribute to a critique of the prevailing values and attitudes in a society. The problem is that while art has this utopian impulse, it is not available to the masses; what they have in its place are the products of the culture industry. These are manufactured on an assembly line and, as a result, they have a 'constant sameness' and fit into 'cyclically recurrent and rigidly invariable types' (Horkheimer and Adorno, 1977:359).

The products of the culture industry carry hidden messages relating to the support and maintenance of conventional values. They contain 'ideals of conformity and conventionalism...clear-cut prescriptions of what to do and what not to do' (Adorno, 1957:478). These hidden messages are more important than the overt or surface messages because they escape the normal mental barriers that we erect to protect ourselves against overt propaganda, such as advertising.

According to Adorno, these messages can be identified in two ways, and the first is by looking at the way people are treated in programmes. In comedy shows, for example, the humorous situations revolve around the attempts of the characters to negotiate with (and accommodate to) humiliating circumstances. These are presented as situations that should be adjusted to rather than resisted or changed. 'Fun', Horkheimer and Adorno (1977:364) assure us, 'is a medicinal bath'; 'The pleasure industry never fails to prescribe it. It makes laughter the instrument of the fraud practised on happiness.'

The second strategy involves the examination of stereotypes. According to Adorno (1957:484), these are not inherently bad and 'no art can entirely dispense with them'. They are necessary to tell stories within limited time constraints. They are used to quickly establish characters and situations, which can then be developed and elaborated. The problem with the stereotypes of mass culture, he argues, is that they are out of touch with the complexities of the real world. They simplify complex social issues by reducing them to issues of personality.

He gives the example of a film on totalitarianism (Charlie Chaplin's *The Great Dictator*). This portrays fascism as a product of the ambitions of a number of psychiatrically disturbed individuals and so as something that can be overcome by well-intentioned, well-meaning and courageous people. As such it distracts attention from the social issues and from the social forces behind the rise of totalitarianism. It also, according to Adorno, suggests that we can understand what is happening in the world by dividing it between 'us', the normal, and 'them', the disturbed, who cause all the problems.

In this way the function of mass culture is control. It encourages people to buy into the success myths of mass society, while at the same time the world view that it proposes undermines their ability to resist and oppose it. Thus mass culture performs a conservative and conserving role in contemporary society.

The diversity of television: the views of Douglas Kellner

For Douglas Kellner television cannot be characterised as simply a 'monolithic tool of a unified ruling class' or as performing a control function in society (Kellner, 1981:45); its role is much more complex. It is caught in the contradictions of the society of which it is a part and these conflicts are reflected in the content of its programming. This means that there is always space for criticism and for progressive change within the media system. The television industry may be seen in broad terms as a defender of the status quo, but it is an unreliable one. The media culture that is carried by television is a 'contest of representations' (Kellner, 1995:56) and there is no guarantee that conformist and conservative ideologies will predominate.

This is because the industry is, according to Kellner (1995), subject to and caught within a series of contradictory imperatives. The most basic of these is 'the contradiction between capitalism and democracy' (Kellner, 1981:38). The democratic ideal of television is that it is a public resource to be used in the public interest; the capitalist notion is that it is a private commercial resource to be used to accumulate profits for its owners. This broad contradiction manifests itself in a number of specific conflicts.

There is, for example, a conflict between the profit motive and the role that the Frankfurt School attribute to the media in the engineering of consent. The media must hold an audience to maximise profits, but to do this they have to deal with controversial issues and crucial problems that audiences are concerned about and that they want to see dramatised on television, even if this conflicts with its role in the maintenance of the status quo.

As a result television series can carry both progressive and regressive messages, and alternative depictions of the world can find their way into media culture. Kellner (1995) cites the development of what he calls 'loser television' as an example. Until the late 1980s and early 1990s the world of American television was primarily that of rich middle-class families whose stories presented advertisers with a suitable environment in which to sell their products. However, the reality of downward social mobility, the marginalisation of the working class, and the growing divide between rich and poor in the 1990s created the space for programmes that articulated the anger of the economic losers. The MTV show *Beavis and Butthead* gave voice to disaffected youth, and it became popular largely because of 'its ability to articulate inchoate social anger' (Kellner, 1995:134).

The Simpsons, initially at least, was much the same thing for grown-ups. It gave expression, in a comic and cartoon fashion, to the experiences of working-class families, dismissed by experts as dysfunctional, yet distinctly recognisable to viewers as having certain correspondences to their own. It broke (and continues to break) many taboos in its depiction of its main characters and its portrayal of their attitudes and behaviour. The father, Homer, is incompetent as a father, selfish in his pursuit of personal pleasure, weak on issues of morality and personal hygiene, and less than expert as a technician, and sometimes safety officer, in a nuclear power plant. His son, Bart, is a reluctant and disrespectful pupil whose capacity to aggravate adult figures of authority is deeply imbedded and considerably over-developed. The nature of the advice that he receives from his father is not much help. It consists largely in the encouragement of cheating and the promotion of the virtues of cowardice. Bart's sister Lisa is, by contrast, the aspiring pupil, resident intellectual, and voice of conventional morality. As a result she is often a derided figure. Marge is the much put-upon and under-rated mother, but also a strong and decisive figure. Finally there is the baby, Maggie, whose childrearing does not follow recognised manuals and whose main contribution is to fall over at appropriate moments.

The themes and jokes of the show are generally at the expense of established figures and institutions of power. The town mayor is corrupt, the police chief is a buffoon, and the nuclear industry is in the hands of a millionaire and miser called Burns. Through this it gives voice to issues and ways of relating to the world that are not normally heard or seen in mainstream television culture; yet there are clear limits to its transgressiveness. Certain values are affirmed at the end of each episode, most notably the centrality of love of family and, unlikely as it may seem, the love of country. Thus an episode in which Bart gets involved with other disreputables in taking the head off the statue of a local patriot ends with him regretting the decision and trying to make up for it with an appropriate display of national fervour. Similarly the losers are conceptualised in populist rather than class terms, allowing the bulk of the audience, 'us', to identify with the Simpsons against the rich and successful 'them'.

Television as a cultural forum: Newcomb and Hirsch

Newcomb and Hirsch (2000) have argued that the role of television, in American society at least, is not about the transmission of dominant and controlling messages; instead it acts as a cultural forum in which the range of views and ideologies in American society are aired and discussed. It offers 'a way of understanding who and what we are, how values and behaviour are adjusted, how meanings shift'. To achieve this it provides 'a multiplicity of meaning rather than a monolithic dominant view' (Newcomb and Hirsch, 2000:564). Issues and problems may not be resolved in the sense of clear solutions being offered in programmes, but this is not the point. 'The raising of issues is', they claim (Newcomb and Hirsch, 2000: 565), 'as important as the answering of them'.

The idea of a cultural forum has important similarities to the notion of public service broadcasting. They both see the media as reflecting and bringing together the range of viewpoints in a society; where they differ is in how these ideals are to be achieved. The public service model requires an element of state intervention, state ownership, and state regulation to achieve its cultural ends. By contrast, Newcomb and Hirsh see the same end being achieved under the American commercial system. They acknowledge that there are limits to the cultural forum. These are the system of political pluralism and the economic system of monopoly capitalism. But despite these limits television is effective in presenting 'a mass audience with the range and variety of ideas and ideologies in American culture' (Newcomb and Hirsch, 2000:566).

Value analysis: the empirical work

We have outlined three arguments about the nature and content of mass culture and of the relationship of this culture to the dominant values of the society that produces it. We now need to ask, which of these best summarises the perspective of television fiction? How can its value orientation be best characterised: is it conservative, is it open to alternative visions or is it an open forum?

Unfortunately there is not a great range of research material to draw from to illuminate these issues. This is partly because many studies are based on limited samples, such as the analysis of single episodes or a single series of programmes. Few have tried to be more wide-ranging, either because of the difficulties of getting access to comprehensive samples of programmes or because of a disdain for this kind of methodological approach (see Murdock, 1997). The material that is available is also somewhat dated. However, we can outline two relevant pieces and we deal with these now.

The core values of television: the research of Gary Selnow. Selnow (1990) took a sample of prime-time shows on the major American networks over two months in 1987. Many of these, such as *Cheers*, would be familiar to international audiences. He found that the values highlighted in them were 'the personal values that are endemic to American culture' (Selnow, 1990:72). These included the importance of personal integrity, having the courage of one's convictions, a sense of pride in one's work, and a sense of the rights of others.

His analysis of problem solving in television fiction substantiates this (Selnow, 1986). He found that success in dealing with problems was portrayed as achieved through hard work, honesty, truthfulness and being good. Such solutions typically drew on a limited range of positive cultural themes such as 'good wins out over evil' and 'honesty is the best policy'. 'Evil' triumphed in only 4 per cent of resolutions.

He concluded that there was a limited range of moral lessons in television programmes, and that these lessons tended to be rather simple and very much in the terrain of mainstream values. Television fiction predominantly highlights the core business, educational and religious values of American society.

Televising Terrorism: Elliott, Murdock and Schlesinger.   Elliott, Murdock and Schlesinger (1983) deal with the media's treatment of political terrorism. They suggest that there are three discourses through which such terrorism can be understood. The 'official' discourse denies any political motivation to acts of terror and portrays those involved as criminals. The 'alternative discourse' highlights the social factors that create situations of violence and consequent terrorism such as the use of violence and repression by governments. This is extended in the 'oppositional discourse', in which the use of violence to achieve political ends is justified in situations where the state is a repressive one that uses terror against its citizens.

They examined fictional programming in the British media to see the extent to which the various discourses were represented. They found that for the most part series aimed at mass audiences operated within the official discourse. These presented terrorism as evil, with violent consequences for its victims, and as committed by ruthless people who concealed their criminal intentions behind political rhetoric. Other forms of television fiction, such as one-off dramas, often dealt with the alternative or oppositional discourses on terrorism. The problem is that there tended to be a lot of one kind of representation and few of the others. For every one presentation of terrorism from an alternative or oppositional viewpoint, there were considerably more from within the official discourse. In this respect, then, the official discourse predominated in television fiction.

Conclusion

In this chapter we have examined the various methods through which sociologists research television fiction and drama. We have looked also at the kinds of conclusion that they have reached. The argument is that television fiction is entertaining, but that it also contains persuasive messages. These messages are not random and isolated but are systematic and patterned. They promote and reinforce certain kinds of values, lifestyles and modes of behaviour and personality and, by implication, the irrelevance and undesirability of other values, lifestyles and modes of being.

This does not mean that programmes remain essentially un-changed and unchangeable; their content must change to keep in touch with the dispositions and perspectives of the audiences they are trying to reach. Social and cultural conflicts could be ignored in the television of the 1950s, but it is less possible to do so in the 2000s. The key question relates to the manner in which television accommodates to them. The main way in which conflicts such as racial discrimination and homosexuality get into prime-time tele-vision is, as Goldman (1982) has shown, through their domesti-cation in situation comedies. Once suitably sanitised they can migrate into mainstream programming.

Assessing the extent of the space for alternative voices is a complex matter. It depends most centrally on the structure of ownership and regulation of the media in different societies. It has been argued that fictional material produced under the com-mercial system that operates in the USA will always tend towards the conservative and the predictable (see Gitlin, 1994). Advertisers are the linchpins of the system and do not for the most part wish to see their products advertised in controversial programmes. If a programme is successful, the rule of thumb says that you make it again, if not as the same series then as a spin-off (but preferably as both). Equally, however, they do not wish to advertise in unpopu-lar programmes, but they will only take risks at times of intense competition and when audiences are changing or proving difficult to reach. Then programme makers will be under pressure to create shows with a wider appeal, and to take programming risks through incorporating themes and representations that are new and even controversial.

By contrast, in those systems with a significant element of public ownership and with an ethos of public service broadcasting, the commitment to reflect the diversity of society should produce a menu of programmes that educate, entertain and provoke. The system with guaranteed revenues through the licence fee facili-tates risk-taking and ensures a greater variety in its fictional pro-gramming. However, this system is currently under pressure and this has important implications for the future of the fictional ma-terial. The likelihood is that it will become less diverse and more homogenised. This issue is taken up in Chapter 8.

CHAPTER 7

Media Audiences: Couch Potatoes or Armchair Intellectuals?

Introduction

The argument in this book is that a key aspect of media power is the potential to shape the nature of social consciousness and the nature of public opinion. Through the 'accounts of reality' that it transmits to audiences, it can influence the views that they form about the nature of the social world. If people's behaviour is related to, and influenced by, their social understanding, then the media also has the potential to shape social and political action.

However, as it stands, there is a missing dimension or connection in the argument. Bennett has identified it in this way. He argues that 'to show that the media propose certain definitions of reality is one thing; but it cannot be inferred from this that such definitions are necessarily accepted in the sense that they are effectively taken for real and acted upon' (T. Bennett, 1982:297–8). In other words, for media power to be translated from a potential to a reality audiences must believe in and accept the social knowledge that the media is carrying to them.

The development of this point requires us to shift our focus from media content and media organisations, and bring audiences under the analytic spotlight. This is the purpose of this chapter. We look at the different ways in which sociologists have accounted for media audiences. These have tended to swing between the view that the media is all-powerful to the view that power rests with the audience, a swing which Katz (1987) has argued occurs about every ten years. An important focus here will be on the latest swing, the one that has placed the audience back in a position of power in its relationship with the media. We begin, however, with a brief excursion into previous swings of the cycle.

Previous swings and roundabouts

From Orson Welles to Joseph Klapper

We can identify three previous swings in views about media audiences. The first came to the fore in the 1920s and 1930s. It saw the audience as an undifferentiated mass that was particularly vulnerable to the media. This view had its roots in the theories of social change and mass society that were popular at the time. These argued that rapid change was dislodging people from their social anchoring in stable, traditional, small-scale communities and reconstituting them in anonymous, urban crowds. The absence of stable ties to family, friends and locality made them particularly vulnerable to the mass media.

This view was not based on detailed empirical research but was supported by a series of incidents that became part of the mythology of media power. One of the most notable of these was the radio version of the *War of the Worlds* broadcast in Los Angeles in 1938 (see Cantril, Gaudet and Herzog, 1940). Based on H. G. Wells's account of the invasion of the world by Martians, it was presented in semi-documentary fashion with the story being interrupted by news flashes detailing the progress of the invaders. Audiences, it was claimed, mistook the story for a real event and many, abandoning the traditional notion of courtesy to visitors, deserted the city in droves. The police had to be mobilised to retrieve them.

This view was formalised into what came to be referred to as 'the hypodermic model of media power' (Gitlin, 1978). The argument was that watching the media and using drugs had something in common. Drug-users lose their self-control and critical judgement when they inject drugs into their veins; in the process, they become prisoners of the substance they abuse and open to its every suggestion. In a similar fashion, the media are capable of injecting ideas and attitudes into vulnerable audiences and in the process making them its prisoners.

This particular view of the media as capable of mass manipulation was effectively killed by research. Paul Lazarsfeld and his associates were major contributors to its demise. In a series of studies, beginning with *The People's Choice* (Lazarsfeld, Gaudet and Berelson, 1944), a study of the role of the media in the 1940 US presidential election, and culminating in *Personal Influence* (Katz and Lazarsfeld, 1955), they succeeded in changing the prevailing view on the power of the media and set in motion a group of ideas that dominated and constrained media studies for almost 30 years.

The conclusion they came to was that the media were not central to the formation of public opinion. In their election study, for example, they showed that political campaigns had only limited success in converting voters from one candidate to another. Similarly, they found that the media had little dramatic effect on people's decisions in areas such as fashion, or what movies to go to.

The conclusions of these and other studies were formalised into a classic statement by Klapper (1960:8). He argued that one of the emerging generalisations from media research was that 'mass communication ordinarily does not serve as a necessary or sufficient cause of audience effects'. This was because the media do not operate on susceptible audiences. Audiences have prior social connections, prior social attitudes and prior opinions, and it is through these that the material from the media was filtered and against which the validity and relevance of its content was assessed. In this way it was argued that 'knowledge of an individual's interpersonal environment is basic to an understanding of his exposure and reactions to the mass media' (Katz and Lazarsfeld, 1955:133, sexism in original). This environment constitutes, as it were, a set of defences against the influence of the media.

These arguments took a lot of the pressure off the media by showing that they do not have the power to exploit audiences; but it was noted, by some at least, that this was a rather peculiar form of justification. As Raymond Bauer (1964:327) pointed out, 'there is a limited range of charges against which impotence may indeed be considered a defense'. Nonetheless it was a conclusion that led Berelson (1959) to suggest that studying the media was no longer a worthwhile exercise and as a field of study it was dead. If the media had little or no power or influence, why bother studying it?

Uses and gratifications: the audience as master

'Uses and gratifications' theorists took the theme of the relative powerlessness of the media a stage further. They felt that the question of media power was always posed in terms of what the media do to audiences, whereas it was more productive to turn the question around and ask what do audiences do with the media? The answer, they argued, is that media audiences are made up of individuals with particular social and emotional needs, and they turn to the media to gratify these needs. Thus the reason they looked at certain programmes was because they wished to satisfy the particular needs that were dominant for them at that point in time. McQuail, Blumler and Brown (1972:144) summarised the central proposition of the model by saying that, 'social experience gives rise to certain needs, some of which are directed to the mass media of communication for satisfaction'.

As a theory it raises a number of issues, most notably what needs do people turn to the media with, and how can we identify them? The best way of identifying these needs, according to these theorists, was simply to ask people what they get from watching particular programmes. On this basis McQuail, Blumler and Brown (1972) identified four sets of needs that are gratified by watching television. The first and most obvious one was the need for diversion and the need to escape the constraints of everyday life. Watching particular programmes helped people get away from the pressure of immediate problems and frustrations in their lives. The second was the need for what they termed 'para-social interaction'. Certain kinds of television programmes provided people with companionship in that they entered into vicarious relationships with the characters, and acted as if they were on friendly and knowing terms with them.

The third set of gratifications provided by the media was the need for personal identity. People used television programmes to reflect on or to confirm certain aspects of their life circumstances or sense of personal identity. Thus, for example, the interest in quiz shows related to people's desire to see how clever they are by comparison with the contestants. The final set of gratifications was the surveillance one: people needed information about what was happening in the world and they turned to the media to find this.

A noteworthy aspect of this research is the complexities of the relationships that it revealed between the needs of people and the programmes they used to satisfy them. People may need information (say, about crime), but it does not necessarily follow that they will fulfil this need by looking at factual programmes such as news and current affairs programmes about crime; instead, they may gratify it through watching crime dramas.

The implication here is that the relationship between the overt content of a programme and the response that it elicits from the audience is a complex one. Audiences can, and regularly do, use programme content for purposes other than what might be predicted from their content, and they do this because of their particular needs at the time they are watching television. Overall the response to particular programmes is not one that is in the control of programme makers, but it is a function of the needs of audience members.

In this way 'uses and gratifications' affirms the power that the audience holds in its relationship with the mass media; but it has been criticised on a number of grounds (see Elliott, 1974). One is the problem concerning the identification of audience needs. Each particular set of researchers seems to come up with their own set of needs which television satisfies so that in practice there seem to be as many needs as there are researchers asking about them. Attempts to reduce these to a manageable and universally accepted typology have not been entirely successful.

It is also argued that there is confusion in many versions of the model between needs and gratifications. So, for example, when researchers talk about the escapist function of the media, are they saying that escapism is what people want or what they get from the media? The distinction is important because it raises the question of whether this model is capable of asking critical questions about the role of the media. If the model asks about the needs people come to the media with, then it is possible to ask whether these needs are fully satisfied. If, on the other hand, the argument is saying that these are the particular satisfactions that people get from the media, then there can be no question of improving the media as it is already providing adequate levels of gratification for its audience.

However, the most fundamental criticism is that if the theory is valid then audiences must be active in their choice of programmes, selecting the ones that will most adequately gratify the particular expectations that they bring to television viewing. The problem here is that research on audiences indicates that, for the most part, they are not selective in their choice of viewing. Generally speaking, people turn on the television and simply watch what everyone else is looking at. In this sense the audience's use of television seems to depend on availability and viewing habit rather than on need.

Back to hypodermics? Screen theory

What has been described as a return to the hypodermic model of the media (see Morley, 1992:59) emerged in the late 1970s and early 1980s. It brought together a range of French social and psychoanalytic theorists in a model that became known as screen theory, after the British film journal in which many of the leading contributions to the theory were published. As a theory it does not lend itself easily to succinct synopsis (see G. Thompson, 1979).

It has its roots, primarily though not exclusively, in the theory of ideology developed by Althusser (1971). He challenges the notion that people are distinguishable and autonomous individuals, capable of thinking and acting in a manner of their own choosing. Drawing on the work of Jacques Lacan, he argues that human subjectivity is created by language, essentially because of the possibility that it offers to identify ourselves as individuals, and most notably through the capacity that it offers to say 'I'. In other words, our sense of individual subjectivity is only possible because we accept language and because we accept the assumptions that underlie language. We do not exist as individuals without the capacity to refer to ourselves as such, and this capacity is given to us through the adoption of language. Moreover, we cannot participate in society unless we accept its language and the assumptions that are inherent in it.

In this way it is language that constructs us as individual and as autonomous. But it does so in a society that is capitalist in nature and, as such, one of domination and exploitation rather than freedom and autonomy. Hence a language, which constructs us as autonomous in a society in which we are not, is an ideological tool. It creates the illusion that we are free subjects and so it enables us to enter 'freely' into relations of domination. Language limits the range of ways in which we can think and act, while appearing to facilitate them.

How is this relevant to the study of the media? The argument is that language and media products have certain similarities. Just as language creates us as subjects, media products also create us as audience members. And just as language limits the range of what we can think and say, so too do television programmes or media texts limit the ways in which we can respond to them. In the formal language of screen theory, the media text imprisons the viewer in its structures.

Programmes address audiences as if they were made up of particular kinds of people. They offer what screen theory describes as 'subject' positions, through which or from which the programmes should be viewed; and through a range of presentational devices such as script, camera angles, editing and music, they encourage audience members to 'occupy' these subject positions. So the way in which programmes speak to us as spectators encourages us to understand them in particular ways and makes it impossible for us to step outside their intended meaning. In this sense, media texts have the power to create the manner in which they will be understood.

What this means is that in studying media messages we need to focus on the communication and not on the audience. If the meaning of the message is in the text, then the responses of audience members do not require independent study: they can be deduced from the structure and characteristics of the film or television programme. The viewer, according to Stephen Heath (quoted in Moores, 1993:13), 'has no option but to make ... the meanings the film makes for it', and these meanings can be read off from the characteristics of the text.

If this argument is accepted, then the audience ceases to be of interest or concern to students of the media. The analysis of the media becomes confined to the study of programmes and to the examination of their inherent meaning. Studying the audience, in effect, becomes redundant.

The 'new audience' studies: getting off the roundabout?

Introduction

Screen theory established the text as dominant in the study of the media. However, this perspective was challenged from a number of different directions and it is this turn of the roundabout that we wish to consider in this section. What is common to these challenges is that they do not accept that the meaning of a media message is given in, and confined by, the manner in which it is produced and presented. They argue that the process of message production by media professionals, and the process of message reception by audiences, must be disconnected and studied separately. There is, as Morley (1983:105) argues, a 'potential disjunction between the codes of those sending and those receiving messages through the circuit of mass communication'. It is out of the study of this disjunction that the new audience studies have emerged.

Media messages need to be analysed at two distinct levels, the first being that of media production. We need to analyse the meaning that the programme producers intend audiences to receive, and to examine the means that they use to encourage and persuade viewers to read programmes in this way. For example, we need to look at how programme makers try to establish points of identification with 'us', the audience, and through these to 'suggest' a way of looking at the programme. We also need to analyse the range of influences that lead to particular messages being encoded into particular media texts. Readers will be familiar with these through the material considered in previous chapters.

At the second level we have to look at how audiences interpret and make sense of programmes. This involves us in a series of considerations: we need to establish what interpretative frameworks audiences bring to their viewing; we need to establish what impact these have on the ways in which audiences make sense of what they view; and, if they result in what Eco (1977) called 'aberrant decodings', we need to know the social characteristics of those whose readings are significantly different from those intended by programme makers. Let us begin with the issue of the interpretative codes used by audiences.

Finding the Active Audience

A number of pieces of research show the diversity of ways in which viewers make sense of television programmes and the ways in which viewers are active in their interpretations of media texts. They have two things in common: one is that they 'reveal the degree to which viewers may negotiate meanings and thereby mitigate against the power of television to impose its "preferred" meaning' (Livingstone, 1990:73); the other is that extent to which they ignore the reception and interpretation of messages from media other than television.

Workers in dispute: the research of David Morley.   Morley (1980) was interested in the manner in which different groups interpreted the treatment of industrial relations in a news magazine programme on British television. The typical approach or discourse that the programme adopted to the issue was a populist one: it was cynical towards politicians and trade unions, it treated the notion of a collective national self-interest as self-evident and it blamed industrial disputes on workers.

He looked to see if audiences adopted the same approach in their interpretation of the programmes. He conducted interviews with different groups of people. They viewed episodes of the programme and he asked them a series of questions about what they had seen. On the basis of the answers he argued that viewers decoded in three principal ways:

- hegemonic: viewers used the same dominant code or interpretation as the programme producers;

- negotiated: viewers accepted the general frame of the media message but felt that it did not apply to their specific circumstances, so they were able to accept the anti-union attitude of the programme but combined it with support for and justification of the activities of their particular trade union;

- Oppositional: viewers recognised the frame of interpretation proposed by the programme but rejected it and used an alternative framework, (such viewers, for example, rejected the notion of national identity being proposed by the programme because it was one they saw as excluding people like them).

There was a fourth category of response among those viewers who saw no connection between their concerns and their lifeworld, and the cultural framework of the programme. They had no points of identification with the world of the programme and could not connect with it. Morley included them in the third category and said that they offered a 'critique of silence'.

Different kind of suds: a study of soap opera.   The second example is from the work of Livingstone (1990). She showed a group of viewers – mostly white-collar workers – a particular sequence from a popular British soap opera, *Coronation Street*. This involved a daughter who has an affair with a man 20 years older than her. She subsequently marries him. Initially her father refuses to attend the wedding and has a fight with her intended husband but eventually, under pressure from his son, he attends the wedding.

According to Livingstone, this sequence is open to two possible interpretations, both of which can be supported by the events of the story. One is the traditional romantic one in which true love triumphs over adversity; the other is that of the unsuccessful attempt of a father to prevent his naive daughter from making a fool of herself with an older man. However, when she analysed the results of a questionnaire she gave to viewers she found four clusters of interpretation. The 'cynics' were strongly on the side of the father and felt the daughter was making a fool of herself. The 'romantics' were on the side of the lovers and felt they had done the right thing. The 'negotiated cynics' agreed with the cynics but felt that the father was right to oppose the marriage. Finally, the 'negotiated romantics' agreed with romantics but had some sympathy for the dilemma of the father.

Birds of a feather flock together: the work of Tamar Liebes. Liebes (1992) looked at how Israeli television treated the protests by the Palestinians in what has become known as the Intifada. She found that it tended to depoliticise the conflict, presenting it as violent unrest and as urban riots rather than as a civil war. The violence of the protesters was emphasised through the way in which the demonstrations were filmed from behind police lines. This made them seem stronger, more dangerous, and a significantly larger threat than they actually were. By contrast, the brutality by the police, which often provoked these disturbances, was not considered to be news. Similarly, the families of victims of the violence of protesters were interviewed whereas the families of those who suffered violence at the hands of the police were not.

However, her audience research showed that viewers decoded this news in a variety of ways. The key factor appeared to be their particular political stance. Those whom she characterised as 'hawks' followed the media framing. They used the same terms as the media to describe the conflict, though they felt that the media were biased simply because they showed the conflict. 'Doves', by contrast, were unhappy with the media presentation. They felt that the media was framing the conflict as a series of violent incidents, whereas it should have been presented as protesters making a legitimate political statement.

Freeing the prisoner: the work of Hodge and Tripp. Hodge and Tripp (1986) looked at the responses of children to a television soap opera called *The Prisoner* (shown in Britain and the USA as *Prisoner Cell Block H*). It dealt with the lives of women in a female prison and as such was aimed at an afternoon audience of housewives,

yet market research showed that schoolchildren formed a significant part of its audience.

Their research showed that the young people were making
connections between their own lives and those of the women in
prison, and it was through this connection that they understood
and enjoyed the programme. Thus, both the women in prison and
the young people in school were there unwillingly. Some of the
prison warders victimised particular individuals; some prisoners
were like fellow students and went along with the system; others
fought it, and considerable numbers pretended to go along with
the institution and its petty rules but underneath continued to
resent (and, where possible, to resist) it.

The prison regime was repressive and surveillance was tight,
but it was possible to create niches in which this could be evaded.
This was similar to the ways in which it was possible, through
the use of the toilets and the space behind the bicycle shed, for
school children to escape the attention, and relax from the pressures, of adult authority. Thus the programme provided them
with a means through which they could articulate and discuss
these feelings about school. This may well have been admirable
but it had no relationship to the intentions of the programme
makers.

Giving the active audience a purpose: Fiske and semiotic democracy

Reception theorists see these findings as an indication that audiences are free to interpret programmes in whatever manner they
choose. The media may try to control the meanings of programmes
and to impose certain ways of interpreting them on viewers, but
this is not necessarily successful. Audiences 'read' and understand
programmes in a diverse range of ways. Reception theorists see
the fact that they do as a form of political resistance to the dominant power that programme makers embody and represent.

Fiske (1987) is the major representative of this tradition. He has
taken these kinds of finding as an indication that we now live in
what he terms a 'semiotic democracy' (Fiske, 1987:95). This is one
in which the power to produce meanings and pleasures from
media texts lies with audiences. He argues that we need to distinguish between the financial economy and the cultural one. In the
financial economy goods are produced, circulated and sold. In

the cultural economy meanings, pleasures and social identities circulate. In this economy, cultural products such as television programmes do not in themselves contain or carry meaning. They are, as Fiske (1987:313) puts it, 'provokers of meaning and pleasure'. Programmes provide, as it were, the raw material from which meaning can be created. Turning this material into concrete meanings is the work of audiences. Indeed Fiske and others, such as Radway (1984), argue that the capacity to 'create' meaning in this manner is one of the most important pleasures the media have to offer audiences.

The ability of audiences to make meaning has a further dimension. There are, Fiske argues, two forms of resistance in societies in which power is unequally distributed, and these are related to the two kinds of economy. One is social power, and it is linked to the financial economy (this is the power to resist at a social and political level and, as such, it is resistance as conventionally understood, through political and industrial action). The other is semiotic power, and this is linked to the cultural economy. Resistance here is 'the power to construct meanings, pleasures, and social identities that differ from those proposed by the structures of domination' (Fiske, 1987:317). The cultural economy is the site of resistance to dominant meanings and interpretations.

However, the relationship between the kind of resistance that is implicit in semiotic power and radical oppositional political action is an indirect one; there is, after all, little evidence of people storming the barricades after watching *Coronation Street* or *Dawson's Creek*. But this does not mean, Fiske claims, that that semiotic resistance lacks political effectiveness. It is a source of huge insecurities for the powerful and the dominant, and it exposes dangerous contradictions in society. The dominant require a strong economic return from their investments in the media business, but they can only get this by making programmes that are sufficiently open to allow for oppositional readings. The contradictory logics of the financial and semiotic economies coerce them into making programmes that create legitimation problems for the system from which they gain their power and their profits.

Thus, the central contention of this perspective is that the audience and not the media have the power. Audiences use media material to make meaning and in doing so make meanings that are both subversive and critical of those with political and cultural power in society. This contention has important implications for the analysis of issues such as media ownership and media imperialism.

If we accept this perspective then it is a matter of indifference whether the media are owned by industrial conglomerates, by rich monopolists, or (for that matter) by local neighbourhood organisations since they will have no control over the ways in which their audiences interpret the material they produce. It also means that the degree to which the global television is dominated by material that originates in the USA is not a problem.

It is argued by development theorists (see Preston, 2001) that this material celebrates the values and lifestyles of developed countries and so may be inappropriate for many of the poor, developing countries in which the programmes are shown. They can aggravate the developmental problems of such countries by encouraging an expansion of values and expectations that are unrealisable in their current stage of growth. Thus the materialism and consumerism that is taken as a matter of course in such programmes may devalue the virtues of saving on which development depends, and may encourage the kind of consumer spending that increases levels of foreign indebtedness. They may also create aspirations that such societies cannot satisfy.

However, Fiske contests this view. He argues that this assumes that homogeneity of programming produces a narrow, bland and homogeneous range of readings among the audience. Diversity is not produced by programmes, he argues, but by audiences. A single, widely distributed television programme is in effect a menu from which viewers choose the reading that they wish. In this way culture in developing countries can be created from media material, but only by its consumers and not by its producers. The whole world may well be watching them.

Prisoners or escapees?

Fiske's work establishes that audiences are not prisoners of the media. They bring their own frames of reference and interpretation to the programmes they watch, and in this sense the programmes they 'see' are not necessarily the ones the programme producers 'make'. As Radway (1984:17) puts it, 'opportunities exist within the mass-communication process for individuals to resist, alter and re-appropriate the materials designed elsewhere for their purchase'.

However, while these opportunities exist, their significance for arguments about media power remains to be fully determined.

Critics accept that the capacity for aberrant decoding is important, and they also accept that opportunities exist for audiences to exercise this capacity; but they argue that the mere existence of a cultural economy does not guarantee that it will be full of entrepreneurial and radical decoders. Simply because the opportunities exist for aberrant or resistant decoding exist does not mean that these will be used.

These concerns lead to two important questions, one being the proportion of the viewing population that takes advantage of the opportunities for aberrant or alternative decoding. How many decode in a manner different from that used in the encoding process? Unless it can be established that a significant proportion of the audience decodes in an aberrant way then those people's capacity to do so has little relevance to the issue of media power. The second relates to the nature of alternative decodings: audiences are capable of alternative readings, but is it the case that these readings are oppositional or radical in any political sense of that term?

How many alternative decoders?

Both Lewis (1991) and Kitzinger (1997) argue that there is a tendency to over-state the extent of alternative readings. This comes from a failure to distinguish between the comprehension of a media text and the interpretations and reactions to it. In most cases audiences agree on what happens in particular episodes of programmes and on what is said in particular news bulletins: that is, they comprehend them in the same way. But they did not always agree in their interpretation and evaluation of what went on. When Kitzinger (1997:195) looked at audience reception of information on AIDS, she found that 'people often shared a common interpretation of an article or TV programme, but differed in the meaning they took away with them'. They could clearly see and agree on the nature of the messages the media were trying to convey, but they disagreed over the cultural value and social appropriateness of these messages. Thus audiences can agree on the meaning of a media text, but disagree on its value. So when Schroder (1987:19) asks the question, 'Do people who watch the same programme actually see the same programme?', the answer is yes. What they disagree over is the quality, value, and social and moral validity of what they are watching.

Aberrant or resistant readings?

In a similar way Livingstone (1990) has cautioned against the tendency to see alternative readings as necessarily radical or oppositional. She found that while audiences were capable of a variety of readings of a media text, these were variations on conventional accounts and not alternatives to them. Her analysis of the narrative sequence in the British soap opera, *Coronation Street*, showed that while there was a range of readings of this text, these drew for the most part on conventional morality and the dominant rhetoric about the conduct of interpersonal relationships. 'Much of the difference in interpretations', she concluded (Livingstone, 1990:83), 'seems to reflect conventional rather than radical positions'.

The notion that media texts set parameters to the range of audience interpretations is also confirmed in the research of Roscoe, Marshall and Gleeson (1995). They looked at the responses of viewers to a programme about the Birmingham Six. This was the name given to a group of Irishmen imprisoned in England for a crime they did not commit. A number of television programmes highlighted deficiencies in the case against them. The programme that the researchers showed steered viewers towards a particular understanding of the plight of the six, and it set parameters within which the debate about their guilt or innocence could be conducted. The researchers found that the majority of viewers did not go beyond these parameters in their discussion and interpretation of the programme.

Why so few resisters?

The suggestion of the previous sections is that while the extent of alternative readings is by no means clear, they are not as widespread or as common as many reception theorists would wish us to believe. Equally, although alternative readings go on, it is by no means clear that they are necessarily critical or politically resistant in nature. Critics of reception theory have advanced a number of reasons for this, and two in particular are important.

The first is that the construction of oppositional readings requires considerable investment of time and energy by viewers and they may not have such resources to spare. It is also difficult work, and can result in a significant reduction in the pleasure that readers derive from their television viewing. This may encourage resistant readers to turn off the set or simply go with the flow of the programme. This latter course of action is facilitated by what Condit (1989:116) terms 'the disengaged character' of television viewing. Most viewers are doing other things while they are watching television, so it does not have their total attention.

The second reason lies in what Morley (1996:286) calls 'the distribution of cultural competencies' or the range of 'decoding strategies' (Morley, 1980:117) that are available in the audience. The best-documented examples of alternative decoding are among audiences or sections of audiences that are relatively advantaged in relation to the media: that is, among those who have most access to groups and organisations that promote alternative and oppositional interpretations of the world, among those whose culture is radically different from that in which the programmes were produced, or among those with personal experience of the issues covered by the media.

Roscoe, Marshall and Gleeson (1995), for example, found that those viewers whose political activity gave them access to alternative understandings of politics were most likely to be critical of the programme that they were shown. Conversely, those with the weakest access to group organisation were least likely to produce oppositional interpretations. Cultural background is also important. Liebes and Katz's (1986) research on audiences for *Dallas* in Israel, and Hodge and Tripp's (1986) work on aboriginal children's comprehension in Australia of Western movies, showed very clear and basic disagreements over the meanings that readers thought these texts were trying to convey; but this level of aberrant decoding appeared to depend on the massive cultural differences between the senders of the messages and those receiving them.

Similarly, the role of personal experience can be crucial. The Glasgow University Media Group devised a research technique which they termed a 'news game'. Participants were given sets of still photographs from television coverage of a particular issue or event. These included the miners' strike of 1983–84 in Britain (Philo, 1990), the media coverage of AIDS and mental illness (Glasgow University Media Group, 1997; Miller, Kitzinger, Williams and Beharell, 1998), and the content of media coverage of child abuse in Britain (Kitzinger and Skidmore, 1995). They were then asked to write a script or 'imaginary news story' (Philo, 1990:12) for a number of issues. These scripts drew on, and reflected fairly closely, the original media coverage. Thus the researchers found clear connections between the dominant themes in media coverage and 'what is recalled, understood, and sometimes believed by audience groups' (Eldridge, Kitzinger and Williams, 1997:161).

The research participants who responded differently were those with personal experience of having either seen or been on a picket line, knowing someone who had AIDS or was mentally ill, or being an abuse survivor. These were important bases from which the dominant messages of media reporting could be resisted. However, while personal experience may shape how people respond to the media, it is equally the case that personal experience can be shaped (and in some cases over-ridden) by the media.

Kitzinger (1997:208) found that media images of the signs of AIDS 'formed the template for many people's perceptions of the "look" of those with HIV/AIDS'. This became the resource through which they interpreted their personal interaction with victims of AIDS. It was also found that audiences were not always able to reject the media messages they may, on the basis of personal experience, have wished to. A gay man told Kitzinger (1997:208) that he knew that people with AIDS do not look any different to other people, but he had a 'residual mental image' of them as dirty and scruffy; he attributed this to the media.

How active is the audience? summary

In this section we have considered the critical responses to theories that stress that active role of media audiences in the creation of meaning from their use of the media. We have seen that while most of the critics would argue that audiences are not prisoners of the media, they would also say that the degrees of freedom allowed to them by theorists such as Fiske are excessive. They would argue that aberrant, alternative or resistant readings of media material are the exception rather than the rule. As Eldridge, Kitzinger and Williams (1997:167) put it, 'most of us, most of the time go along with what the media tells us to be the case'.

They would also argue that there are good reasons why we do. These are rooted in the nature of the knowledge and the life experience that people bring to their viewing, and the contexts in which viewing typically goes on. This latter concern has directed the attention of researchers to the conditions under which people use the media and the effects that these have on the nature of the viewing experience.

The consumption of television

Introduction

One of the criticisms that has been made of the 'new' audience studies is that the context within which viewers watch and subsequently discuss the programmes is one which has been created for them by researchers (Schroder, 1987). As such, it is divorced from the contexts in which audiences routinely watch television and routinely construct meaning from the material that they view. This has led to the desire among audience researchers to place the viewing activities of audiences back into the context in which it generally occurs (namely, the domestic one). As Silverstone (1990:186) puts it, 'the starting point for such study is the household or the family, for it is here that the primary involvement with television is created'.

The challenge has been to devise ways of studying the patterns of television use in a naturalistic way, and two different research strategies have been formulated to achieve this. The first is the use of video cameras to record the activities of families as they go about their domestic routines. Bectel, Achezpohl and Akers (1972) placed a television camera on top of the television set in 20 houses in Kansas, and placed microphones around the room to record behaviour patterns and conversations around the use of television. Collett (see Root, 1986) adopted a somewhat similar practice in the UK. He had a television set constructed with a video camera, recording devices and a set of timers in it. He persuaded 20 families to accept this in their homes for a period of a week each. In effect, the television watched them as they watched it, hence confirming every paranoid's view that we are never alone.

The second strategy is represented by the tradition of ethnography. This is a research technique that seeks to understand the lives of people as they themselves experience them, and it works to gain access to, and an understanding of, the ways in which they live in and view the world. Applied to the study of audiences, it involves observing family members in their everyday use of the media. It also involves intensive interviews with them to check the reliability of the researcher's observations against the interpretations of the family members.

Both strategies have the same objective and the same problems: they seek to understand how people use television in the normal context of living, but there is the concern that the presence of the observer or a television camera changes the behaviour of those being observed. Lull (1990), for example, claims that the families in his research told him that they did not change the way they behaved because he was with them. Similarly, members of the families that Collett (1986) researched indicated that they got used to the new television cabinet in their living room and after a short period of time forgot that it was recording their behaviour. The intimate nature of some of the material captured by the videos would suggest that this claim has some substance.

Yet this has to be placed beside a concern about the sort of families that would allow such a level of intrusion into their homes and the problems of representativeness that this creates. For most of us a six-pack and popcorn are essential accessories for viewing television, but being watched by a television camera is not normally regarded in the same light. Despite these reservations, however, this research has established a number of important features of television viewing.

Modes of viewing and the attentive audience

The first relates to our notion of an attentive audience. The research shows that audience members engage in a wide range of behaviour when in front of the television, much of which has little to do with television viewing. Thus Collet (see Root, 1986:26) and Bectel, Achezpohl and Akers (1972) found that viewers eat, argue, kiss, read books and newspapers, write letters, do homework, sort and iron clothes, play musical instruments, and vacuum the carpet while the television is on. If asked by researchers what they are doing, they are likely to say that they are watching television.

Other studies confirm that television viewing is a busy activity and it is accompanied by other (apparently unrelated) activities. Television may, for example, facilitate family communication and talk, but the content of the talk and conversation often has little relationship to what is on the screen. It has led Lindlof and his colleagues (reported in Lull, 1988:165) to offer a typology of viewing modes. These include focused viewing, where watching the television is the primary activity; monitoring, where television viewing is secondary to some other activity; and idling, where attention is low and the television is merely a momentary distraction for viewers. Where these modes differ is in the level of attention directed to the television.

Morley (1986) has suggested that modes of attention and styles of viewing are influenced by gender. He found that men and women watch television in very different ways. Men watch attentively and in silence so that they will not miss anything. By contrast, women talk and hold conversations while looking at the screen, including keeping up a running commentary on the programmes. This can often be a source of tension in relationships as men have difficulty accommodating to their partner's viewing styles.

Taste in programmes: a weapon in domestic warfare?

It has also been established that men and women have different tastes in programmes. Men prefer action films, sports programmes and factual television generally. Women, by contrast, tend to prefer programmes that deal with the emotional lives of people, such as soap operas. These are programmes that foreground 'emotional' rather than strictly 'empirical' realism. Morley (1986) has developed this to suggest that men can use the television as a means to assert their cultural and social power in the domestic sphere, which happens in two ways.

One is through control of programme choice. In his interviews Morley found that men control the pattern of viewing in households and settle conflicts over viewing choices by acting as the final arbiters of programme selection. Their choices are supported by the styles of cultural legitimation that adhere to different kinds of programme. Watching factual programmes has a level of cultural legitimacy and what van Zoonen (1994:125) calls an 'assumed general superiority', that watching fictional ones does not. It can be justified and defended by reference to the notion that watching the news is the responsibility of a 'good citizen' (Alasuutari, 1999). By contrast, watching fictional television is harder to defend and the justifications are often couched in apologetic or 'guilty' terms.

The second way in which cultural power can be demonstrated and enforced is through control over the technology. This is seen most immediately in the possession of the remote control. Morley (1996:147) found that this was typically 'on the arm of Daddy's chair'. Similarly, the use of Video recorders is largely a male domain in that operating this technology is seen as men's work and so becomes men's responsibility. As a result, it is not surprising to find that women make little contribution to, or have little control over, the renting or purchase of videotapes. Given that women can operate machines such as washing machines which have a level of complexity that often baffles men, gender expectations and controls are clearly at work here.

Gray (1987), for example, claims that many women's attitude to video recorders is one of 'strategic ignorance'. They pretend to a naïveté with the technology so that it will not become another domestic task for which they are expected to assume responsibility. Lull (1988:169) has also suggested that some women view video recorders as yet another embodiment of under-developed human interaction and as an impediment to genuinely human communication.

Summary

When television viewing is put into and studied in the context of the domestic and hence into the context within which it is routinely viewed, it allows for the study of the ways in which television is used as a resource in social interaction. It also allows us to see the ways in which this interaction is structured by power and gender relationships within the family. Families, it appears, use and integrate television into their everyday routines, but the nature of this integration reflects the play of wider forces. Television viewing has, in this way, come to be bound up with the intricacies and complications of family life. It has become part of what David Morley referred to as the politics of family life.

Modifying the domestic: television as a thief of time and community

The research in the previous section indicates that television has been integrated into domestic routines, but it has also modified them. Lull (1988) has pointed out several of these changes, including the way in which many domestic routines have been restructured around television programmes. Meal times have, for example, been altered by television in that the timing of meals, their preparation, their duration, and their consumption are now increasingly dictated by, and scheduled around, the times of favourite television programmes. Another is the way in which television has facilitated the privatisation of the family. Increasingly the evening entertainment for families involves sitting at home watching television. This process has been encouraged by other social changes, such as having both parents working (which reduces their willingness to go out after work), increased suburbanisation (which increases distances from centres of entertainment), and fear of the city (which reduces the desire to travel there).

This has been characterised as the 'theft of time' or as the 'colonisation of leisure' (Lodziak, 1986:128). Research suggests that while there is some variation between social groups, average viewing times for individuals can be around 20–30 hours per week. This figure appears to have been rising over the last two decades. But more critically for its social significance, this increase has occurred against a background of a decline in the amount of leisure time available to audiences over the last 20 years, in the USA at least (see Schor, 1992). The consumption of significant portions of time by television viewing has social consequences, if only because the increased time spent in front of television must reduce the time that is available for other forms of social activity, especially those outside the home. It is possible to combine a range of domestic activities with television viewing but it is by no means clear that this is possible for many other social activities. Whether this is a positive or a negative development is a matter of some dispute.

Some writers, such as Curran and Tunstall, (quoted in Lodziak, 1986) argue that television use has displaced less attractive activities, though as their list of such activities includes 'doing nothing', 'sitting' and 'resting' there was not a lot of competition. For others, such as Putnam (1995), its implications are predominantly negative. He argues that a certain level of social connection and civic engagement is necessary to a healthy society. By this he means membership of, and involvement in, public activities such as attending political meetings, school board meetings, trade union meetings, meetings of voluntary associations such as the Boy Scouts and the Red Cross, and participation in bowling leagues. More Americans, he claims, are now bowling alone than at any time in the past. This has an immediate effect on the income of owners of bowling alleys as those who bowl alone eat and drink less. But the broader social significance is the loss of the kind of social interaction and conversation that group bowling implies. Its loss is part of the erosion of the social capital and the vibrant civic life on which a democratic society depends.

The causes for this decline are complex and varied, but one factor that Putnam sees as significant is the way in which leisure has been transformed by new communications technology and most obviously by television. It has most dramatically individualised the use of leisure time and so undermined what he calls the 'opportunities for social capital formation'. 'Television viewing', he argues (Putnam, 1996), 'comes at the expense of nearly every social activity outside the home, especially social gatherings and informal conversations'. Television as a form of technology and as a resource for leisure is producing what Vallelly (1996) called 'couch potato citizens'.

Putnam's analysis has been the source of vigorous dispute (see, for example, Schudson, 1996). This debate has centred around issues such as the measures that he uses of civic participation (it may well have changed its nature rather than declined as such), and around the precise point at which this decline may have started: for some it can be dated to the 1930s, which reduces the contribution that television could have made to its demise. However, there can be little doubt that whatever else may be true in the relationship between television and its audience, it has undoubtedly altered and restructured the use of leisure time.

Beyond the domestic?

It is important to give attention to the context within which the media are used as it represents the cultural space within which media messages are received and interpreted. However, there are a number of limitations on research that uses the domestic context as its research site. The main one is the assumption that television viewing is typically a collective familial experience. The proliferation of television sets in many households has enabled family members to break free of the constraints set by the single set and by the opportunities that this presented for the exercise of domestic power. Having a set in one's bedroom allows children, and particularly teenagers, to evade the imposition of adult tastes and freely indulge their own. Similarly a television in the kitchen allows women to escape the tyranny of Monday night football.

Another problem is the way in which the research has been limited generally to what might be regarded as a conventional and increasingly less typical family type, namely, two adults and some children. This is recognised by Morley (1986) and Livingstone (1993). They argue that there is a need to know more about different kinds of domestic context such as those involving single-parent families, childless couples living together, and adults living alone. It may have been possible in the past to argue that these could be considered as stages in the life cycles of families, but increasingly this is not the case. The number of women, for example, who live alone and who do so by choice is growing as a percentage of the population. The effects of context on viewing would be different in this situation from how it might be in other domestic settings.

Finally there is the more general concern that the domestic, however this is conceptualised, may be about to be displaced as the typical viewing location. The proliferation of sets in diverse settings such as bars, hotels, doctors' waiting rooms, airports and shopping centres means that television has become difficult to escape. In the course of an average day people are never far from the opportunity to see what is being broadcast. So far, we know little about the effects of this kind of exposure on attitudes and responses to television.

The knowledgeable viewer

The integration of television into everyday life and the routine familiarity that people have with the medium has one final conse-quence, and this concerns the level of the 'television knowledge' that is present among audiences. The term refers to the know-ledge that people have of the medium with which they are inter-acting. This knowledge comes in two forms.

One is what might be regarded as the more technical kinds of media literacy. This covers the understanding of a range of aspects of the medium, including editing conventions, the devices through which programmes are separated from advertising breaks, the pacing of programmes, the movement between scenes within them, the use of flashbacks, slow motion, laughter tracks, and the use of background music. Though at one level these are tech-nical, they also have a social dimension in that it requires consider-able experience of the medium to understand the significance of many of these technical features; thus the ability to understand that a sudden upsurge in background music can signify an impending and significant change in the action in a programme is an important viewing skill. The understanding that the shot-reverse-shot sequence in camera work conveys the sense of the flow of conversation is also an essential skill for television viewing.

The other kind of television knowledge is more explicitly social in nature. Viewers bring sets of expectations, skills and understandings to their viewing, and this means that they do not approach all programmes as if they were the same or as if they were new to them. They know the conventions of particular genres, and they expect that the programmes will conform to these. They have explicit knowledge and clear expectations about what should happen in particular programmes and what will not. Thus while they expect marital disharmony to be a part of soap operas, they do not expect extreme violence to be. They also have clear expectations of the kind of 'technical' features that will be used in particular genres. They know that blurred camera shots and fast editing have no place in soap operas, and hence if they are used they are experienced as a form of dissonance and significantly reduce audience pleasure.

These kinds of knowledge are significant in the responses of audiences to television. Collett (1986) found, for example, that children could engage in a range of activities while the television was on in the background; but if the music changed or if they heard music that was familiar to them, then they would turn their attention to the screen with the knowledge and expectation that certain kinds of things were about to happen. Similarly Grispud (1995) found that when viewers approached a programme in expectation that it was a serial, when it fact it was intended to be a series, they were confused and disappointed. They looked at the soap opera, *Dynasty*, expecting it to be a serial and so expected a resolution of the issues at the end of the episode. When it did not, and the story line continued over into the next episode, they were confused and disappointed. Finally Michaels (quoted in Wilson, 1993:104) found that Aboriginals in Australia were unfamiliar with the conventions and genres of American television and film, and so were unable to assess the truth-value of programmes. They were, for example, unable to distinguish between documentaries and fiction.

Consuming the technology: what happened to the menu?

In these sections we have been considering the range of research that has arisen out of a concern with the conditions under which people use the mass media. They provide important considerations and insights that must be recognised in the study of the mass media, but it is also important to acknowledge their shortcomings. Their current focus is for the most part on television, and other media (such as the press) are ignored. Newspapers are equally resources for conversation and also likely to be read in a distracted manner.

Furthermore, they emphasise the use of the technology at the expense of a consideration of its content. While such use is important, its implications for the reception of media messages have not been spelled out. It may be attractive to assume that because audiences are less attentive, they are less open to the influence of media messages; but that may be also be premature. The fact that audiences are less attentive could just as easily mean that their viewing is less critical and they are in these circumstances less likely to read against the grain of media meanings. Similarly, the notion that audiences come to the media with certain kinds of technical and social knowledge is illuminating: the problem is that it tells us what they bring to the media and not what they take away from it.

Summary and conclusion

In this chapter we have seen how two opposing perspectives have dominated and influenced the study of the media audience. One sees the media as dominant and the audience as, in varying degrees, its prisoner; the other sees the audience as dominant in the creation of meaning and the media as merely a menu from which viewers select ingredients and create their own views and interpretations. In the first, the media control the audience, while in the other the audience control and use the media. This contrast has certain elements of simplification to it. Each of these positions has more nuanced versions, yet the primary opposition is significant.

We have also seen how the study of media effects swings between the notions of a powerful media and that of a powerful audience. Katz (1987) has pointed out that media studies move from one to the other about every ten years. A consequence of this is the constant rediscovery of old issues and the regular retrieving of old solutions. Curran (1996), for example, has argued that many of the insights of reception theory were present in the work of researchers in the 1940s in the USA. There were, as he says (Curran, 1996:267), 'considerable points of affinity' between the earlier and the later work.

This means that one of the tasks of future media research must be, as Livingstone (1993:6) puts it, 'to transcend the old polarities'. Rather than reverting to one or other model of media effects, there is a need to combine perspectives into a new model of the relationships between media and audiences. This issue is taken up in Chapter 8.

Conclusion: The Future for Media Sociology?

In the preceding chapters we discussed a series of themes that are central to the sociological study of the mass media. We argued that attempts to find the power of the media in terms of direct effects of content on audiences are misconceived. A more complete treatment requires us to take account of three central aspects of the mass communication process: these are the content of the media (what is on the screen, what is in the papers) its production, how the media gets the particular content that it has, and its reception (how audiences receive and respond to media content). There are two issues that we need to address more fully in the conclusion. The first is the relationship between media content and audience response, and the second is the issue of diversity and representativeness in the media.

The way forward? The views of Sonia Livingstone

It has become clear that it is not possible or productive to infer audience reception of media material from the content of the media. We cannot assume that simply because the media has a particular content it automatically has a particular effect. We also cannot assume that audiences have a total freedom in the manner in which they respond to media material. This means that, as Livingstone (1998) puts it, we need to find a path between the dominant and contrasting views of powerful media and powerful audiences. We need to construct a theory that takes account of two central components in the complex relationship between media and audience.

Text messages

The first is textual factors, or what she terms 'the operation of textual constraints' (Livingstone, 1993:10). Audience interpretations can be influenced and structured by factors in the media text that encourage or point to particular ways in which the text should be interpreted and viewed. Some media texts are less open than others, and this is a direct intention of their producers. The news is, for example, less open to diverse readings because of the way in which it addresses and positions viewers. It treats audiences as passive and attentive recipients of information and, as such, it does not leave itself open to diverse interpretations.

Television fiction, by contrast, often incorporates a range of possible interpretations into its structure. Programmes are often planned by their creators to be capable of carrying multiple meanings and multiple pleasures. Television comedies, such as *The Simpsons*, have jokes and sketches that can be understood and accepted as funny in their own terms, but they can also operate at another level as parodies of cultural products (such as popular films and other television shows). The producers insert these layers of meaning, and they are seen as the source of the programme's wide appeal. This means that a more complete theory must take account of the manner in which media texts are structured and framed to facilitate or convey particular interpretations.

Personal experience and cultural capital

The second component is the way in which the social and personal experiences that audiences bring to the media influence their interpretations of its content. We need to understand more extensively and more precisely the effects that cultural capital, social class, cultural context and personal experience have on the ways in which audiences respond to and understand media material.

Cultural capital in this context refers to the social and media knowledge that groups and individuals bring to their encounter with the media. The importance of social knowledge in audience interpretations is illustrated in William Gamson's (1992) work. He found that the media are a primary resource of information and interpretation for many people but this is largely on issues of which they have little or no direct personal experience. The role of the media is a secondary and supportive one on those issues that were part of their direct experience. Similarly Iyengar (1991) found that people draw on cultural resources – such as experiential knowledge and popular wisdom – to understand and to interpret what the media are telling them. Hartmann (1979) found a much closer correspondence between the accounts of industrial disputes given by his middle-class respondents and those in the media than was the case with those from working-class backgrounds. He attributed this to the more direct knowledge that working-class people had of such disputes. Thus it is the case that if particular issues and events are part of people's experience then their attitudes and opinions are less likely to be derived from external sources, such as the mass media.

The media knowledge, and more specifically the television knowledge, that viewers bring includes their level of genre knowledge and their level of trust or scepticism in the media. These influence the expectations with which they approach particular programmes, their level of attention while viewing, and their level of involvement in the narratives and truth claims of programmes. If we add cultural context to the package the scenario gets more complicated as media knowledge is sensitive to cultural background. Liebes and Katz (1986), for example, have pointed to the differential distribution of what they term 'distancing skills'. This refers to the capacity of audiences to see fictional programmes as artistic creations rather than realistic portrayals of the world. In their study, Americans in Los Angeles saw soap operas as fictional while Arabs living in Israel were more likely to see them as having significant realistic elements. As a result they got more involved with programmes and were more open to be challenged and moved by them.

The essential elements

The complex interaction between media and audience means that the model must combine textual and social determinants in what Livingstone (1998:249) calls 'the text–reader balance'. It must be a model that respects and includes both dimensions, rather than one that exclusively privileges either the media text or the media audience. As such this suggestion is not necessarily novel but its implementation is a task of some complexity. The precise nature of the interactions between media content and audience interpretations remains to be determined although, as we have seen, the indications are that media texts have considerable influence on audience interpretations (Eldridge, Kitzinger and Williams, 1997:160–80).

The overall import is that the analysis of media content in isolation from a consideration of the responses of audiences can no longer be considered as sufficient in media sociology, and the study of media audiences separately from media content is equally deficient. It is no longer possible to study the mass media from a perspective that treats media content or the media audience in isolation from each other. It is also no longer acceptable to make statements that privilege one or other as the site of media power. The nature of media power is a complex interaction between the two. The elaboration of this interaction needs to be a focus for the next generation of media studies.

The future of diversity?

A model of text–reader balance is essential but it needs to be supplemented by a consideration of media content and of what it is audiences are responding to. We need to look at media texts and at the factors that are shaping their diversity and the representativeness of their content. This concern is present in Habermas's (1989) discussion of the public sphere. He says that this is in the effective control of large bureaucracies and global corporations. As a result the media is an instrument for the manipulation rather than for the creation of a democratic public opinion. It is also present in the work of Gitlin (1994), who claims that when the media are in commercial ownership their output is inevitably limited, repetitive and uninspiring.

It is in this context that the fate of public service broadcasting assumes an importance. It is often represented as the defence of the democratic ideal against the commercial one. This means that it has been seen as the somewhat imperfect means through which the broadcast media in many European countries (including Britain) have managed to be more reflective of the diverse concerns of increasingly complex nations. It is based on addressing its audience as citizens rather than as consumers, and so has a mandate to tell them what they want to hear as well as what they do not. The question that arises is whether it can continue to function in this manner.

The end of public service broadcasting?

There are a number of reasons why its future is in doubt. These are political and economic and revolve around the twin processes of globalisation and conglomerisation. In an increasingly complex and interdependent world the concept of a nation is an increasingly fragile one, and globalised processes of cultural homogenisation make national distinctiveness and national identity difficult to determine and hence difficult to protect. This creates a crisis of legitimacy for public service broadcasting, as it is unclear what public it is supposed to represent. This is connected to (and certainly exacerbated by) the drift of audiences away from public service channels. Combine this with changes in the regulation of broadcasting, with increased competition from new channels, and with the reluctance of national governments to subsidise and you have public service broadcasters facing a crisis of financial sustainability.

These changes have produced what Preston (2001:203) calls 'striking sets of convergences' between television in the USA and in Europe. One of these is at the level of ownership. There has been a huge growth in television channels in Europe, up from 55 terrestrial channels in 1980 to 213 terrestrial and 403 satellite channels in 1995. The majority are privately owned and supported by advertising and subscription revenues. In 1980, around 75 per cent of European channels were public service ones; in 1995, less than 25 per cent were. Another convergence is at the level of content. European television is heavily dependent on the importation of programmes from the USA, as it does not produce enough of its own to meet what Preston (2001:204) describes as 'the expanding appetite of the multiplying distribution system'. Increasingly media content in Europe mirrors that in the USA.

The state of the union

This would not be a problem if these imports were coming from a system that was noted for its creation and maintenance of diversity, but this is not the case. According to Gitlin (1994), the three major networks in the USA are continuing to lose audiences. They are down from 92 per cent of the national audience to 60 per cent in 1993, a level they have hovered around since then. The audience has not gone to public service broadcasting stations but to the new Fox Channels and to cable stations. The Fox network has shown some capacity to provide innovative programming, such as *The Simpsons*, but this capacity is severely constrained. Faced with a choice between the important and the inconsequential, its solutions are depressingly predictable.

In late 1999 the then American president, Bill Clinton, and other world leaders were under siege from anti-globalisation protesters in Seattle. The protesters were in turn under siege from a combined show of police and military strength, the likes of which had not been seen since the Vietnam protests in the late 1960s. It was, one would have thought, a story of immense political significance. The Fox News Channel interrupted its programmes for a special live on-the-spot report. The subject of the story was not Seattle, but an update on the activities of the parents of a murder victim, five-year-old JonBenet Ramsay (Nichols and McChesney, 2000:24).

The move to cable can also be seen as positive in terms of diversity and quality and, as Gitlin (1994:x) puts it, 'the gain to diversity is correspondingly real'. Coupled with the development of satellite television, it has had a dramatic impact on the number of available channels. The problem is that as cable fees are expensive it is beyond the resources of the less well off. Consequently the 'class-cum-taste' division in American culture has been accentuated. Moreover, cable is not entirely independent from established media interests. One of the responses of the major networks has been to buy controlling interests in the new stations. In addition, although cable has shown some innovation at the level of programme making, most cable companies go for the lowest common denominator in their respective niche markets. Nichols and McChesney (2000:33) says that this has promoted the use of a 'rehashing of tried-and-true formulas, as well as the use of sex, violence' and what they term 'shock' or 'gross-out' fare to attract audiences. Gitlin (1994:xi–xii) concludes that while 'the networks have lost many of their recent battles' they have won the 'war over culture'. 'Their principles' of what television is 'are what prevails' even (and, indeed, especially) in the world of cable television.

The experience of the USA is unhelpful in another way. Despite the scale of the changes in the media industry, the issue of ownership is, according to Nichols and McChesney (2000:29), 'off-limits' in American public and political discourse. There has also been a collapse in the commitment of the federal government to regulate the industry. The 1996 Telecommunications Act was the turning point. The act was written, in large part, by lobbyists for the media industry and it allows a level of cross-ownership in the industry that 'had previously been unthinkable' (Nichols and McChesney, 2000:29).

This has been accompanied by an increase in the dominance of advertising. More broadcast time is now given over to commercial advertising. In 1999 the four networks had almost 16 minutes advertising per hour and ran over 6000 commercials a week (Nichols and McChesney, 2000), a large increase on what had been possible ten years before. Advertisers have also found new ways to merge advertising into programming. Direct placement of products in the programmes is one tactic, but the Fox Network tried another: they ran commercials at the bottom of the screen during prime-time programmes. These are not the kinds of development that produce or guarantee media diversity.

Going digital: more channels, more choice?

The issue of digital television brings these issues clearly into focus. This new technology has the capacity to give viewers access to hundreds of different channels, each aimed at specific segments of the audience and each catering for particular audience interests. It also (more crucially) allows for new and different methods of financing such as pay-per-view. When this is combined with the ability of such stations to outbid public service broadcasters for premium material, such as major sporting events and new Hollywood films, the implications for universal access become apparent. Audiences will become fragmented along the dimension of ability to pay. Public service broadcasters will find it difficult to survive in this new environment.

The options: (1) going political

There are, broadly speaking, two survival options available to them. One is to reassert the legitimacy of the public service ideal, to defend the notion of the broadcasting media as a universally available public good, and to pressure governments into supporting it. Though there continues to be considerable public concern about the dominance of television by commercial interests, this has yet to be translated into political terms. Nichols and McChesney (2000) see signs on a world-wide basis of an emergent movement for the democratisation of television and the addition of a significant public service sector to it, but at the moment it remains a somewhat faint hope.

There is a need to force the issue on to the political agenda and this requires a political party to carry it there. But as the process of globalisation increases the parties that would in the past have done this, those on the left, appear in many European countries to have come to an ideological and political accommodation with large media organisations. The British Labour Party is a case in point. They now see these companies in a more positive light, as a necessary force to get maximum national benefit from developments in the 'multi-media' revolution. The issue has passed to a series of new political groupings which Nichols and McChesney call the 'Third Left'. This is a loose amalgam of environmentalists, community activists and feminists who are concerned about media concentration and conglomerisation. So far they have failed to capture the pubic imagination and remain somewhat marginal in terms of influence and impact. They have yet, as Nichols and McChesney (2000:37) put it, to 'reach critical mass in any nation'.

The options: (2) doing business with the beast

The other option is to reach an accommodation with the new forces, particularly at an economic level. Recent accounts would suggest that a corporation such as the BBC, often regarded as the exemplar of the public service model, has chosen this option. According to Steemers (1998:183), the BBC believes its survival is in going 'commercial globally in order to subsidize their domestic public service activities'. To this end it has set up BBC World Service Television, a global commercial company to offer worldwide services. It has also entered into an alliance with two global corporations – Flextech and the US Discovery Communications – to create over 12 commercial television channels for the world market.

This has been accompanied by a series of innovations at the domestic level, not all of which are unquestioningly positive. One of these is changes in programming strategies, with more competitive scheduling and the development of new programmes to compete with commercial channels. An example is the quiz show, *The Weakest Link*, to challenge the dominance of *Who Wants to be a Millionaire?* It may be good broadcasting, but what have quiz shows to do with public service? Another is co-production with other broadcasters. This has the benefit of spreading the risks with new programmes but results in the dilution of content (the addition of a more explicit sexual content to television versions of classic English novels to facilitate success in international markets is a case in point). The third option is the opening of access to additional sources of revenue through, for example, sponsorship from the National Lottery.

These strategies do not automatically solve the problem. The BBC World Service channel has not, for example, been particularly successful and is under pressure to become fully commercial. Moreover these moves have been accompanied by a series of rationalisation strategies designed to make the national broadcaster more efficient and streamlined. These have, by some accounts at least, produced massive demoralisation in the organisation (see Eldridge, Kitzinger and Williams, 1997). Whatever happens, however, Steemers (1998:241) says that 'one certainty remains ... publicly funded public service television will always be financially vulnerable'.

If we expect public service broadcasting to be the guarantor of cultural diversity, then it is unlikely to be able to perform that function. In the absence of a political commitment to public funding, its future is one of increased commercialisation, increased marginalisation, or both.

A blessing in disguise, or radical desperation?

This is the pessimistic scenario; there are other possibilities. Morley and Robins (1994) have outlined one. It is based on an acceptance that public service broadcasting is in decline and on a recognition that global corporations increasingly shape and structure international informational and cultural flows. They accept that this has produced strong tendencies towards cultural homogenisation. They also accept that these global developments have surpassed the capacity of nation states to control or regulate the communication process.

However, there are other tendencies present in the situation, the most important being localisation. Media technology may facilitate global processes but it also creates the space through which a sense of the local can be articulated. In this context it opens up what Hagerstrand (quoted in Morley and Robins, 1994:36) calls the 'possibility space' of local media 'to establish localized arenas for public debate and cultural expression, to elaborate meaningful public spheres'. The technology makes possible the development of decentralised and local programme-making capacities and in this way opens up 'the possibilities of local media spaces'.

There are risks that these kinds of media spaces could sentimen-talise the local and they could 'degenerate into introverted and nostalgic historicism and heritage fixation' (Morley and Robins, 1994:42), but this is unlikely. The attachment to the local in the modern world of movement and mobility is a matter of rational choice and not an inevitable consequence of birth. There is a decision involved in living in, and identifying with, the local. Moreover, local cultures cannot survive without entering into dialogue with the global one; the local no longer means the insular and the insulated. Modern communication technologies do not inevitably mean a global media and its associated homogeneity. They can have a positive role to play in articulating a sense of the local.

There are a number of problems with this formulation, one being that it is not clear what the local is or what entity the term is intended to refer to. Is it as large as Europe or as small as a local town or city? If it is the former, then it is one to which there is no strong or inevitable sense of attachment. If it is the latter, then it is subject to the forces that were outlined in the discussion of local news. These are the increasing monopolisation of local stations by larger organisations and the standardising effects that this has had on the structure of local news broadcasting. Increasingly these are dominated by crime and human-interest stories in a bid to attract audiences.

Moreover it has become clear that the large broadcasting corpor-ations are aware of the 'local' and its potential as a market. This is captured in the Disney slogan, 'think globally, act locally' (Herman and McChesney, 1997:42). Along with corporations such as CNN, Sky and MTV they have recognised the importance of local markets and are beginning to differentiate content, both in terms of pro-gramming and in terms of advertising, to incorporate elements of cultural specificity into their schedules. So while the process of globalisation may create opportunities at the local level, the space for distinctive local material may not be as great as that created for local variations on global culture and for opportunities that global corporations have a critical edge in exploiting.

Lying down with the beast?

Overall there are important questions about the capacity of broad-casting systems to avoid the globalising tendencies of the new media order and to maintain diversity in the face of what appear to be overwhelming odds. Preston (2001:205) agues that the implication of these trends is that 'the production of diverse and quality programming (or "content") will not match the impending expansion of delivery systems'.

There is one final possibility, and this is to suggest that the kind of concerns we have raised here about ownership structures and their relationship to diversity may increasingly be irrelevant. Ang (1996) has argued that we now live in a new era of 'capitalist postmodernity'. This is one of constant flux and perpetual change and as such it is, she argues, a truly chaotic system. It is also the paradoxical result of the 'hegemonizing, globalizing, integrating forces of the modern capitalist order'. These produce a 'surplus of meaning' that the system cannot contain and that it is impossible to domesticate. Each attempt to impose a new social, political or economic order is a temporary and self-defeating one. Notwithstanding the social and political powers involved, 'uncertainty', Ang (1996:162) claims, 'is a built-in feature' of the new capitalist order.

When this perception is applied to the media two features are important. One is the sheer and indigestible volume of programming coming at us from all directions, whether this is from terrestrial, cable or satellite channels or from video. The second is the universality of television: television is simply everywhere. This, in her phrase, 'makes it bleed into every corner of day-to-day social life' (Ang, 1996:175). Together these produce an enormous variety of styles and locations of viewing. They also mean that the media is where the dynamic of perpetual change that characterises capitalist post-modernity gets worked out. Like other consumer goods, cultural products and social meaning come with the built-in obsolescence that is characteristic of the system. Meaning is never final; it is always in the process of being constructed or deconstructed.

Thus a media event such as the O. J. Simpson trial begins to acquire a meaning through its initial televised presentation, but before that meaning acquires some level of acceptance it is challenged, contested and undermined either through diversity of audience response or through books, newspaper articles, or other television programmes that offer radically different accounts. The implication is that it is no longer possible to tell a 'single, total story about the world' (Ang, 1996:177). The chaos of the system means that the imposition of a dominant meaning or the telling of an event from one side or the other is no longer possible. Multiple representations and infinite interpretations are, irrespective of ownership structures, the order of the day.

This may well be the new terrain within which media sociology must operate. A key question will be whether the analytical concerns outlined in this book – the study of media content, media production and media reception – are adequate to an understanding of the media in this new and chaotic system.

References

Abt, V. and Mustazza, L. (1997). *Coming after Oprah: cultural fallout in the age of the TV talk show*, Bowling Green, OH: Bowling Green State University Popular Press.

Adorno, T. (1957). 'Television and the Patterns of Mass Culture', in B. Rosenberg and D. M. White (eds), *Mass Culture: The Popular Arts in America*, New York: Free Press, pp. 474–88.

Alasuutari, P. (1992). ' "I'm Ashamed to Admit it but I have Watched Dallas": The Moral Hierarchy of television programmes', *Media, Culture and Society*, Vol. 14, pp. 561–82.

Alasuutari, P. (1999). 'Cultural Images of the Media', in P. Alasuutari (ed.), *Rethinking the Media Audience*, London: Sage, pp. 86–105.

Alcock, B. and Robson, J. (1990). 'Cagney and Lacey Revisited', *Feminist Review*, No. 35, pp. 42–53.

Altheide, D. L. and Rasmussen, P. K. (1976). 'Becoming News: A Study of Two Newsrooms', *Sociology of Work and Occupations*, Vol. 3, pp. 223–46.

Althusser, L. (1971). *Lenin and Philosophy and Other Essays*, London: NLB.

American Psychological Association (1993) *Violence and Youth: Psychology's Response*, Washington, DC: American Psychological Association.

Anderson, A. (1993). 'Source–Media Relations: the production of the environmental agenda', in A. Hansen (ed.), *The Mass Media and Environmental Issues*, Leicester University Press, pp. 51–68.

Anderson, D. and Sharrock, W. (1979). 'Biasing the News: technical issues in "media studies" ', *Sociology*, Vol. 13, pp. 367–85.

Ang, I. (1996). *Living Room Wars: Rethinking Media Audiences for a Post-Modern World*, London: Routledge.

Arthurs, J. (1994). 'Women and Television', in S. Hood (ed.), *Behind the Screen*, London: Lawrence & Wishart, pp. 82–101.

Bagdikian, B. (1993). *The Media Monopoly*, Boston, MA: Beacon Press.

Bantz, C., McCorkle, S. and Baade, R. (1997). 'The News Factory', in D. Berkowitz (ed.), *Social Meaning of News* London: Sage. pp. 269–85.

Barker, M. and Petley, J. (1997). 'Introduction', in M. Barker and J. Petley (eds), *Ill Effects*, London: Routledge, pp. 1–11.

Barker-Plummer, B. (1995). 'News as a Political Resource: Media Strategies and Political Identity in the U.S. Women's Movement, 1966–1975', *Critical Issues in Mass Communication*, Vol. 12, pp. 306–24.

Barkin, S. M. (1984). 'The Journalist as Storyteller: An Interdisciplinary Perspective', *American Journalism*, Vol. 1, pp. 27–33.

Barnett, S. (1997). 'New Media, Old Problems: New Technology and the Political Process', *European Journal of Communication*, Vol. 12, pp. 193–218.

Barrat, D. (1986). *Media Sociology*, London: Tavistock.

Bauer, R. A. (1964). 'The Obstinate Audience', *American Psychologist*, Vol. 19, pp. 319–28.

Baylor, T. (1996). 'Media Framing of Movement Protest: The Case of American Indian Protest', *Social Science Journal*, Vol. 33, No. 3, pp. 241–55.

Baym, N. (1998). 'The Emergence of On-Line Community', in S. Jones (ed.), *Cybersociety 2.0*, London: Sage, pp. 35–68.

Beck, U. (1992). *Risk Society: Towards a New Modernity*, London: Sage.

Beckett, K. (1996). 'Culture and the Politics of Signification: The Case of Child Sexual Abuse', *Social Problems*, Vol. 43, No. 1, pp. 57–76.

Bectel, H., Achezpohl, P., and Akers, R. (1972). 'Correlates between observed behaviour and questionnaire responses on Television viewing', in E. A. Rubenstein, G. A. Comstock and J. P. Murray (eds), *Television and Social Behaviour 4*, Washington: Government Printing Office.

Beirne, P. and Messerschmidt, J. (1991). *Criminology*, New York: Harcourt Brace Jovanovich.

Bennett, T. (1982). 'Theories of the Media, Theories of Society', in M. Gurevitch, T. Bennett, J. Curran and J. Woollacott (eds), *Culture, Society and the Media*, London: Methuen, pp. 30–56.

Bennett, W. L. (1996). *News: The Politics of Illusion*, New York: Longmans.

Bennett, W. L. and Lawrence, R. C. (1995). 'News Icons and the Mainstreaming of Social Change', *Journal of Communication*, Vol. 45, No. 3, pp. 20–39.

Bennett, W. L., Gressett, L. and Halton, W. (1985). 'Repairing the News: A Case Study of the News Paradigm', *Journal of Communication*, Vol. 35, No. 2, pp. 50–68.

Berelson, B. (1959). 'The State of Communication Research', *Public Opinion Quarterly*, Vol. 23, pp. 1–6.

Blumler, J. G. (1969). 'Producers' Attitudes Towards Television Coverage of an Election Campaign: A case Study', in P. Halmos (ed.), *The Sociology of Mass Media Communicators*, Keele University Press, pp. 85–116.

Blumler, J. G. and Gurevitch, M. (1986). 'Journalists' Orientations to Political Institutions: The Case of Parliamentary Broadcasting', in P. Golding, G. Murdock and P. Schlesinger (eds), *Communicating Politics: Mass Communications and the Political Process*, Leicester University Press, pp. 67–92.

Bondebjerg, I. G. (1996). 'Public Discourse/Private Fascination: Hybridization in "true-life" genres" ', *Media, Culture and Society*, Vol.18, pp. 122–45.

Boorstein, D. J. (1962). *The Image*, Harmondsworth: Penguin.

Bosso, C. J. (1989). 'Setting the Agenda: Mass Media and the Discovery of Famine in Ethiopia', in M. Margolis and G. Mauser (eds), *Manipulating Public Opinion*, Pacific Grove, CA.: Brooks/Cole, pp. 153–74.

Bourdieu, P. (1998). *On Television*, London: Polity Press.

Bradford, S. (1993). 'The Big Sleaze', *Rolling Stone*, 13 February.

Brown, B. (1984). 'Exactly What We Wanted', in M. Barker (ed.), *The Video Nasties*, London: Pluto, pp. 68–87.

Brunsdon, C. (1983). 'Crossroads: Notes on Soap Opera', in E. Ann Kaplan (ed.), *Regarding Television*, New York: American Film Institute, pp. 76–83.

Brunsdon, C. (1985). 'Writing about Soap Opera', in L. Masterman (ed.), *Television Mythologies*, London: Comedia, pp. 82–7.

Buie, J (1999). 'How the Internet is Changing Politics', http:/www.us.net/indc/column2.html/.

Burgelin, O. (1972). 'Structuralist Analysis and Mass Communication', in D. McQuail (ed.), *The Sociology of Mass Communications*, Harmondsworth: Penguin, pp. 313–29.

Butler, D. and Kavanagh, D. (1983). *The British General Election of 1983*, London: Macmillan – now Palgrave.

Butler, M. and Paisley, W. (1980). *Women and The Mass Media*, New York: Human Sciences Press.

Cantril, H., Gaudet, H. and Herzog, H. (1940). *The Invasion from Mars*, Princeton, NJ: Princeton University Press.

Carey, J. W. (1989). *Communication as Culture*, Cambridge University Press.

Carpignano, P., Andersen, R., Aronwitz, S., Difazio, W. (1990). 'Chatter in the Age of Electronic Reproduction: Talk Television and the "Public Mind"', *Social Text*, Vol. 9, pp. 33–55.

Carter, C. (1998). 'When the "Extraordinary becomes "Ordinary"', in C. Carter, G. Branston and S. Allen (eds), *News, Gender and Power*, London: Routledge, pp. 219–32.

Carveth, R. (1992). 'The Reconstruction of the Global Media Marketplace', *Communications Research*, Vol. 19, No. 6, pp. 705–23.

Castells, M. (1996). *The Rise of Network Society*, Oxford: Basil Blackwell (1st edn).

Castells, M. (2001) 'Information Technology and Global Capitalism', in W. Hutton, and A. Giddens, (eds), *On the Edge: Living in Global Capitalism*, London: Jonathan Cape, pp. 52–74.

Cavender, G. and Bond-Maupin, L. (1993). 'Fear and Loathing on Reality Television', *Sociological Inquiry*, Vol. 63, pp. 305–17.

Chibnall, S. (1975). *Law-and-Order News*, London: Tavistock.

Chomsky, N. (2001). 'Introduction: Project Censored 25th Anniversary', www.projectcensored.org/c2001stories.

Cloud, D. (1998). *Control and Consolation in American Culture and Politics: Rhetoric of Therapy*, London: Sage.

Cohen, S. and Young, J. (eds) (1981). *The Manufacture of News*, London: Constable (rev. edn).

Coleman, S. (1999). 'Can the New Media Invigorate Democracy', *Political Quarterly*, Vol. 7 No. 70, pp. 16–22.

Collett, P, (1986). 'Watching People Watching Television', Report to Independent Broadcasting Authority, London.

Condit, M. (1989). 'The Rhetorical Limits of Polysemy', *Critical Studies in Mass Communication*, Vol. 6, No. 2, pp. 103–22.

Connell, I. (1988). 'Fabulous Powers: Blaming the Media', in L. Masterman (ed.), *Television Mythologies: Stars, Shows and Signs*, London: Comedia.

Connell, I. and Galasinski, D. (1996). 'Cleaning up its act: the CIA on the Internet', *Discourse and Society*, Vol. 7, No. 2, pp. 165–86.

Cook, T. D., Kendzierski, D. A. and Thomas, S. V. (1983). 'The Implicit Assumptions of Television Research: An Analysis of the 1982 NIMH Report on Television and Behaviour', *Public Opinion Quarterly*, Vol. 47, pp. 161–201.

Corner, J. (1995). 'Editorial', *Media, Culture and Society*, Vol. 18, pp. 5–9.

Cottle, S. (1993). 'Mediating the Environment: modalities of TV news', in A. Hansen (ed.), *The Mass Media and Environmental Issues*, Leicester University Press, pp. 107–33.

Coward, R. (2000). *Sacred Cows*, London: HarperCollins.

Cracknell, J. (1993). 'Issue Arenas, Pressure Groups and Environmental Agendas', in A. Hansen (ed.), *The Mass Media and Environmental Issues*, Leicester University Press, pp. 1–21.

Craig, S. (1996). 'More (Male) Power: Humor and Gender in *Home Improvement*', *The Mid-Atlantic Almanack*, Vol. 5, pp. 61–84.

Croteau, D. (1999). 'Examining the "Liberal Media" Claim: Journalists' Views on Politics, Economic and Social Policy and Media Coverage', *International Journal of Health Services*, Vol. 29, pp. 627–55.

Croteau, D. and Hoynes, W. (1997). *Media/Society*, London: Pine Forge Press.

Cumberbatch, G. and Howitt, D. (1989). *A Measure of Uncertainty*, London: John Libby.

Curran, J. (1990). 'Culturalist Perspectives on News Organisations: Reappraisal and Case Study', in M. Ferguson, *Public Communication: The New Imperatives*, London: Sage, pp. 114–34.

Curran, J. (1996). 'The New Revisionism in Mass Communication Research: A Reappraisal', in J. Curran, D. Morley and V. Walkerdine (eds), *Cultural Studies and Communications*, London: arnold, pp. 256–78.

Daley, P. with O'Neill, D. (1991). ' "Sad is Too Mild a word": Press Coverage of the Exxon Valdez Oil Spill', *Journal of Communication*, Vol. 41, pp. 42–57.

Danner, L. and Walsh, S. (1999). ' "Radical" Feminists and "Bickering" Women: Backlash in U.S. coverage of the United Nations Fourth World Conference on women', *Critical Studies in Mass Communication*, Vol. 16, pp. 63–84.

Deacon, D. and Golding, P. (1991). 'When Ideology Fails: The Flagship of Thatcherism and the British Local and National Media', *European Journal of Communication*, Vol. 6, pp. 291–313.

Dunwoody, S. and Griffin, R. (1993). 'Journalistic Strategies for Reporting Long-term Environmental Issues: a case study of three Superfund sites', in A. Hansen (ed.) *The Mass Media and Environmental Issues*, Leicester University Press, pp. 22–50.

Durkin, K. (1985). 'Television and Sex-role Acquisition 1: Content', *British Journal of Social Psychology*, Vol. 24, pp. 101–13.

Dyer, G. (1987). 'Women and Television: an overview', in H. Baehr and G. Dyer (eds), *Boxed-In: Women and Television*, London: Pandora Press, pp. 6–16.

Eco, U. (1977). *A Theory of Semiotics*, London: Macmillan – now Palgrave.

Edelman, M. J. (1988). *Constructing the Political Spectacle*, Chicago, IL: University Press.

Ehrenreich, B. (1995). 'In Defense of Talk Shows', *Time Magazine*, Vol. 124, No. 23 (Internet edn).

Eldridge, J., Kitzinger, J. and Williams, K. (1997). *The Mass Media and Power in Modern Britain*, Oxford University Press.

Elliott, P. (1974). 'Uses, and Gratifications Research: a critique and a Sociological Alternative', in J. G. Blumler and E. Katz (eds), *The Uses of Mass Communication*, London: Sage, pp. 249–68.

Elliott, P., Murdock, G. and Schlesinger, P. (1983). ' "Terrorism" and the State: a case study of the discourses of television', *Media, Culture and Society*, Vol. 5, pp. 155–77.

Entman, R. (1991). 'Framing U.S. Coverage of International News: Contrasts in Narratives of the KAL and Iran Air Incidents', *Journal of Communication*, Vol. 41, No. 4, pp. 6–27.

Entman, R. (1993). 'Framing: Toward Clarification of a Fractured Paradigm', *Journal of Communication*, Vol. 43, No. 4, pp. 51–8.

Epstein, E. J. (1974). *News from Nowhere: Television and the News*, New York: Vintage Books.

Ericson, R. V. (1994). 'Mass Media, Crime, Law, and Justice: An Institutional Approach', *British Journal of Sociology*, Vol. 31, pp. 219–49.

Ericson, R. V., Baranek, M. and Chan, J. (1987). *Visualizing Deviance: A Study of News Organization*, Milton Keynes: Open University Press.

Ettema, J. S. and Whitney, D. C. (eds) (1994). *Audiencemaking: How the Media Create the Audience*, London: Sage.

Faludi, S. (1992). *The Undeclared War against American Women*, New York: Anchor.

Fejes, F. (1992) 'Masculinity as Fact: A Review of Empirical Mass Communication Research on Masculinity' in Steve Craig (ed.), *Men, Masculinity, and the Media*, Newbury Park, CA: Sage, pp. 9–22.

Ferguson, M. (1990). 'Images of Power and the Feminist Fallacy', *Critical Studies in Mass Communication*, Vol. 7, No. 3, pp. 215–30.

Fishman, M. (1980). *Manufacturing the News*, Austin, TX: University of Texas Press.

Fiske, J. (1987). *Television Culture*, London: Methuen.

Fiske, J. and Glynn, K. (1995). 'Trials of the Post-Modern', *Cultural Studies*, Vol. 9, No. 3, pp. 505–21.

Franke, G. (1996). 'Participatory Political Discussion on the Internet', *Votes and Opinions*, Vol. 2, pp. 22–5.

Franklin, B. (1997). *Newszak and News Media*, London: Arnold.

Freedman, J. (1984). 'Effects of Television Violence on Aggression', *Psychological Bulletin*, Vol. 96, pp. 227–46.

Friedland, L. A. (1997). 'Electronic Democracy and the New Citizenship', *Media, Culture and Society*, Vol. 18, pp. 185–212.

Friedrich-Cofer, L. and Huston, A. C. (1986). 'Television Violence and Aggression: The Debate Continues', *Psychological Bulletin*, Vol. 100, pp. 364–71.

Fuchs, C. (1993). 'The Buddy Politics', in S. Cohan and I. R. Hark (eds), *Screening the Media*, London: Routledge.

Galtung, J. and Ruge, M. (1973). 'Structuring and Selecting News', in S. Cohen and J. Young (eds), *The Manufacture of News*, London: Constable, pp. 62–72.

Gamson, J. (1995). 'Do Ask, Do Tell: Freak Talk on TV', *American Prospect*, No. 23, pp. 44–50.

Gamson, W. (1989). 'News as Framing: Comments on Graber', *American Behavioural Scientist*, Vol. 33, No. 2, pp. 157–61.

Gamson, W. (1992). *Talking Politics*, New York: Cambridge University Press.

Gamson, W. and Modigliani, A. (1987). 'Media Discourse and Public Opinion on Nuclear Power: A Constructionist Approach', *American Journal of Sociology*, Vol. 95, No. 1, pp. 1–37.

Gamson, W. and Stuart, D. (1992a). 'Media Discourse as a Symbolic Contest: The Bomb in Political Cartoons', *Sociological Forum*, Vol. 7, No. 1, pp. 55–86.

Gamson, W., Croteau, D., Hoynes, W. and Sasson, T. (1992b). 'Media Images and the Social Construction of Reality', *Annual Review of Sociology*, Vol. 18, pp. 373–93.

Gans, H. (1978). 'Some Additional Proposals', *Journal of Communication*, Vol. 28, pp. 100–5.

Gans, H. (1979). *Deciding What's News*, New York: Pantheon.

Gauntlett, D. (1995). *Moving Experiences: Understanding Television's Influences and Effects*, London: John Libby.

Geertz, C. (1973). *The Interpretation of Culture*, New York: Basic Books.

Gerbner, G. (1992). 'Violence and Terror in and by the Media', in Marc Raboy and Bernard Dagenais (eds), *Media, Crisis and Democracy*, London: Sage, pp. 94–107.

Gerbner, G. (1994). 'The Politics of Media Violence: Some Reflections', in C. Hamelink (ed.), *Mass Communication Research*, Norwood, NJ: Ablex, pp. 133–46.

Gerbner, G. (1995). 'Television Violence: The Power and the Peril', in G. Dines and J. M. Humez (eds), *Gender, Race, and Class in Media: A Text-Reader*, London: Sage, pp. 547–57.

Gilbert, J. (1986). *A Cycle of Outrage*, New York: Oxford University Press.

Gitlin, T. (1978). 'Media Sociology: The Dominant Paradigm', *Theory and Society*, Vol. 6, pp. 205–53.

Gitlin, T. (1980). *The Whole World is Watching: Mass Media in the Making & Unmaking of the New Left*, Berkeley, CA: University of California Press, 1980.

Gitlin, T. (1994). *Inside Prime Time*, London: Routledge (rev. edn).

Gitlin, T. (1998). 'The Clinton–Lewinsky Obsession: How the Press made a Scandal of Itself', *Washington Monthly*, Vol. 30, No. 12, pp. 1–19.

Glasgow University Media Group (1997). *Media and Mental Distress*, London: Longmans.

Goffman, E. (1974). *Frame Analysis: An Essay on the Organization of Experience*, New York: Harper & Row.

Golding, P. and Murdock, G. (1991). 'Culture, Communication, and Political Economy', in J. Curran and M. Gurevitch (eds), *Mass Media and Society*, London: Edward Arnold, pp. 15–33.

Golding, P. and Murdock, G. (1996). 'Culture, Communication, and Political Economy', in J. Curran and M. Gurevitch (eds), *Mass Media and Society*, London: Edward Arnold, pp. 11–31.

Goldman, R. (1982). 'Hegemony and Managed Critique in Prime-Time Television: a critical reading of "Mork and Mindy"', *Theory and Society*, Vol. 11, No. 3, pp. 363–88.

Graber, D. (1980). *Mass Media and American Politics*, Washington, DC: Congressional Quarterly.

Graber, D. (1996). 'The "New" Media and Politics: What Does the Future Hold?', *PS: Political Science and Politics*, March, pp. 33–6.

Gray, A. (1987) 'Behind Closed Doors: Video Recorders in the Home', in H. Baehr and G. Dyer (eds), *Women and Television*, London: Pandora Press, pp. 38–54.

Greenberg, P. S. (1975). *Life on Television*, New York: Oxford University Press.

Greenberg, B. S., Sherry, J. L., Busselle, R. W., Hnilo, L. R. and Smith, S. W. (1997). 'Daytime Television Talk Shows: Guests, content and interactions', *Journal of Broadcasting and Electronic Media*, Vol. 41, pp. 412–26.

Grindstaff, J. (1998). 'Trashy or Transgressive? "Reality TV" and the Politics of Social Control', *T:VC*, Vol. 9 (Internet edn).

Grispud, J. (1995). *The Dynasty Years: Hollywood Television and Critical Media Studies*: London: Routledge.

Grossberg, L. (1995). 'Cultural studies vs. Political Economy: Is Anybody Else Bored with this Debate?', *Critical Studies in Mass Communication*, Vol. 12, pp. 72–81.

Grossman, W. (1997). *Net. Wars*, New York: University Press.

Gunter, B. and Wober, M. (1988). *Violence on Television: What the Viewers Think*, London: John Libby.

Habermas, J. (1989). 'The Public Sphere', in S. Seidman (ed.), *Jürgen Habermas on Society and Politics: A Reader*, Boston, MA: Beacon Press, pp. 56–60.

Habermas, J. (1998). *Between Facts and Norms: Contributions to a Discourse Theory of Law and Democracy*, London: Polity Press.

Hacker, K. (1996). 'Missing Links in the Evolution of Electronic Democratization', *Media, Culture and Society*, Vol. 18, pp. 213–32.

Hackett, R. (1984). 'Decline of a Paradigm? Bias and Objectivity in News Media Studies', *Critical Studies in Mass Communication*, Vol. 1, No. 3, pp. 229–59.

Hackett, R. (1991). 'A Hierarchy of Access: Aspects of Source Bias in Canadian News', *Journalism Quarterly*, Vol. 62, pp. 256–65.

Hagen, I. (1999). 'Slaves of the Ratings Tyranny? Media Images of the Audience', in P. Alasuutari (ed.), *Rethinking the Media Audience*, London: Sage, pp. 130–50.

Hall, S. (1973). 'The Determination of News Photographs', in S. Cohen and J. Young (eds), *The Manufacture of News*, London: Constable, pp. 270–84.

Hall, S. (1977). 'Culture, the Media and the "Ideological Effect" ', in J. Curran, M. Gurevitch and J. Woolacott (eds), *Mass Communication and Society*, London: Edward Arnold, pp. 315–48.

Hall, S. (1980) 'Encoding and Decoding', in S. Hall, D. Hobson, A, Lowe and P. Willis, (eds), *Culture, Media and Society*, London: Hutchinson, pp. 128–39.

Hall, S. (1982). 'The Return of "Ideology": return of the repressed in media studies', in M. Gurevitch, T. Bennett, J. Curran and J. Woolacott (eds), *Culture, Society and Media*, London: Methuen pp. 56–90.

Hallin, D. (1984). 'The Media, the War in Vietnam and Political Support', *Journal of Politics*, Vol. 46, pp. 2–24.

Hallin, D. (1987). 'From Vietnam to El Salvador: Hegemony and Ideological Change', in D. Paletz (ed.), *Political Communication Research*, Norwood, NJ: Ablex, pp. 3–25.

Hallin, D. (1992). 'Sound Bite News: Television Coverage of Elections, 1968–1988', *Journal of Communication*, Vol. 42, pp. 5–24.

Hallin, D. C., Mankoff, R. D. and Weddie, J. K. (1993). 'Sourcing Patterns of National Security Reporters', *Journalism Quarterly*, Vol. 70, pp. 753–66.

Halloran, J. D. (1978). 'Studying Violence and the Media', in C. Winick (ed.), *Deviance and the Mass Media*, London: Sage, pp. 287–305.

Hansen, A. (1993). 'Greenpeace and Press Coverage of Environment Issues', in A. Hansen (eds), *The Mass Media and Environmental Issues*, Leicester University Press, pp. 150–78.

Hansen, A. and Murdock, G. (1985). 'Constructing the Crowd: Populist Discourse and Press Presentation', in V. Mosco and J. Wasko (eds), *The Critical Communication Review*, Norwood NJ: Ablex, Vol. 3, pp. 227–57.

Harms, J. D. and Dickens, D. (1996). 'Post-modern Media Studies: Analysis or symptom', *Critical Issues in Mass Communication*, Vol. 13, pp. 210–27.

Hart, R. P. (1994). 'Politics and the Virtual Event: An overview of the Hill–Thomas Hearings', *Political Communication*, Vol. 11, pp. 263–75.

Hartmann, P. (1979). 'News and Public Perceptions of Industrial relations', *Media, Culture and Society*, Vol. 1, No. 3, pp. 253–70 .

Harrison, M. (1997). 'Politics on the Air', in D. Butler and D. Kavanagh (eds), *The British General Election of 1997*, London: Macmillan, – now Palgrave, pp. 133–56.

Hedley, R. A. (1999). ''The Information Age: Apartheid, Cultural Imperialism or Global Village'', *Social Science Computer Review*, Vol. 17, pp. 78–87.

Hellman, H. (1999). 'Legitimations of Television Programme Policies', in P. Alasuutari (ed.), *Rethinking the Media Audience*, London: Sage, pp. 105–29.

Hellman, H. and Sauri, T. (1994). 'Public Service Television and the Tendency towards Convergence', *Media, Culture and Society*, Vol. 16, pp. 47–71.

Herman, E. (1985). 'Diversity of News: ''Marginalizing'' the Opposition', *Journal of Communication*, Vol. 35, pp. 135–46.

Herman, E. (1998). 'The Propaganda Model Revisited', in R. W. McChesney, E. M. Wood and J. B. Foster (eds), *Capitalism and the Information Age: The Political Economy of the Global Communication Revolution*, New York: Monthly Review Press, pp. 191–206.

Herman, E. and Chomsky, N. (1988). *Manufacturing Consent: The Political Economy of the Mass Media*, New York: Pantheon.

Herman, E. and McChesney, R. (1997). *The Global Media: The New Missionaries of Global Capitalism*, London: Cassell.

Himmelstein, H. (1994). *Television Myth and the American Mind*, London: Praeger.

Hitchens, C. (1999). *Nobody Left to Lie To*, London: Verso.

Hodge, B. and Tripp, S. (1986). *Children and Television*, Cambridge: Polity Press.

Horkheimer, M. and Adorno, T. (1977). 'The Culture Industry: Enlightenment as Mass Deception', in J. Curran, M. Gurevitch and J. Woollacott (eds), *Mass Communication and Society*, London: Edward Arnold, pp. 349–83.

Huberman, B. A. and Lukose, R. M. (1997). 'Social Dilemmas and Internet Congestion', *Science*, No. 277, pp. 535–7.

Hughes, J. N. and Hasbrouck, J. E. (1996). 'Television Violence: Implications for Violence Prevention', *School Psychology Review*, Vol. 25, No. 2, pp. 134–51.

Humphries, D. (1981). 'Serious Crime, News Coverage, and Ideology', *Crime and Delinquency*, Vol. 27, pp. 191–206.

Ignatieff, M. (1998). *The Warriors' Honour: Ethnic Wars and the Modern Conscience*, London: Chatto & Windus.

Iyengar, S. (1991). *Is Anyone Responsible: How Television Frames Political Issues*, Chicago, IL: Chicago University Press.

Jeffords, S. (1989). *The Remasculinization of America*, Bloomington: Indiana University Press.

Jhally, S. and Lewis, J. (1992). *Enlightened Racism: 'The Cosby Show', Audiences, and the Myth of the American Dream*, Boulder, CO: Westview Press.

Joyner Priest, P. and Dominick, J. R. (1994). 'Pulp Pulpits: Self-Disclosure on "Donahue", *Journal of Communication*, Vol. 44, No. 4, pp. 74–97.

Katz, E. (1987). 'Communication Research since Lazarsfeld', *Public Opinion Quarterly*, Vol. 51, pp. 25–45.

Katz, E. and Lazarsfeld, P. F. (1955). *Personal Influence*, New York: Free Press.

Kellner, D. (1981). 'Network Television and American Society', *Theory and Society*, Vol. 10, No. 1, pp. 31–62.

Kellner, D. (1995). *Media Culture*, London: Routledge.

Kieran, M. (1997). 'News Reporting and the Ideological Presumption', *Journal of Communication*, Vol. 47, No. 2, pp. 79–95.

Kilborn, R. (1994). '"How Real Can You Get?": Recent Developments in "Reality Television" ', *European Journal of Communication*, Vol. 9, pp. 421–39.

Kilborn, R. (1998). 'Shaping the Real: Democratization and Commodification in UK Factual Broadcasting', *European Journal of Communication*, Vol. 13, No. 2, pp. 201–18.

Kirkham, P. and Skeggs, B. (2000). 'Absolutely Fabulous: Absolutely Feminist?', in H. Newcomb, (ed.), *Television: The Critical View*, New York: Oxford University Press, pp. 306–18.

Kitzinger, J. (1997) 'Resisting the Message: The Extent and Limits of Media Influence', in D. Miller, J. Kitzinger, J. Williams, and P. Beherell (eds), *The Circuit of Mass Communication*, London: Sage, pp. 192–212.

Kitzinger, J. (1998). 'The Gender-Politics of News Production: silenced voices and false memories', in C. Carter, G. Branston and S. Allen (eds), *News, Gender and Power*, London: Routledge, pp. 186–205.

Kitzinger, J. (2000). 'Media Templates: Patterns of association and the (re)construction of meaning over time', *Media, Culture and Society*, Vol. 22, pp. 61–84.

Kitzinger, J. and Reilly, J. (1997). 'The Rise and Fall of Risk Reporting', *European Journal of Communication*, Vol. 12, No. 3, pp. 319–50.

Kitzinger, J. and Skidmore, C. (1995). *Child Sexual Abuse and the Media; Summary Report to the ESRC*, Glasgow Media Group.

Klapper, J. (1960). *The Effects of Mass Communication*, New York: Free Press.

Knightley, P. (1975). *The First Casualty: The War Correspondent as Hero, Propagandist, and Mythmaker from the Crimea to Vietnam*, London: Deutsch.

Kramarae, C. (1998). 'Feminist Fictions of Future Technology', in S. Jones (ed.), *Cybersociety 2.0*, London; Sage, pp. 100–28.

Lawrence, R. (1996) 'Accidents, Icons, and Indexing: The Use of Dynamics of News Coverage of Police Use of Force', *Political Communication*, Vol. 13, pp. 437–54.

Lazarsfeld, P., Gaudet, H. and Berelson, B. (1944). *The People's Choice*, New York: Columbia University Press.

Leurdijk, A. (1997). 'Common Sense versus Political Discourse: debating racism and multicultural society in Dutch talk shows', *European Journal of Communication*, Vol. 12, pp. 47–168.

Lewis, J. (1991). *The Ideological Octopus*, London: Routledge.

Lewis, J. (1997). 'What Counts in Cultural Studies', *Media, Culture and Society*, Vol. 19, pp. 83–97.

Lichter, S. R., Noyes, R. E. and Kaid, L. L. (1998). 'No News or Negative News: How the Networks Nixed the '96 Campaign', in L. L. Kaid and D. Bystrom (eds), *The Electronic Election*, New York: Lawrence Erlbaum, pp. 3–13.

Lichter, S., Rothman, S. and Lichter, S. (1986). *The Media Elite*, Bethseda: Adler & Adler.

Lichter, S., Rothman, S., Rycroft, R. and Lichter, S. (1990). *Nuclear News*, Center for Media and Public Afairs.

Liebes, T. (1992). 'Decoding Television News: The Political Discourse of Israeli Hawks and Doves', *Theory and Society*, Vol. 21, pp. 357–81.

Liebes, T. and Katz, E. (1986). 'Patterns of Involvement in Television Fiction: A Comparative Analysis', *European Journal of Communication*, Vol. 1, pp. 151–71.

Liladhor, J. (2000). 'From the Soap Queen to the Aga-Saga: different discursive frameworks of familial femininity in contemporary "women's genres"', *Journal of Gender Studies*, Vol. 9, pp. 5–12.

Linne, O. (1993). 'Professional Practice and Organization: environmental broadcasters and their sources', in A. Hansen (ed.) *The Mass Media and Environmental Issues*, Leicester University Press, pp. 69–80.

Livingstone, S. (1990). 'Interpreting a Television Narrative: How Different Viewers See a Story', *Journal of Communication*, Vol. 40, No. 1, pp. 72–85.

Livingstone, S. (1993). 'The Rise and Fall of Audience Research: An Old Story with a New Ending', *Journal of Communication*, Vol. 43, No. 4, pp. 5–12.

Livingstone, S. (1998). 'Relationships between Media and Audiences: Prospects for Audience Reception Studies', in T. Liebes and J. Curran (eds), *Media, Ritual and Identity*, London: Routledge, pp. 237–54.

Livingstone, S. and Liebes, T. (1995). 'Where have all the Mothers gone – Soap Opera Relaying the Oedipal Story', *Critical Studies in Mass Communication*, Vol. 12, No. 2, pp. 155–75.

Livingstone, S. and Lunt, P. (1994). *Talk on Television: Audience Participation and Public Debate*, London: Routledge.

Lodziak, C. (1986). *The Power of Television*, London: Frances Pinter.

Loshitzky N. (1991). 'Framing Images of Intifada Television News: The Case of Nahalin', paper read to Fourth International Television Studies Conference, London.

Lowry, D. T. and Shidler, J. A. (1995). 'The Sound Bites, the Biters, and the Bitten', *Journalism and Mass Communication Quarterly*, Vol. 72, pp. 33–44.

Lull, J. (1988). *World Families Watch Television*, London: Sage.

Lull, J. (1990). *Inside Family Viewing: Ethnographic Research on Television's Audiences*, London: Science Paperbacks.

Lynch, F. (1993). 'Whose Diversity? Whose Consensus?', *Society*, July/August, pp. 36–40.

MacDonald, M. (1995). *Representing Women: Myths of Femininity in the Popular Media*, London: Arnold.

Marvin, C. (2000). 'On Violence in the Media', *Journal of Communication*, Vol. 50, No.1, pp. 142–9.

Marx, G. T. (1995). 'The Road to the Future', *Scientific American*, Web Issue.

Masciarotte, G. (1991). 'C'mon Girl: Oprah Winfrey and the Discourse of Feminine Talk', *Genders*, No. 11, pp. 81–110.

McAnany, E. G.and Wilkinson, K. T. (1992). 'From Cultural Imperialists to Takeover Victims?', *Communication Research*, Vol. 19, No. 6, pp. 724–48.

McChesney, R. (1998). 'The Political Economy of Global Communication', in R. W. McChesney, E. M. Wood and J. B. Foster, *Capitalism and the Information Age: The Political Economy of the Global Communication Revolution*, New York: Monthly Review Press, pp. 1–26.

McCombs, M. E. and Shaw, D. L. (1972). 'The Agenda Setting Function of the Press', *Public Opinion Quarterly*, Vol. 36, pp. 176–87.

McEachern, C. (1994). 'Bringing the Wildman Back Home: television and the politics of masculinity', *Australian Journal of Media and Culture*, Vol. 7, No. 2 (Internet edn).

McLaughlin, L. (1998). 'Gender, Privacy and Publicity in "Media Event Space"', in C. Carter, G. Branston and S. Allen (eds), *News, Gender and Power*, London: Routledge, pp. 71–90.

McLean, A. (2000). 'Media Effects: Marshall McLuhan, Television Culture and the X-Files', in H. Newcomb (ed.), *Television: The Critical View*, New York: Oxford University Press, pp. 253–65.

McLeod, J., Kosicki, G. and Pan, Z. (1991). 'On Understanding and Misunderstanding Media effects', in J. Curran and M. Gurevitch (eds), *Mass Media and Society*, London: Edward Arnold, pp. 235–67.

McManus, J. P. (1992). 'What Kind of Commodity is News', *Communication Research*, Vol. 19, No. 6, pp. 787–805.

McQuail, D, Blumler, J. V. and Brown, J. (1972). 'The Television Audience; A Revised Perspective', in D. McQuail (ed.), *Sociology of Mass Communications*, Harmondsworth: Penguin, pp. 135–65.

Merelman, R. (1995). *Representing Black Culture: Racial Conflict and Cultural Politics in the United States*, New York: Routledge.

Meyers, M. (1997). *New Coverage of Violence against Women: Engendering Blame*, London: Sage.

Miliband, R. (1973). *The State in Capitalist Society*, London: Quartet.

Miller, D. (1994). *Don't Mention the War: Northern Ireland, Propaganda and the Media*, London: Pluto Press.

Miller, D. (1998). 'Public Relations and Journalism', in A. Briggs and P. Cobley (eds), *The Media: An Introduction*, London: Longman, pp. 65–81.

Miller, D. and Beharrell, P. (1998). 'AIDS and Television News' in D. Miller, J. Kitzinger, K. Williams, and P. Beharell (eds), *The Circuit of Mass Communication*, London: Sage, pp. 68–91.

Miller, D. and Reilly, J. (1995). 'Making an Issue of Food Safety: the media, pressure groups and the public sphere', in D. Maurer and J. Sobal (eds),

Eating Agendas: Food, Eating and Nutrition as Social Problems, New York: Aldine de Gruyer.

Miller, D., Kitzinger, J., Williams, K. and Beharell, P. (1998). *The Circuit of Mass Communication*, London: Sage.

Milne, K. (1988). 'Analysis of Violence', *New Statesman*, 19 February, p. 22.

Molotch, H. L. and Lester, M. J. (1974). 'Accidental News: The Great Oil Spill as Local Occurrence and National Event', *American Journal of Sociology*, Vol. 81, No. 1, pp. 235–60.

Moores, S. (1993). *Interpreting Audiences: The Ethnography of Media Consumption*, London: Sage.

Morley, D. (1980). *The Nationwide Audience: Structure and Decoding*, London: British Film Institute.

Morley, D. (1983). 'Cultural Transformations: the politics of resistance', in H. Davis and P. Walton (eds), *Language, Image, Media*, Oxford: Basil Blackwell, pp. 104–17.

Morley, D. (1986). *Family Television*, London: Comedia.

Morley, D. (1992). *Television, Audiences and Cultural Studies*, London: Routledge.

Morley, D. (1996) 'Populism, Revisionism and the "New" Audience Research', in J. Curran, D. Morley and V. Walkerdine (eds), *Cultural Studies and Communications*, London: Arnold, pp. 279–91.

Morley, D. (1999). ' "To Boldly Go ..." ': The Third Generation of Reception studies', in P. Alasuutari (ed.), *Rethinking the Media Audience: The New Agenda* London: Sage, pp. 195–205.

Morley, D. and Robins, K. (1994). *Spaces of Identity: Global Media, Electronic Landscapes and Cultural Boundaries*, London: Routledge.

Morrison, D. E. (1999). *Defining Violence: The Search for Understanding*, Luton: Luton University Press.

Mosco, V. (2000). 'The Web', in G. Browning, A. Halcli and F. Webster (eds), *Understanding Contemporary Society: Theories of the Present*, London: Sage, pp. 343–55.

Muncie, J. (1984). *'The Trouble with Kids Today': Youth and Crime in post-war Britain*, London: Hutchinson.

Murdock, G. (1982). 'Large Corporations and the Control of the Communications Industries', in M. Gurevitch (ed.), *Culture, Society and the Media*, London: Methuen, pp. 118–50.

Murdock, G. (1990). 'Redrawing the Map of the Communications Industries', in M. Ferguson (ed.), *Public Communication: The New Imperatives*, London: Sage, pp. 1–15.

Murdock, G. (1994). 'Visualizing Violence: Television and the Discourse of Disorder', in C. Hamelink (ed.), *Mass Communication Research*, Norwood, NJ: Ablex, pp. 171–87.

Murdock, G. (1997). 'Reservoirs of Dogma' in M. Barker and J. Petley (eds), *Ill Effects*, London, Routledge, pp. 67–86.

Murdock, G. and McCron, R. (1979). 'The Television and Delinquency Debate', *Screen Education*, Vol. 30, p. 51–67.

Murphy, D. (1991). *The Stalker Affair and the Press*, London: Unwin Hyman.

Musso, J., Weare, C. and Hale, M. (2000). 'Designing Web Technologies for Local Governance Reform: Good Management or Good Democracy?', *Political Communication*, Vol. 17, pp. 1–19.

Nakhaie, M. R. and Pike, R. M. (1998). 'Social Origins, Social Statuses and Home Computer Access and Use', *Canadian Journal of Sociology*, Vol. 23, pp. 427–50.

Negrine, R. (1998). 'Media Institutions in Europe', in A. Briggs and P. Cobley (eds), *The Media: An Introduction*, London: Longman, pp. 224–37.

Newcomb, H. and Hirsch, P. (2000). 'Television as a Cultural Forum', in H. Newcomb (ed.), *Television: The Critical View*, New York: Oxford University Press, pp. 561–73.

Nichols, J. and McChesney, R. (2000). *It's the Media, Stupid*, New York: Seven Stories Press.

Norris, P. (2001). *A Virtuous Circle: Political Communication in post-industrial Societies*, Cambridge University Press.

Norris, P., Curtice, J., Sanders, D., Sammel, M. and Semetko, H. (1999). *On Message: Communicating the Campaign*, London: Sage.

Oliver, M. B. (1994). 'Portrayals of Crime, Race, and Aggression in "Reality-based" Television Shows', *Journal of Broadcasting and Electronic Media*, Vol. 38, pp. 179–92.

Page, B. I. and Tannenbaum, J. (1996). 'Populistic Deliberation and Talk Radio', *Journal of Communication*, Vol. 46, No. 2, pp. 33–54.

Palmer, J. (1998). 'News Production', in A. Briggs and P. Cobley (eds), *The Media: An Introduction*, London: Longman, pp. 377–91.

Parenti, M. (1981). *Inventing Reality*, New York: St Martin's Press.

Parks, L. (1996). 'Special Agent or Monstrosity: finding the feminine in the X-Files', in D. Lavery (ed.), *Deny All Knowledge: Reading the X-Files*, New York: Syracuse University Press, pp. 121–34.

Patterson, P. (1988). 'Reporting Chernobyl: Cutting the Government Fog to Cover the Nuclear Cloud', in L. M. Wilkins (ed.), *Bad Tidings: Communication and Catastrophe*, New York: Erlbaum, pp. 131–47.

Patterson, T. E. (1994). *Out of Order*, New York: Vintage Books.

Patterson, T. E. and Donsbach, W. (1996). 'News Decision: Journalists as Partisan Actors', *Political Communication*, Vol. 13, pp. 455–68.

Patterson, T. E. and McClure, R. D. (1976). *The Unseeing Eye: The Myth of Television Power in National Politics*, New York: Paragon Books.

Pearson, G. (1983). *Hooligan: A History of Respectable Fears*: London: Macmillan – now Palgrave.

Peckham, M. (1998). 'New Dimensions of Social Movement/Counter Movement Interaction', *Canadian Journal of Sociology*, Vol. 23, pp. 451–70.

Penley, C. and Willis, S. (1993). *Male Trouble*, Minnesota: University of Minnesota Press.

Pfau, M. and Eveland, W. P. (1996). 'Influence of Traditional and Non-Traditional News Media in the 1992 Election Campaign', *Western Journal of Communication*, Vol. 60, pp. 214–32.

Philo, G. (1990). *Seeing and Believing*, Routledge: London.

Postman, N. (1986). *Amusing Ourselves to Death*, London: Heinemann.

Postman, N. and Powers, S. (1992). *How to Watch TV News*, New York: Penguin.

Preston, P. (2001). *Reshaping Communications*, London: Sage.

Purdy, J. S. (1998). 'The God of the Digerati', *The American Prospect*, No. 37, pp. 86–90.

Putnam, R. (1995). 'Bowling Alone: America's Declining Social Capital', *Journal of Democracy*, Vol. 6, pp. 65–78.

Putnam, R. (1996). 'The Strange Disappearance of Civic America', *The American Prospect*, Vol. 7 (Internet edn).

Radway, J. (1984). *Reading the Romance*, Chapel Hill, NC: University of North Carolina Press.

Rakow, L and Kranich, K. (1991). 'Woman as a Sign in Television News', *Journal of Communication*, Vol. 41, pp. 8–23.

Ranney, A. (1983). *Channels of Power*, New York: Basic Books.

Reese, S. D., Grant, A. and Danielian, H. (1994). 'The Structure of News Sources on Television', *Journal of Communication*, Vol. 44, pp. 84–107.

Reiner, R. (1997). 'Media Made Criminality', in M. Maguire, R. Morgan and R. Reiner (eds), *The Oxford Handbook of Criminology*, Oxford: University Press, pp. 189–231.

Robinson, C. and Powell, L. A. (1996). 'The Post-modern Politics of Context Definition; Competing Reality Frames in the Hill-Thomas Spectacle', *Sociological Quarterly*, Vol. 37, No. 2, pp. 279–305.

Rockler, N. (1999). 'From Magic Bullets to Shooting Blanks: Reality, Criticism, and *Beverly Hills, 90210'*, *Western Journal of Communication*, Vol. 63, No. 1, pp. 72–94.

Rogers E. and Dearing, J. (1988). 'Agenda Setting Research: where has it been? Where is it going?', in J. A. Anderson (ed.), *Communication Yearbook*, Vol. 11, pp. 555–94.

Root, J. (1986). *Open the Box*, London: Comedia.

Roscoe, J., Marshall, H. and Gleeson, K. (1995). 'The Television Audience: A Reconsideration of the Taken-for Granted Terms "Active", "Social" and "Critical"', *European Journal of Communication*, Vol. 10, No.1, pp. 87–108.

Ross, K. (1998). 'Making Race Matter: an overview', in B. Franklin and D. Murphy (eds), *Making the Local News: Local Journalism in Context*, London: Routledge, pp. 228–40.

Rowland, W. (1982). 'The Symbolic Uses of Effects: Notes on the Television Violence Inquiries and the Legitimation of Mass Communication Research', *Communication Yearbook*, Volume 5, New Brunswick N.J.: Transaction Books, pp. 385–404.

Sabato, L. J. (1991). *Feeding Frenzy: How Attack Journalism has Transformed American Politics*, New York: Free Press.

Sachs, H. (1995). 'Computer Networks and the Formation of Public Opinion: an ethnographic study', *Media, Culture and Society*, Vol. 17, pp. 81–99.

Sakkas, L. (1993). 'Politics on the Internet', *Interpersonal Computing and Technology, Electronic Journal for the 21st Century*, Vol. 1, No. 2.

Scammell, M. and Harrop, M. (1997). 'The Press', in D. Butler and D. Kavanagh (eds), *The British General Election of 1997*, London: Macmillan – now Palgrave, pp. 120–33.

Scannell, P. (1989). 'Public Service Broadcasting and Modern Public Life', *Media, Culture and Society*, Vol. 11, pp. 135–66.

Schiller, H. (1983). *Information and the Crisis Economy*, Norwood, NJ: Ablex.

Schlesinger, P. (1990). 'Rethinking the Sociology of Journalism: Source Strategies and the limits of Media-Centricism', in M. Ferguson (ed.), *Public Communication: The New Imperatives, Future Directions for Media Research*, London: Sage, 1989, pp. 61–83.

Schlesinger, P., Dobash, R. E., Dobash, R. P. and Weaver, C. K. (1992). *Women Viewing Violence*, London: British Film Institute.

Schor, J. (1992). *The Overworked American: The Unexpected Decline of Leisure*, New York: Basic Books.

Schroder, K. (1987). 'Convergence of Antagonistic Traditions? The Case of Audience Research', *European Journal of Communication*, Vol. 2, pp. 7–31.

Schudson, M. (1986). 'Deadlines, Datelines, and History', in R. K. Mankoff and M. Schudson (eds), *Reading the News*, New York: Pantheon, pp. 79–108.

Schudson, M. (1992). 'The Limits of Teledemocracy', *The American Prospect*, No. 11, pp. 41–5.

Schudson, M. (1996). 'What if Civic Life Didn't Die?', *American Prospect*, Vol. 7, No. 25 (Internet edn).

Schultz, T. (2000). 'Mass Media and the Concept of Interactivity', *Media, Culture and Society*, Vol. 22, pp. 205–21.

Schutz, A. (1997). 'Self-presentational Tactics of Talk-show Guests: a comparison of politicians, experts, and entertainers', *Journal of Applied Social Psychology*, Vol. 27, pp. 1941–52.

Selnow, G. (1986). 'Solving Problems on Prime-Time Television', *Journal of Communication*, Vol. 36, pp. 63–72.

Selnow, G. (1990). 'Values in Prime-time Television', *Journal of Communication*, Vol. 40, pp. 64–74.

Semetko, H. and Valkenburg, P. M. (2000). 'Framing European Politics: A Content Analysis of Press and Television News', *Journal of Communication*, Vol. 50, No. 1, pp. 93–109.

Semetko, H., Scammell, M. and Goddard, P. (1997). 'Television', *Parliamentary Affairs*, Vol. 50, No. 4, pp. 609–15.

Seymour-Ure, C. (1997). 'Editorial Opinion in the National Press', *Parliamentary Affairs*, Vol. 50, No. 4, pp. 586–608.

Shattuc, J. (1997). *The Talking Cure*, New York: Routledge.

Shields, M. (1996). *Cultures of Internet: Virtual Spaces, Real Histories, Living Bodies*, London: Sage.

Sigal, L. V. (1986). 'Sources Make the News', in R. K. Mankoff and M. Schudson (eds), *Reading the News*, New York: Pantheon, pp. 9–37.

Sigelman, L. (1973). 'Reporting the News: an Organizational Analysis', *American Journal of Sociology*, Vol. 79, pp. 132–51.

Silverstone, R. (1990) 'Television and Everyday Life: Towards an Anthropology of the Television Audience', in M. Ferguson (ed.), *Public Communication: The New Imperatives – Future Directions for Media Research*, London: Sage, pp. 170–89.

Smart, C. (2000). 'Post-Feminism', in G. Browning, A. Halcli, and F. Webster, *Understanding Contemporary Society: Theories of the Present*, London: Sage, pp. 46–56.

Soderbund, W. C., Wagenburg, R. H. and Pemberton, I. C. (1994) 'Cheerleader or Critic? Television News Coverage in Canada and the United States of the US invasion of Panama', *Canadian Journal of Political Science*, Vol. 27, No. 3, pp. 581–604.

Stabile, C. A. (1995). 'Resistance, Recuperation and Reflexivity: the Limits of a Paradigm', *Critical Studies in Mass Communication*, Vol. 12, pp. 403–22.

Steele. C. A. and Barnhurst, K. G. (1996). 'The Journalism of Opinion: Network News Coverage of U.S. Presidential Campaigns, 1968–1988', *Critical Issues in Mass Communication*, Vol. 13, pp. 187–209.

Steemers, J. (1998). 'Broadcasting is Dead: Long Live Digital Choice', in H. Mackay and T. O'Sullivan (eds), *The Media Reader: Continuity and Transformation*, London: Sage, pp. 231–49.

Strodtheff, R. P., Hawkins, R., and Schonfeld, A. C. (1992). 'Media Roles in a Social Movement: a model of ideology diffusion', *Journal of Communication*, Vol. 35, No. 2, pp. 134–53.

Stubbs, P. (1998). 'Conflict and Co-operation in the Virtual Community: eMail and the Wars of the Yugoslav Succession', *Sociological Research Online*, Vol. 3, No. 3, http://www.socresonline.org.uk/socresonline/3/3/7.html.

Sumner, C. (1979). *Reading Ideologies*, London: Academic Press.

Surgeon General's Scientific Advisory Committee on Television and Social Behaviour (1972). *Television and Growing Up: The Impact of Televised Violence*, Washington, DC: Government Printing Office.

Sutherland, J. (1998). 'The Fight for Eyeballs', *London Review of Books*, Vol. 20, No. 19, pp. 13–16.

Tasker, Y. (1993). 'Dumb Movies for Dumb People', in S. Cohan and I. R. Hark (eds), *Screening the Male*, London: Routledge, pp. 230–44.

Tedesco, J. C., Miller, J. L. and Spiker, J. A. (1998). 'Presidential Campaigning on the Information Superhighway', in L. L. Kaid and D. Bystrom (eds), *The Electronic Election*, New York: Lawrence Erlbaum, pp. 51–63.

Thompson, G. (1979). 'Television as Text: Open University "Case Study" Programmes', in M. Barrett, P. Corrigan, A. Kuhn and J, Wolff (eds), *Ideology and Cultural Production*, London: Croom Helm, pp. 160–97.

Thompson, J. (1990). *Ideology and Modern Culture*, Oxford: Polity Press.

Thussu, D. K. (2000). 'Legitimizing "Humanitarian" Intervention', *European Journal of Communication*, Vol. 15, No. 3, pp. 345–61.

Traube, E. (1990). 'Transforming Heroes: Hollywood and the Demonization of Women', *Public Culture*, Vol. 3, pp. 1–28.

Tuchman G. (1978). *Making News: A Study in the Construction of Reality*, New York: Free Press.

Tunstall, J. (1996). *Newspaper Power*, Oxford: Clarendon Press.

Turkle, S. (1996). 'Virtuality and Its Discontents: Searching for Community in Cyberspace', *The American Prospect*, No. 24, pp. 50–7.

Turow, J. (1992) 'The Organizational Underpinnings of Contemporary Media Conglomerates', *Communication Research*, Vol. 19, No. 6, pp. 682–704.

Valelly, R. M. (1996). 'Couch-Potato Democracy?', *The American Prospect*, No. 25, pp. 25–6.

van Zoonen, L. (1991). 'A Tyranny of Intimacy? Women, femininity and Television News', in P. Dahlgren and C. Sparks (eds), *Communication and*

Citizenship: Journalism and the Public Sphere in the New Media, London: Routledge & Kegan Paul, pp. 217–35.

van Zoonen, L. (1994). *Feminist Media Studies*, London: Sage.

van Zoonen, L. (1998). 'One of the Girls: The Changing Gender of Journalism', in C. Carter, G. Branston and S. Allen (eds), *News, Gender and Power*, London: Routledge, pp. 33–46.

van Zoonen, L. and Meijer, I. C. (1998). 'Gender: from Pamela Anderson to Erasmus', in A. Briggs and P. Cobley (eds), *The Media: An Introduction*, London: Longman, pp. 295–307.

Vattimo, G. (1992). *The Transparent Society*, London: Polity.

Vincent, R. C. (2000). 'A Narrative Analysis of US Press Coverage of Slobodan Milosevic and the Serbs in Kosovo', *European Journal of Communication*, Vol. 15, No. 3, pp. 321–44.

von Feilitzen, C. (1998). 'Media Violence – four research perspectives', in R. Dickenson, R. Harindranath and O. Linne (eds), *Approaches to Audiences*, London: Arnold, pp. 88–103.

Wasko, J. (1994). *Hollywood in the Information Age*, Cambridge: Polity Press.

Webster, F. (1995). *Theories of the Information Society*, London: Routledge.

Wilson, C. and Gutierrez, F. (1995). *Race, Multiculturalism, and the Media: From Mass Communication to Class Communication*, London: Sage.

Wilson, T. (1993). *Watching Television: Hermeneutics, Reception and popular Culture*, London: Polity Press.

Winn, M. (1985). *The Plug-In Drug*. New York: Viking Press.

Winston, B. (1998). *Media Technology and Society: A History from the Telegraph to the Internet*, London: Routledge.

Wittig, M. A. and Schmitz, J. (1996). 'Electronics Grassroots Organizing', *Journal of Social Issues*, Vol. 52, pp. 53–69.

Wober, M. (1984). 'Review Article', *Media, Culture and Society*, Vol. 6, pp. 65–71.

Zha, J. H. (1992). 'Issue Competition and Attention Distraction: A Zero-Sum Theory of Agenda-Setting', *Journalism Quarterly*, Vol. 69, pp. 825–36.

Index